IN THE SHADOW OF
BREAST CANCER

11020-LEAT

IN THE SHADOW OF

BREAST CANCER

Maria's 7-Year War, From Lump

Discovery to Final Peace

ROBIN R. LEATHERMAN

HUSBAND AND HELPMATE OF 50 YEARS

To order additional copies of this book, contact:
Xlibris Corporation
1-888-7-XLIBRIS
www.Xlibris.com
Orders@Xlibris.com

CONTENTS

To the memory of my beloved wife Maria, who shared 50 years of my life before losing her battle with breast cancer, and

To the thousands of other women who have braved the silent brutality of that insidious invader, and

To the millions of women who, by frequent self-examination, hopefully will avoid such struggles.

CHAPTER 1

"Oh, no, Daddy! I'm going to die!" the words burst forth, and a flood of tears washed Maria's cheeks. I moved quickly to her side and threw my arm around her, squeezing her closely to me. I fought back my own tears as I struggled to find my suddenly panic-stricken voice.

At last I was able to speak. "No, no, Maria, you aren't going to die," I comforted her. "Doctor Coe won't let that happen. Whatever that little lump is, he will take care of it, won't you, Doctor?"

"I most certainly will, Maria," Dr. Coe spoke soothingly.

"But cancer kills almost everyone it strikes!" Maria protested through her tears, and slumped on my shoulder to sob deeply. Then slowly, over a period of several minutes, my wife regained her composure, her tears abated, and I dried her cheeks with my handkerchief.

We were in Doctor Coe's examining room in St. Petersburg. Maria was the Brazilian girl I had met in Bahia in 1943, and married in Recife in 1944 while serving on an American Naval Repair Base in each of those cities during World War II. We were retirees now, living in Florida. We had an engineer son, Bobby living in Rochester, New York with his wife, Judy and three daughters; and a daughter, Kathy in Oak Harbor, Washington with her husband, Charlie a Navy A-6 pilot, and their son and daughter.

I was retired on a monthly income under $2,000, and Maria and I had lived in our modest condominium for about five years. Maria's pet name in her family was Nini, pronounced

"Knee-KNEE." I often called her that, and will use both names in this story.

The time had rolled around for Nini's annual physical. Her appointment was for Tuesday, so Monday she had a chest x-ray, EKG, blood tests et cetera preparatory to the doctor's check up. I hated the hours we spent in one waiting room after another, but I always accompanied Maria, for I knew the importance of annual physicals, especially for women. I also recognized Nini's need for me at her side to offer support at such times.

Maria's already voluptuous breasts had increased in size down the flow of years, so that nurses and doctors now referred to them politely as 'generous'. She self-examined her breasts from time to time, looking for a telltale lump, but never found anything to disturb her peace of mind. Now, on the very morning of her physical, I heard her finish her shower. A few minutes later she called to me. "Daddy, come here a minute, please."

"What can I do for you?" I asked, heading into the bathroom. She was standing before the mirror wearing slacks and smelling sweetly of talcum powder, nude from the waist up and gently touching her right breast.

"Can you feel a lump here?" she asked, and took my hand to place my fingers over a spot on her breast slightly above the areola.

I palpated the area gently under her coaching, until for a moment I seemed to feel a firmness. "I *thought* I felt something . . . at first," I said, "but it's very elusive. I can't feel anything now."

"That's exactly what happened to me!" she said, apprehension ringing in her voice. "I thought I felt a lump, but it disappeared. "Then after a while, I found it again." She looked at me steadily for a moment—and in those few seconds I saw deep anxiety lurking in her brown eyes.

I tried to control my reaction so as not to alarm her further. If a lump in Maria's breast gave *me* the shakes, how much worse it must be for her? I dared not let her know how much that small lump worried me.

"Be sure to tell Doctor Jones about this when we get there," I spoke as calmly as my voice permitted.

"I'll tell the nurse when I go to the room," Maria said. She felt easier telling the nurse instead of the doctor, for Maria was shy about her body in general, and even more demure about her breasts. Ever since her pre-teens the admiring glances of boys and men had been an embarrassment to her.

After sitting an extra half hour in the doctor's waiting room, which overflowed with mostly older people such as Maria and I, the nurse called her and put her in a cubicle to wait for the doctor some more. Finally the doctor arrived, checked her over, reported that all her tests appeared satisfactory, and said she was looking great. Then he checked for the lump she had found that morning. Within seconds he had the fugitive hardness beneath his fingers, and was instantly alert to its significance.

Maria and I were well aware of that lump's ugly implication ourselves, but neither of us had dared to mention the 'C' word. Instead, I prayed that it might be merely a lipoma, a lump of benign tissue. Maria came into the waiting room and I rose to accompany her out. "What did the doctor say?" I asked, as we left the office.

She related the doctor's actions and words. "He wants me to have a mammogram," she continued, and moved close against me, as though for physical support. But I knew it was emotional support my beloved Nini really sought at that moment.

Several wild thoughts pursued one another through my mind, but I tried to be calm. "I'm sure that's a good idea," I said. "Then we can know for sure nothing is wrong." I used the words, *nothing is wrong*, rather than saying, *what it is*. I didn't want to mess with the issue of what it was! "When do you have it?"

"The nurse made an appointment for me at the hospital for Friday," she said. As my mind grasped the full significance of that appointment, I grew so choked up I could scarcely breathe as we made our way to the parking lot. But I did my best to present a cheerful mien to Nini, who was obviously deeply disturbed.

We both forced the thought of the small lump from our minds as we fixed supper that evening. How can I lie like that? Of course we didn't force the thought from our minds! How could we, when 1 out of 9 women develops breast cancer during her lifetime, and 20% of 'lumps' in women's breasts are cancerous? What we did—or at least what *I* did—was consider the fact that, mathematically, the odds were in our favor.

The horrible thought which flooded my mind was that when any woman develops a lump in her breast, she quickly becomes one of the medical profession's greatest cash contributors. The number of hospitals, nursing homes, laboratories, pharmacies, drug companies, doctors, nurses and specialists who become involved with her is astronomical. And so are their fees and prices—even when they aren't cheating the insurance company, Medicade or Medicare, which some of them blatantly do. My files contain the proof of such instances, although, when challenged, the perpetrator always insisted it was an accident, a mistake.

Friday we checked in at the hospital's x-ray department. I knew Maria was frightened, but the nurse had explained that a mammogram was merely an x-ray of her breast, taken with a specially-designed machine. We were barely seated when a technician came to escort Maria to his diabolical device to shoot pictures. It didn't take long; Nini soon rejoined me.

"How did it go, honey?" I asked.

"It hurt quite a bit," she complained. "They squeezed my breast down too hard to take the x-rays. It was very painful!" "My poor darling," I sympathized, and gave her an embrace, surprised by the vigor of her responding hug, especially if she harbored any residual soreness in her breasts. "Now what happens?" I asked as we left the hospital.

"They will send a report to my doctor, and he'll let me know the results," she replied. So we were floating in limbo, scared stiff, or worried sick or both. I did my best to convince Maria that she probably had nothing to worry about, while chill fingers of fear seized my own heart, making my chest ache—literally.

That afternoon the doctor's nurse called to inform Maria the mammogram had revealed a small lump in her breast. I listened in on the extension. "I've made an appointment for you with Doctor Coe. He's a surgeon who can help you if necessary." I saw Nini turn tense at the news, and my own pulse went ballistic. Even though we both *knew* she had a lump in her breast, to have that confirmed by the mammogram suddenly turned the alien knot into something more baneful, more threatening, more sinister.

I took Maria in my arms, and told her not to be preoccupied, yet my own mind and emotions were in turmoil, a flood of unhappy thoughts seething within me, like the lava in Hawaii's Kilauea volcano—angry, hot and threatening to overflow without notice or provocation. Since I had to exercise tremendous effort to keep from breaking down, I could imagine the tumult within Nini's heart and soul.

We had recently been at the side of my lifelong buddy for his last few days as he died a horrible death from prostate cancer out in Oregon. Now, just the word 'cancer' gave me the shivers. It was Friday, and Maria's appointment with the surgeon was Monday. I prayed it would not be an ominous conference.

Hadn't I been worried once that I had a cancer in my left

side? And hadn't it turned out to be nothing more than a fatty tumor? Why shouldn't it be the same for Maria? After all, the odds were in her favor, according to everything I'd learned; for after my pal's death, I began to pay attention to anything in the papers, magazines or on TV concerning that devastating malignancy.

It was a horribly long weekend. It seemed we'd never get through it. Although the power of positive thinking can be strong and uplifting, it's a tough discipline to practice under such vitiating circumstances. We sat up late that Sunday night, watching television and reading, not talking much, wrapped in our own thoughts. It seemed neither of us was eager to go to bed, but we finally turned in and kissed a lingering goodnight.

Monday drug by in fits and starts with the reluctance of a big toboggan sliding on patchy snow, but finally we were in Doctor Coe's office for our 3:15 appointment. We were surprised to see how many patients he had waiting, for the room was full. Of course, just as in our case, only about half the people were patients. The others were spouses, relatives or friends providing transportation, and/or moral support.

Maria went in alone when the nurse called her name, and I waited behind, disinterestedly turning old magazine pages, and praying the doctor would have comforting words for Nini. Half an hour later, the nurse came and asked me to join Maria, for the doctor was about to enter her examining room. All that time, Nini had been waiting in a consultation room by herself! I went in to find her sitting uneasily on the examining table, clad only in a paper nightgown.

Doctor Coe came in, introduced himself, shook hands warmly with Maria and me and moved to palpate her right breast. Having just studied her x-rays, he quickly found what he sought. He looked at Maria. "Mrs. Leatherman, the mammogram you took Friday definitely reveals a small growth in your breast, right here," and he touched the area lightly. "I'm sorry," he said gently, "but it *appears* to be cancerous."

Maria disintegrated. "Oh, no, Daddy! I'm going to die!" she cried in anguish, and I rushed to her side to clasp her to me, as I have previously described.

11020-LEAT

CHAPTER 2

Once Maria's tears stopped flowing, and we became a semblance of our normal selves, I began to discuss our situation with Doctor Coe. I sat beside Nini and held her close, her head on my shoulder and both her hands in my left hand as I embraced her with my right arm to give her strength. "We know there's a lump, doctor," I said, "but can't it be merely a benign tumor?"

"The odds are in favor of that," he said. "But I would urge her to have a biopsy. For if it's cancer, you don't want to lose any time before removing it." I felt the shudder which passed through Maria—an involuntary quiver she could not suppress.

"So how do we approach this?" I asked the question for Nini, who was still in no condition to converse.

"I've checked with the hospital, and they have an operating room available next Thursday. Maria can check in on Wednesday afternoon to prepare for surgery the next morning," he replied.

My beloved still quivered in my embrace. *Lord Jesus, why should this evil be visited upon such an innocent, faithful wife?* I wondered, as wild thoughts and fears rushed through my head with the velocity and commotion of African lions chasing zebras. The ugliest thought of all concerned the articles I'd read on the needless surgery performed every day in America; unnecessary hysterectomies, heart by-pass operations of questionable need or value, and yes, even mastectoomies, surely as physically deforming and as mentally excruciating as any type of surgery. I forced my mind to quit spining so I could raise the questions I had to ask. "Isn't Maria's lump a small one?" "Yes, it is," he replied, "about the size of a small olive."

"And isn't it possible it's benign?" I insisted once more.

"Yes, the odds are in favor," he said calmly. He was a man in his 40s, about my average height, but considerably plumper, with burnt-red hair and a reassuring, pleasant nature. I had the deep-seated feeling he knew what he was doing.

"I have read a lot lately about lumpectomies," I said. "If the biopsy *does* show malignancy, would you consider removing the lump rather than doing a mastectomy?"

"Of course that is a possibility to consider. But as a surgeon who has treated many women for this condition, I would be averse to doing only a lumpectomy if the tumor's appearance indicates possible further complications."

"I understand what you're saying doctor," I said. "But God help you if you go the whole distance and I ever learn it wasn't necessary. Almost every week we read in the papers about the great number of unnecessary operations surgeons perform—and I don't want one performed on my wife unless you are damned sure it has to be done!" I looked him straight in the eye. Maria gasped, and the doctor recoiled slightly.

But he recovered quickly. "Mister Leatherman, I understand your feelings. I assure you that my practice is such that I don't have to operate when it's not essential. But my professional opinion is that if Mrs. Leatherman's lump proves to be malignant, it would be far better to perform a modified radical mastectomy immediately rather than a lumpectomy . . . it's a safer procedure, and offers a better prognosis for the future.

I turned to Maria. "Of course, Nini, you are the one who has the final say in the matter. I don't mean to intrude, only to ask questions to clarify the options." There was also the partial language barrier, for Maria had learned English after coming to America during World War II; and grammar, pronunciation and vocabulary would throw her a curve now and then.

I looked at the doctor. "*I'm* satisfied, doctor," I said, "but what do *you* think, darling?" I asked, and squeezed Maria close, for she was still in my arms. "Do you want to take a few days to discuss this together . . . to think through the pros and cons of the options before you decide?"

For a woman who had just had a terrible shock, her reply amazed me. "What has to be done, has to be done, Daddy. I'm scared to death, but I don't think we should wait," she said quietly and stoically.

At that moment I absolutely adored my dark-eyed little wife! She really had what it takes: a woman to ride the trail with, as the cowboys used to say in Colorado; a woman a Skipper would '*ask* to have on board his ship' as the Navy used to rank an officer. As a Marine, she'd have been in the first wave to hit the beach at Iwo Jima. Beyond question, she was a strong, gallant incredible woman. Pushing past her earlier shock, she was now ready to deal with reality, come what may, with more courage than a Christian awaiting the lions in the Colosseum.

"So how do we go about this?" I asked the doctor.

"We can handle it two ways," Doctor Coe said. "One way is for Maria to go in for a biopsy, go home to await the results, and then decide what she wants to do if the lesion proves cancerous. The other approach is for me to take a sample of the lump and send it to the laboratory to be checked immediately by a pathologist who will stand by, and, if it proves malignant, to go ahead and perform the modified mastectomy right away. That approach is less expensive . . . and would be easier for you, Maria."

My god, what an anguishing decision to have to make! My mind revolted against the idea—not because my darling might lose her breast, but because of the apprehension she must feel in standing up to such a terrible decision. But again, I underestimated my sweetheart.

She faced the doctor. "I'd rather do everything at once," she said, "for I hate anesthesia. If the growth is malignant, we'll do the whole operation right away."

Her courage in the face of such a traumatic choice gave me strength. But I still wanted to know exactly what had to be done, so I asked another question. "Doctor, what do you mean by *modified* total mastectomy?" I was thankful that he did not rush us like most doctors do.

"In the past, a total mastectomy meant the removal of the breast and the underlying muscle tissue. But nowadays we normally don't remove the chest muscles. Instead, we remove the breast and the nodules under that arm. We send the lymph nodes to the lab to check for cancer ... if it has spread, the lymph nodes usually are the first place it reaches."

So those were the basic options: a lumpectomy to remove only the growth; a mastectomy, to remove the breast, or a radical, or total, mastectomy, to remove the breast and the tissue beneath it.

Doctor Coe had recommended No. 2, and Maria had agreed, without any further questions. The nurse made a couple of calls, and Nini was set to check into the hospital Wednesday and start the chain of preparations for Thursday's 'exploratory' surgery. We signed the papers authorizing the procedures, the doctor left us, I helped Maria dress and we were on our way out.

Maria and I didn't know it at the time, but a medical study of lumpectomies which led to their increased usage in lieu of the disfiguring mastectomies was a study which was said to contain flawed data, either accidentally or deliberately, a fact which would not become known for several years down the road. So Maria's surgeon was correct in his approach, despite the then-current trend to remove a lump rather than the entire breast.

21

I wondered bitterly if the people in the doctor's waiting room could sense the fear and apprehension and insecurity which engulfed the two of us as we made our way, half blindly, into the corridor. I was too choked up to say anything to Maria, for the realization of what she was facing had sunk deeply into my heart, and I had to struggle to maintain control over my emotions.

We had not seen the radiologist's interpretation of Maria's mammogram. Perhaps it was best that way, for it said:

> On the right breast, fairly central in location is a 2 cm irregular density with spiculated borders . . . Radiographically, this has the appearance of a malignant lesion. To palpation, the lesion was quite firm and felt larger than was visualized on x-ray, again suggesting malignancy. IMPRESSION: probably malignant neoplasm centrally located in right breast.

Malignant neoplasm means malignant tumor, meaning cancer. The only escape hatch remaining now was the word 'probably'. Perhaps it was not a malignant neoplasm, but still I brooded.

I thought of cancer as a malicious, secretive, despicable monster which attacked *other* people: not the sweetheart I'd wooed and won so long ago in the charming old city of Bahia on the Bay of All Saints in languorous Brazil; not my dear wife of 42 years and the mother of my precious children; not the partner who was sharing my golden years of retirement and without whom I would have no real reason to live.

There was one good thing: by the time we left the doctor's office, I was confident that, regardless of what had to be done, Doctor Coe's work would be excellent. There was little more we could ask, except that the biopsy prove the lump to be benign—not malignant.

One other situation soon arose which added confusion to

an already panicky string of events. Doctor Jones, Maria's 'family' physician informed her that he was going away for a few days and would not be able to see her while she was in the hospital. "But don't you worry," he comforted her, "I have asked Doctor Y to keep an eye on you in my absence. He's a very capable doctor, and will take good care of you."

We had never met Doctor Y, nor the radiologist who 'read' her x-rays, nor the anesthesiologist nor the pathologist. We would get bills for days and days from people we didn't know. We had given no thought to all of those separate entities who would have their fingers in the pie.

These were the people whose fees seemed awfully high for what they did, and over whom we had absolutely no control. They were selected by someone else, and according to a recent article in the news, were the prime factor in the 16% increase in the cost of a hospital stay. Medicare tried to run a tight ship as to hospital costs, but they had yet to tighten up on the charges inflicted by these many 'auxiliaries' including anesthesiologists, laboratory and x-ray technicians, pathologists and radiologists.

We drove home almost in silence, Maria with a small pamphlet entitled 'Breast Lumps' tucked in the outer pocket of her purse. That same afternoon, we called Kathy out in Oak Harbor, Washington to apprise her of her mother's coming operation, explaining that we didn't know yet exactly what the operation would be, whether only a biopsy or a total mastectomy. "Daddy will call you as soon as we know," Nini told her.

"Oh, Mama, this worries me so much!" Kathy cried, compassion ringing in her sweet voice. "Daddy, you be sure to call me right away and let me know all about everything!" she ordered, her past command experience as a Navy lieutenant showing through.

"I will, I promise," I said.

"Have you called Bobby?" she asked.

"No, not yet," Maria said. "I think maybe we'll wait to see how everything goes first."

"I think you should call him today," Kathy argued.

"We'll think about it," Nini replied. "But remember, his wife hasn't been exactly friendly lately."

"But this is different, Mama," Kathy exclaimed.

It *was* a dilemma, but we resolved to wait until after the operation before calling Bobby. Then instead of alarming him, and making him await the results, I'd give him the full story.

We had requested a private room for Maria, because of the nature of her operation, and the room was reserved when we checked into the hospital to sign a bale of papers; releases, waivers, Medicare forms *ad infinitum*. They had to know who was going to foot the bills, of course. And they seemed quite pleased that Maria had both Parts A and B of Medicare, plus supplementary coverage with Prudential Insurance.

"Our private rooms are very, very nice," the counselor assured us. "If you wish, you may have TV and a telephone for only $2.50 a day, for they are not furnished by the hospital."

"That sounds fair," I nodded agreement, although at a rate of $75 a month it wasn't *very* fair.

"You should be ready to pay for them when Maria checks out," she continued. "They're not covered by Medicare or insurance."

"That's fine," I agreed. The surgeon had said Maria probably would not stay in the hospital more than five days, in either eventuality, so the charges would be only a dozen dollars.

"You also have to pay the extra charge for the private room at the time of your wife's discharge," the lady explained. "Medicare doesn't cover that expense. It will be fifty-five dollars per day." I multiplied that by five to determine the $275 I'd have to pay the day Nini checked out—*if* she had to have a mastectomy. "Our private rooms are on the west end of the second floor, and have a nice view of the water," were her parting words.

The room was comfortable and clean, with a private bathroom, but it was so small the bed and one chair crammed it so tightly a nurse or a doctor had trouble getting in and out! It wasn't a private room, it was a private cubbyhole. To charge $55.00 extra for *that* was scandalous. People have doghouses which are bigger!

With the financial arrangements made, and a private 'room' reserved, we made our way home, the shadow of the dreaded morning of the 17th draped across our thoughts like a dirty curtain. We fixed a light supper early, and spent the evening watching TV. I stayed at Maria's side constantly. I knew she was nervous and worried about the operation, especially the anesthesia. Beyond that, she had to be terribly preoccupied about what the biopsy would show.

As for myself, I tried to put the entire thing out of my mind, striving to avoid thinking about the operation or its significance. If I let my thoughts dwell on the matter, even momentarily, I'd find tears sliding down my cheeks. The whole thing just wasn't fair to my little *Brasileira*, a girl who had never done anything to hurt anybody.

Although I was already married when I met Maria, I had been thinking of a divorce because of certain actions of my wife while I was overseas; so I never felt my divorce was brought on by Maria. Rather, she protested it. But she fit my ideal as a wife so well that I just *had* to marry her. So my divorce was of my own instigation. Maria was innocent of any blame for that.

I was thankful the tall table-lamp with its thick ceramic base blocked off Maria's view of my face as she sat in her chair and I sat on the sofa nearby. I was positive she'd break down if she caught me with tears in my eyes. Each time I hugged her during that nerve-wracking day, I could feel that she was on the edge, and the slightest sensing on her part that *I* was worried might send her into a deluge of tears. I had to keep my upper lip just as stiff as hers at all cost; but the mental strain required to do so was almost as much as I could bear.

Concerning my own emotions, I'm obliged to say that I am no sissy. I grew up around coal mines, sawmills, and cattle ranches in the Colorado Rockies, and then on farms in Oregon during the Depression. I spent my summer vacation, beginning at age 11, working ten hours a day, six days a week in strawberry fields and fruit orchards. At 16 I worked with grown men in an Oregon sawmill, turning huge Douglas fir logs into lumber and railroad ties.

Then I did nine years in the Navy, including all of World War II. I was a shipfitter and hard-hat diver, and saw duty against the Germans in the North Atlantic and against the Japanese at Iwo Jima and Okinawa. Until my 30s I was nothing but muscle, and had settled many a personal dispute with my bare fists—losing about as often as I won. This sketch of my background should help the reader to better understand the true depth of my pain and anguish any time I say that I could not hold back the tears.

CHAPTER 3

I beg the reader's indulgence for using a few lines here for a quick orientation before plunging more deeply into our story of real life, real people and real problems.

At the time our story begins, the author, me, Robin Leatherman, also called Bobby by my family as I grew up, was 68 years old. I kicked the scales up to 175 pounds and was but 5'9", so I had a modest layer of baby fat over my muscular frame. Possessed of a ready wit, a wide smile, steady gray eyes and thinning gray hair, I was born in Cheyenne, Wyoming in 1918, the year WWI ended. By the time I'd reached the period in which our story transpires, I'd lived in over 70 houses, apartments, shacks, tents, and Navy ships and stations in several different states in America and in Brazil.

Our heroine, and she truly deserves that title, was two years my junior, was born in Bahia, probably the most romantic city in Brazil, of Portuguese descent with a small dash of German in the mix. She was 66 years old, fair-skinned, with dark, shining eyes, was 5'2"and weighed several pounds more than she should have for her age and height. Her blithe spirit and indomitable courage, coupled with her gregariousness made her a popular lady wherever she went, and a friend of all.

The condominium in which we lived was situated among a flock of condos, some 850 in all, in a heterogeneous collection of buildings ranging from three stories to 20 stories in altitude, spread along three long fingers of land in a pleasant

27

bay off Tampa Bay. There was a sea wall almost all the way around the perimeter, offering a walk of well over a mile to the adventurous, plus a clubhouse, spas, swimming pools and tennis courts. I was a Director at Large on the 20-member Board of Directors which ran Bay Island.

When the Gulf of Mexico was kicking up its heels, Tampa Bay, the large inlet off the Gulf, would be much quieter, and Boca Ciega Bay, in turn opening off Tampa Bay, and on which we were located, might easily be almost serene.

Except when a tropical storm or tornado struck the West Coast of Florida, or the Gulf Coast as it is often called, our weather was something most people would pay dearly for. And most of the year, the comings and goings of tourists by the thousands who did just that, substantiate my comment.

Our own condo was situated on the ground floor on the end of a four story building of 32 units, and had windows on three sides, So our two bedrooms, two baths, kitchen and combined living-dining room was a well-lit, cozy 1.100 square feet of air-conditioned, ceiling-fanned comfort. When a lightning storm knocked out the elevators, we did not have to climb stairs to reach home. We simply opened the door and walked in.

The waters of the bay formed our front yard, ten feet from the door, across the walkway-sea wall. A neatly landscaped area behind our building had streets and our parking under open-sided carports.

We checked Maria into the hospital Wednesday afternoon, as instructed. The boss nurse seemed surprised to see us, but Maria's ticket showed which room was ours, and she led us to it.

Now Pines of Ponderosa is a pretty, for-profit hospital. The exterior of the main building is of mirror glass, much like modern office buildings. The lady downstairs gave us a postcard with a picture of the building, the back of which said, "Pines of Ponderosa is a modern, 310-bed general medical-surgical hospital . . . hub of a . . . medical center overlooking beautiful Boca Ciega Bay."

That description didn't match Maria's extra-charge room. The window of her room overlooked the roof of the Oncology Center, below, with a sprouting clutter of pipes and stacks sticking up, plus the face of the Medical Building across the narrow street. Even by stretching my neck, I couldn't see 'beautiful Boca Ciega Bay'! As the nurse visited a moment with Maria, I walked on down to the end of the section. There were several empty rooms there, all looking out on the bay. Directly across that strip of bay was Bay Island, our condo complex.

Slightly to the left was the causeway of Pasadena Avenue, and beyond that, a lift bridge over the intra-coastal waterway to St. Pete Beach, all in all, a very pleasant vista.

I walked back to the nurse's station. "I want my wife's room changed," I said flatly. The nurse appeared startled, and Maria obviously wondered what had triggered my sudden request.

"I'm sorry, sir, but I have to place your wife in the room which is assigned to her," the nurse attempted to bluff me.

"I understand your duty," I smiled, "but I want you to call whoever assigns rooms, and tell him or her we refuse to accept this room. We want the one right over there on the end of the floor," and I pointed to the room which had a pretty view, Room 212. "We live across there on Bay Island," I added, "and I want to be able to walk on the seawall and see my wife's room while she's here. I'm sure you can arrange that, can't you?" I had put her on the spot. She was in charge of the floor; now she should attempt to prove it.

She picked up the phone, spoke a moment, and said. "I've made arrangements for Mrs. Leatherman to have the room you like," and peace was established between us. Now I could visit Maria, and look out the window at something besides a tarred roof and a forest of vent pipes. For 55 extra bucks a day, we were entitled.

Naturally I would not have complained had Maria been assigned to the only empty room on the floor. But the lady downstairs had given us the worst room on the floor, even though half of the Bayview rooms were empty. I guess we were too polite when we spoke to her, so we looked like pushovers. It was just like having the hostess in a fine restaurant seat you at a dark table between kitchen doors and a bus station, while tables alongside windows with a nice view stand imploringly empty.

"We'll make arrangements for Maria's tests," the nurse said.

"Which tests?" I asked. And the nurse explained them. "She already had all those tests," I exclaimed in surprise. The nurse peered inside the file. Now *she* was surprised. "For heaven's sake, she has!" the lady in white said. "I wonder why they had you check in so early, Maria?" she half-said, half-asked. "You could have come in around four p.m."

"It appears they run this hospital according to the way a person is supposed to give alms: 'Let not thy right hand know what thy left hand doeth'," I said.

"Now that sounds familiar," the nurse said, cocking her head.

"It's from Christ's Sermon on the Mount," I replied gently.

With Maria checked into her room, we visited for half an hour. But Maria was tired and tense. "Let me try to take a nap for a while," she asked and stretched out on the bed. I spread the light blanket over her, kissed her gently and went to the apartment. From our unit, I could drive up our street past the clubhouse, turn left inside our complex, drive across a little, one-way private bridge and come out at the hospital parking lot. To return home, I drove up the side of the hospital to Pasadena Avenue, turned right across the causeway to our main gate, and drove back to the condo. Each trip to the hospital, then, was an easy circle of less than a mile altogether.

By 4:00 p.m. I was back in the hospital to sit with Nini for a couple of hours and help her with her dinner. I was surprised, but they let her eat a regular meal that evening. She'd selected roast turkey with cranberry sauce, mashed potatoes, mixed vegetables and fresh fruit. The only restriction was that her diet was to be low-sodium, as indicated on the little menu which came back to Maria with her food tray. We visited together while she dined royally.

"How does it taste?" I asked, for the aroma was tantalizing.

"Delicious," Nini said, teasing me with a big grin.

I stayed with her through the television news programs. Then we watched a special program on closed-circuit TV, following the nurse's orders. It concerned the process of anesthesia, surgery, post-operative care and the do's and don't's of recuperation, all of which was helpful, though at times alarming.

It reminded me of when Maria went to a diet doctor whose nurse put her in a tiny room with a tape player, and told her to listen to it, and if she had any questions, she *might* get to talk to the doctor . . . otherwise that wasn't necessary. Now, if they could put operations on tape, a person could have one right at home—just play it on the VCR!

The substitute doctor came by to see Maria, looked at her chart, took her blood pressure, offered some comforting words, and departed. Doctor Y had just made the rounds for Doctor Jones, Nini's doctor.

About 8:30 I headed for home as Maria snuggled down for the night. It was nearly 10:00 p.m. by the time I finished dinner that night, for I wanted to spend as much time with Maria as possible. The condo echoed emptily as I rattled around in the kitchen by myself, heating a can of soup and making a bologna sandwich. Maria's operation was scheduled

31

for 9:15 the next morning, but I planned to be at the hospital in time for her breakfast, if she were allowed to eat.

It turned out she couldn't even drink water next morning! She was allowed no food, probably because of the anesthesia. She was awake when I got there at 6:30, and we visited until the anesthesiologist appeared and gave her a preliminary shot to calm and relax her. About 9:00, a male attendant came along with a gurney, gently helped Maria onto it, and I followed down in the elevator and to the operating room entrance on the ground floor.

"I'm afraid this is as far as you can go, Mister Leatherman," he apologized. "You should take a seat in the surgery waiting room, where Doctor can talk with you or send you a message."

"I will, thank you," I said.

My sweetheart was lying quietly on her temporary bed, and she smiled bravely as I bent down to kiss her. Before I could say anything, she spoke up. "Now, Daddy, you take care of yourself, and please don't worry. If I thought you were worrying, I would be very nervous."

"Of course I'll worry . . . a little bit," I added. "But I promise not to overdo it. And you just relax, let these folks take care of you, put your faith in the Lord, and I'll see you in a little while." I bent down and kissed her sweet lips and gave her a squeeze as best I could. The young man wheeled her on through the big door into surgery, and as the door swung shut behind them, I walked dejectedly into the waiting room and took a seat.

My nerves were fairly steady, but I was deeply worried about Maria. What would the small lump turn out to be? I found myself praying to God that it would be nothing more than a cyst. If ever I had been in a blue funk, that was the time. But I kept my hopes up the best I could, and when a tiny, gray-haired volunteer lady offered to fix me a cup of coffee, I accepted eagerly.

Time ticked by in leaden seconds, each successive pulse taking longer to pass than its predecessor. I'd watch the TV for a while, then go out to pace up and down the corridor, staying close to the operating area so the doctor could see me when he came out. To say that I was nervous and worried is like saying billiard balls are round. I tried to calm myself, but that was impossible.

After eons, a gown-clad nurse wearing plastic booties over her shoes and with a face-mask dangling beneath her chin appeared in the doorway. "Mister Leatherman?" she called. My apprehension mounted as I rose and she motioned me into the corridor.

"I'm Rob Leatherman," I said, and glanced at my watch. It was 10:30—an hour and a quarter since Maria entered the operating room.

"Your wife is coming along just fine," she assured me. "But Doctor is so busy he asked me to come speak to you." I waited, almost breathless, though there was a terrible pressure in my temples and an icy hand squeezing my heart.

She continued. "We sent the lesion biopsy to the laboratory, and they froze it and made a section to check it." She reached out and put her arm around me, and with that gesture I knew the sad result before she voiced the words. "I'm sorry, Robin. The tissue was cancerous. We'll continue now with the mastectomy."

The world reeled about me, and a heavy surge of anguish rose from the pit of my belly, thrust upward past my stomach, squeezed my heart and lungs, shoved against my chest wall, and threatened to gag me as it constricted my throat. I fought back the tears, trying to keep my compassion for Maria from totally overwhelming me. I wasn't faint, and the world didn't turn black, but my thoughts were banefully dark, and I sensed the blackness of an alien threat coming at me like a tornado on the horizon. I pulled myself back to reality. *How It must have hurt the nurse to be the carrier of such distressing news,* I thought to myself.

"Thank you," I squeaked out the words, and turned away as my eyes brimmed over. I could no more hold back the tears than Noah could hold back the Flood.

The nurse continued from behind me. "It will probably take an hour or more to finish the operation," she explained, and disappeared back through the fateful door. I groped my way around the corner to the men's room, entered the single stall, and parked on the stool while I tried to regain a semblance of composure. After several minutes I quenched the tears, blew my nose on toilet tissue, went to the basin, splashed cold water on my face and dried with a paper towel.

Damn! Damn! I kept repeating to myself. I was hurting all over for my Maria, my sweetheart, *minha guerida de todas as gueridas*—my darling of all darlings.

There was still an interminable wait, and from the men's room I headed down the long corridor to the cafeteria, found the urns and, half-blind, drew a cup of coffee and took a table, with my back against the wall. I stared absently into the dining area, seeing and hearing nothing, adrift on a sea of gloom.

A lady sitting at the next table moved over beside me on the long bench, and gently laid her arm on my shoulder. "I overheard what the nurse said," she half-whispered. "I'm so very sorry. But you have to be brave, and everything will work out for you both, I'm sure." She gave me a strong squeeze, and slid back to her own table. I tried to say thanks, but the word clogged my throat like a ratty tennis ball. I could only nod my head to acknowledge her kind words.

I stopped annoying my styrofoam cup, dumped it in the barrel, and made my way back to the men's room to wash my face again. Back at the waiting room, there were now several people waiting. I hoped they'd all have better news than I'd had.

CHAPTER 4

It must have been a tedious operation thereafter, for it was 12:30 when Doctor Coe came to interrupt my pacing in the corridor, wafting along with him the odor of operating room air. "We're finished, Mister Leatherman," he said, a strand of brick-red hair poking out from beneath his green sterile cap. "Everything went very well, and Maria is doing just fine. She'll be in the recovery room for about an hour, and then she'll return to her room. You may visit with her then, of course."

"Can't I go see her now?" I asked, my voice in 'begging' mode.

"No, it's better that you wait. The recovery room is sterile. You'd have to be cleaned up and gowned to go in there. She's still asleep, and when she comes to she'll be pretty groggy for a while." He patted my arm. "Don't worry, you'll have her back soon now, with no more worries about that nasty little lump. I've taken care of that for good."

"Thank you, Doctor," I managed, and he turned and went back through the door to surgery. Now I suffered a true dichotomy of feelings: the doctor's words reassured me for the present; but still I feared the possibility of an error in his prognosis, and I worried what *that*, if so, would portend for the future.

When the hour was up, and Nini had failed to appear, I asked the volunteer if *she* could check in the recovery room, and she said 'yes', disappeared inside and returned quickly. "Your wife will be taken to her room in about half an hour,"

11020-LEAT

she said. I looked at my watch. That meant Maria would come out around 2:00. To kill time, I made the trek to the cafeteria again. I drew myself a cola, and let the icy liquid burn its course down my taut throat, then headed back to the corridor to wait for Nini.

But something was amiss in the information given to the volunteer, for now she came out to speak to me. "I think your wife may have been taken to her room already," she informed me. I caught the next elevator upstairs, scooted back to room 212, and there on the high bed lay Maria, the sheet pulled up under her chin as though she were cold. Her dark eyes fixed on me as I walked in and a faint smile touched her dry lips. I was so disgusted I could have shot somebody. Naturally I'd wanted to greet her the moment she appeared in the corridor from surgery!

"Now, *menina* (little girl), how the devil did you get here when I wasn't looking?" I demanded to know.

"That young man delivered me just a minute ago," she said. "He's such a nice boy. When I came to in the recovery room, I was shivering with the cold . . . my teeth were chattering . . . I just couldn't stop shaking. He brought warm sheets from an oven and wrapped them around me to help me get warm. That operating room is *too cold*, honey! I thought I would never stop shivering!"

"Here, let me put this over you," I said, and unfolded the blanket which lay across the foot of the bed and tucked it around her, for it was obvious she was chilled clear through. It seemed strange that neither the young man nor any of several floor nurses had bothered to ask Maria if she were cold, or had offered to put the blanket over her. For $55 a day extra, one might have expected a trifle more of the hospital staff's attention to a lady who had just had a breast removed! But I suppose nurses are just like the rest of us. They've been there and done that, and life has turned boring, and without realizing it, they become less attentive to their work, even disinterested at times. And they do take a lot of crap off people, especially cocky doctors who think theirs doesn't stink.

"That feel better?" I asked as I tucked the cover over her.

"*Much* better," Maria said, and smiled somewhat weakly.

"I'm sorry I wasn't here when you came up," I apologized. "They wouldn't let me in the recovery room, and when the lady volunteer checked, they told her half an hour yet. I went for a cola in the cafeteria, then came right back . . . no more than ten minutes had passed . . . but you were here already in your room!"

Since she'd been unconscious or drowsy until recently, I wasn't sure whether Nini realized yet what had transpired in the operating room. But I couldn't bring myself to say anything. Instead, I bent down to kiss her cold forehead and put my face against hers. She nuzzled her cheek snugly against mine for warmth. We were both silent like that for well over a minute.

"I'm sorry, Daddy," she murmured at last. "They had to remove my breast. It was cancer." Obviously she was aware.

I damned near overflowed again, but I forced the flood back. "I know, honey. The nurse came out to tell me, and then the doctor, after he finished." I gripped her soft hand in mine, avoiding her luminous eyes as I fought back the tears for the umpteenth time that day.

Vaguely I sensed the hand-printed sign at the head of the bed, DO NOT TAKE BLOOD PRESSURE OR DRAW ANY BLOOD FROM THE RIGHT ARM, absent-mindedly noting the drip of the intravenous hose and needle taped to Maria's left hand, 'feeding' her saline solution. "The doctor said he removed the noodles under my arm," Maria added, displaying a wisp of a coy smile.

I was aware that she knew the correct name, but I pretended I didn't. "Not noodles, honey . . . *nodules* . . . lymph

37

nodes." Her grin grew a little stronger, and I bent down to give her another hug and kiss. We visited for half an hour, when Maria dozed off, the after-effect of the anesthesia slipping subtly back to overcome her. I stayed beside her bed, and stared out the window at Boca Ciega Bay and our condo complex across the water. A deep sigh escaped me, like the sighs I used to emit as a Navy hard-hat diver after great exertion under water—a sigh that would have sent a bushel of air bubbles to the surface!

'It's safely done, thank heaven,' I thought to myself. *'Now we'll start getting used to our new situation. I'll do everything within my power to be super-patient and super-helpful, for I know this is something from which Nini won't recover physically nor emotionally for many months'.* As though she sensed my thoughts, Maria stirred slightly on the bed, then became quiet once more.

It was after 6:00 when Maria awoke, complaining of thirst—and hunger. I poured a glass of ice-water and held it while she drank a bit through the bent straw. They soon brought in her dinner, and I held *the* cup for her to sip a few swallows of broth—which was all she got that night! But it was more than enough; she pushed the cup aside before she'd finished it. "That's all I want, *querido* (darling)," she said, and a few minutes later she was off to dreamland again. When Maria awoke, I told her I was starved, and was going down to get a bite.

"Poor Daddy," she sympathized. "Did you eat any lunch?"

"I forgot to eat," I said. "And when I remembered, it was almost time for you to leave surgery, so I just drank a cola." "Then go and eat, while I rest for a while," she ordered. I don't remember now what I ate, but recall vaguely that it tasted better than expected. With some food in me, I returned to Maria's room. About 8:00 p.m. I said perhaps I should head home and call Kathy and Bobby.

"You stay home then, and get some rest, honey," Maria said. "You've had such a long day." Coming from a woman

who'd undergone so many hours of horrible surgery, her remark was whimsical, but far from laughable. We kissed and
hugged a tender, lingering goodnight.

At home, I called Kathy and gave her the sad news. "It
was cancer," I managed to say. "They performed a total mastectomy, and also removed the lymph nodes under Mama's
right arm."

"Oh, Daddy, I'm so sorry," Kathy said in a rising tone of
voice, and disintegrated on the other end of the line.

I let her pull herself together before continuing. "They
say that if a breast cancer spreads, it usually goes to those
nodes first. The doctor sent them to the lab, and tomorrow
we'll know the results of that test. He is confidant the cancer
was caught soon enough, and doesn't think it has spread."

"That's a blessing, at least, Daddy. You give Mama my
love, and take care of yourself. I know this is a heavy strain
on you, too. We don't want *both* of you in the hospital."

"I'm afraid I'll be there most of the time for a few days,
Boneca (Doll)," I teased her.

"I know. But that's not what I meant. You take care, and
don't forget to eat . . . and get plenty of sleep. We'll be praying for both of you," she finished her orders, and we soon
hung up.

Now I had to call our son, who was still completely in the
dark. Thankfully, it was Bobby who voiced a rich, "Hello."

"Hello, Bobby, it's Dad," I said, as though he wouldn't
recognize my voice.

"Dad!" he cried enthusiastically. "Hi, there, how are you?"

"Bobby, I'm calling to tell you about your mother . . . "
and suddenly I was overcome once more by that awful surge
of pressure and pity which boiled up from deep down in my
guts. I absolutely could not speak! There was no way I could
find my voice as the pressure mounted in my throat, squeezing my larynx tighter than a boa constrictor's grip on a tapir.
Not a peep could escape me.

39

"Dad! What is it? Dad!" Bobby cried frantically, while I hung there in suspension, trying to regain my voice! I think that was the first time in my life I wasn't able to say something! While Bobby grew more and more agitated and apprehensive in Rochester, I stretched the phone cord across the kitchen, filled a glass with tap water and gulped down a few swallows.

Finally my voice responded to my will. "I'm sorry I choked up," I managed to squeak out. "Give me a moment to get organized here," and for another half-minute I left Bobby waiting in suspense while I pulled myself together.

At last I could continue. "A few days ago your mother went for her annual physical, and there was a small lump in her right breast. They took mammograms, and the doctor said they should perform a biopsy to see if it was cancer."

My voice tried to elude me again, but I forced it back into the box. That word 'cancer' simply tied my throat and my heart in knots—not simple square knots, but convoluted, double carrick bends. After a few seconds, I went on. "This morning they did the biopsy, and kept Mama under anesthesia while the pathologist ran the test. It was cancer." My salty tears overflowed into the receiver as I struggled to keep my vocal cords functioning.

"Oh, no!" Bobby interjected, his voice filled with anguish.

"Yes, honey. We'd already decided that if it were cancer, the surgeon would perform a total mastectomy. They operated from 9:15 this morning until 12:30 p.m. to remove Mama's right breast." I paused to grab a dishtowel to dry my face and wipe off the slippery phone. "But your mother is very strong, honey. She came through just fine. I was with her until a few minutes ago. She is resting comfortably in the hospital near our condo."

"Oh, sure, I remember it," Bobby said, "lots of glass."

"That's the one. Mama's in room two-twelve, and she has a telephone." I gave him the address, and telephone number. "But I don't think you should try to call her today, she's still very tired and a trifle woozy."

"I can imagine," Bobby said. He gave me a few bits about what Judy and the girls were doing, we hung up, and I toweled off the phone again.

I imagined that by that time of day, Maria's brother in Rio would be home, so I dialed the code for Brazil, then Rio, then Nivaldo's number. After two rings Nivaldo said, "Alo."

"Robin *aqui*, Nivaldo," (Robin here.) I fought to control my voice and emotions once again. *'God, how weak I've turned out to be!'*, I kept thinking as I struggled to speak.

"Robin! *Como vai voce? Estamos todos bem aqui, gracas a Deus.*" (Robin, how are you. We are well here, thank God.) How I wished that were true about my own little family!

Continuing in Portuguese, I told him about his dear sister's operation, and it was evident that he was deeply affected. I explained about the lump, x-rays and mammogram, the biopsy as Nini waited on the operating table and the removal of her right breast and lymph nodes. Naturally he understood what had happened even better than I, for Nivaldo was a doctor who specialized in radiology and skin diseases. Years before, his and Maria's father, Jose, had died of prostate cancer in Rio de Janeiro.

He commiserated with me, and told me to be brave, for with American medical technology, he was certain our dear Nini would soon be home and would have a rapid recovery. Because of high long-distance charges, we stayed on the line only a few minutes. I promised to write, or have Nini write as soon as she could, to give him all the details. That was easier than trying to explain over the phone a lot of things which I, myself, wasn't sure of yet. I gave my love to Dulce, his wife, and Beth, their older daughter, 36 years old and living at home. and hung up.

Next morning I was back at Maria's bedside in time to help her with her breakfast. She was still swathed in bandages, the drain still inserted in her armpit. The IV solution dripped slowly through the tube into her left arm. The head of her bed was raised to a sitting position, and although she was pale, she seemed to be recovering well and was in good spirits, God bless her heart. She was a girl the Spartans would have been proud to call their own!

"Good morning, *querida*. How's my best girl today?" I asked.

"I'm fine, Daddy," she smiled bravely. "Just uncomfortable with this thing in my arm," indicating the IV needle and hose.

I gave her a gentle hug, and kissed her cheeks and forehead, and at last her soft lips. "Are you having any pain?"

"No, I feel okay, really. Just a little tired."

"I can imagine. You were in the operating room a long time. But I must say you are looking very pretty this morning."

"The nurse washed my face and combed my hair," she smiled.

When breakfast arrived, I stood beside the bed and helped Maria hold the cups and glasses of apple juice, chicken soup, gelatin and hot tea. Not very substantial, but even so, she was sated before all the food was gone.

With her breakfast tray back on the dolly in the hall, Nini spoke of her earlier fears. "You know, honey, the thing that scared me most was the anesthesia," she said. "I was so afraid that time in Belem *[the capital of the state of Para in Brazil]* when I came out from under the anesthetic and didn't know where I was and thought I was dead! I never got over that fright. But this time I didn't have any problem, thank heaven. Everything seemed just fine . . . except I was freezing to death!"

"I asked about that, honey," I said. "They told me they keep the room cold on purpose, to slow down the patient's circulation and reduce blood loss. Were you warm enough last night?"

"I was fine as soon as you put the blanket over me."

"Then I think you're well on the way to recovery, Pussycat."

"Oh, I hope so! I keep praying they took everything out, and I won't have to worry about cancer any more. That is the horrible part for me . . . not knowing for sure that everything has been removed and I am truly cured."

Of course that was my terrible worry, too. But I tried to speak reassuringly. "I know, but you have to have faith in the doctor and in the Lord. Let's start right now considering the subject closed. You will not be bothered any more with cancer, right?"

"Right," she murmured, and closed her dark eyes. I bent down close to her sweet face, and saw the traces of moisture seeping from between her eyelids. I put soft, dry kisses on each pretty eye, and gently lifted off the dewy drops.

Doctor Coe and his personal nurse came in shortly after breakfast, read her chart, took her blood pressure and examined the bandages and the drain beneath her arm. "You're getting along just fine, Maria," he said. "There's no infection or fever. You came through very well," and he patted her cheek affectionately.

I had no idea how the wound was closed after a mastectomy, but I was relieved there was no infection. I turned to the doctor as we walked outside. "Will the operation leave a big ugly scar?" I asked, for somehow I felt Maria would be almost as sensitive to a large scar as to the loss of her breast. Stupidly, I feared the scar would cover her chest like a pancake! It's hard for me to believe, now, that I'd had such an abysmal lack of knowledge concerning surgical procedures!

"No, no!" Doctor Coe said. "Her scar will look like a narrow railroad track for a while, until I remove the stitches.

Then it will be only a line across her chest." He smiled, and gave my arm a squeeze.

"It's nice that you bring your nurse along with you," I said. "Maria seems to be quite fond of her."

The nurse laughed, and gave me a quick hug. "You're going to see a lot of me for the next few months, Mister Leatherman, so you better get used to me."

"If you give me a hug like that every time I see you, getting used to you will be very easy to do," I said, and grinned. I was surprised when her cheeks colored slightly as she smiled back.

They left, and I helped Nini turn on the TV so she could watch some of the morning shows. I stayed there until the floor nurse came in around 10:00 to administer a sponge bath. Without waiting for her to ask, I said I'd leave for a while, and take care of things at home. I hugged and kissed Maria goodby and let the nurse take over

Even when it was necessary and proper for me to leave, I was always reluctant to go. I hated to leave Nini alone, even if the nurse were going to be with her.

CHAPTER 5

The condo was terribly empty without Maria bustling around in the kitchen, or sitting in her chair reading a newspaper or book, or doing the Jumble puzzle. I brewed a pot of coffee, and served myself a bowl of cereal, fixed some toast and jam and ate breakfast about an hour before lunch time.

I called my sister, Maxine, and my niece, Robbie, all of whom lived in Pasco County to the north, to let them know Maria had come through her ordeal very well, and was resting in the hospital.

"What time are visiting hours?" Robbie asked, as had Sis.

"She's in a private room, so as long as we don't raise a ruckus we can visit her any time we please. Whatever time or day is convenient for you guys," I replied.

"Then we'll come down tomorrow morning, Uncle Bobby," Robbie said. "And bring Mom with us, of course."

"Bring my darling nieces, too," I replied, just in case they were thinking of leaving Sarah and Laura behind.

Before noon I was back in Maria's room, helping her 'drink' her lunch, which turned out to be about the same as she'd had for breakfast. When it came, I helped her handle cups and bowls, and kept pouring ice water, for her thirst was boundless.

"I asked the nurse to pull off my white stockings for a while," Maria said. "But now I've been thinking . . . I don't want my legs and feet to swell, so maybe I should put them back on."

"Yes, ma'am, right away," I said. I located the long stock-

45

ings, straightened them out, and managed to put them on Maria, whose legs and feet did not appear swollen. Either she didn't have the tendency to swell, or else the stockings did their job.

The nurse came in just as I finished, and said I'd handled it well. "You could make a good nurse," she smiled.

"That's one of the things I've always wanted to do," I said.

"Be a nurse?" she asked in amazement.

"No, *make* one, like you said before," I laughed. She giggled and went back to her station to shuffle pills and papers.

Maria had several nurses during her stay, as the shifts changed. But oddly enough, the finest nurse of them all was a slender woman well into her 50s. She would come into the room, straighten the bed and the sheets, fluff up Maria's pillow, check that she was completely comfortable, replenish her ice water and tidy the whole room with a quick, gentle efficiency that belied her gray hair and veined hands. She was a veritable gem of a nurse, and when we left, I made special mention of her at the check-out desk.

"Everybody says the same thing about her," the lady told us.

'*She would have put a blanket over Nini after her operation!*' I thought.

I went to the cafeteria for lunch, then returned to Maria's side to spend another hour with her. A volunteer appeared with a huge basket of fruit done up in fancy ribbons and bows and bright cellophane. I gave the envelope to Maria.

"It's from Bobby and family!" Nini cried excitedly. "What a gorgeous basket of fruit! Isn't it, Daddy?" As she continued, I knew she was more delighted that Bobby had *sent* her the basket than she was with the basket itself. "I'm so glad Bobby thought of me!" she said, and I watched her relax back onto her pillow, a soft look filling the depths of her flashing dark eyes—for even after such a terrible operation, Nini's eyes were filled with the glow and sparkle they always possessed: beautiful, deep, luminous eyes, like brown opal, if there is such a gem. I stifled a little chuckle as I thought how I used to look at her small round face, with those marvelous dark eyes, and call her 'my little bee-face'.

Bobby and Kathy both called their mother that day, talking with her for several minutes, bringing her great joy and comfort. Kathy called while I was at the condo in the morning, and Bobby called while I was away in the afternoon. But all that mattered was that both had called to wish their Mama a speedy recovery, and to give her some of the latest gossip from Oak Harbor and Rochester. Bobby called from work, so Maria didn't talk with Judy.

I was back at the hospital that afternoon when a lady from 'Reach to Recovery' came by to visit with Maria. She was a volunteer in a program which helps women who've had mastectomies to get back to their normal selves, giving aid and comfort both physically and emotionally. 'Reach to Recovery' was sponsored by the American Cancer Society. There was one printed sheet directed at husbands specifically. While the lady visited with Maria and showed her some exercises she might do each day after she got home, I read the sheet:

> The woman you love has had a mastectomy. Each year, thousands of women and their loved ones are involved in the rehabilitation process following breast surgery.
>
> Recovery from surgery takes time. Your loved one may tire more easily and need physical help with everyday chores. She may have periods of depression. Encourage her to resume her normal activities as soon as her doctor agrees that this is not only indicated but helpful as part of her treatment.
>
> We know that this period of physical and mental ad-

justment is helped by large doses of love and understanding. The key is the demonstration of that love
and understanding in the same familiar ways. Changing behavior now, however subtle, might be interpreted as a rejection. She is adjusting to the change in
her body. Her doubts and fears are to be expected.
It is sometimes difficult to understand how deeply
she may feel that her femininity has been threatened.
Being accepted as the same person she was before is
essential to her recovery. Your awareness of her reactions and your reassurances will help her to dispel any
doubt she may have.

I understood fully the role I had to play in helping my
dear Maria to recover, in letting her know that I loved her
just as much as before, even *more* now, and that the physical
change she had undergone was of no consequence to me
whatsoever, except as it might affect *her* health and well-
being.

All of a sudden my mind swept back through the years to
the day of our wonderful picnic at the beach in Bahia, Brazil,
after I had known Maria for several weeks and we considered ourselves engaged. I could see Maria bending over to
pick up seashells, the swelling of her lovely breasts slightly
exposed to view. I caught my breath now, just with the thought
and the vision. How beautiful she had been that day! And
when we walked in the trees, hidden from sight, what a thrill
it had been taking that first truly lingering kiss, and letting
my hand move up to gently caress her bosom. And how she
had pressed close to me and whispered, *"Roberto, voce esta
demais ousado hoje!"* Robert, you are too bold today!

Pulling my thoughts back to the present, I knew, down
deep inside, that I would always think of Maria's breasts as
they'd been that day in our youth. Whatever might happen
now, or in the future, would never erase that joyous memory,

nor affect my love and admiration for my little Brazilian. Of course I would comfort and assure her. Of course I would help her. Of course I would give her strength to overcome this set-back in her life. For she was my love for eternity.

The lady showed Maria some light exercises to build up the muscle strength in her chest once more. And then gave her a small pillow, about the shape and size of a child's play football, but smooth and soft and cuddly.

"You can place this under your right arm when you're lying down," she said, "and it will make you feel very nice. Nobody knows exactly why, but it does. And later, at night in bed, you can put a soft pillow on that side, next to your body, and it will make you feel very comfortable." She helped Maria place the wee pillow under her arm, and even with the bandages still in place, Maria was delighted by its gentle touch and massage.

"You may even want to pin it inside your bra when you leave the hospital, and you can use it until you are well enough to buy a proper prosthesis," the lady said. She was slender, with a lovely figure—probably in her late 30s. "Most of all, Maria, you just have to tell yourself that you're going to do just great," and she raised her arms above her head. "You see, I had a mastectomy a few years ago, and I've recovered completely. I'm wearing a prosthesis now, and I'll bet you can't tell which breast I lost." In truth, I could not have guessed—even though she was wearing a snug sweater. "It's this one," she said, and pointed to one side of her body. I glanced at Maria, and was sure her eyes brightened after that lady's kindly, unembarrassed demonstration.

Nini saved all the menus from her stay in the hospital, and that evening she had a much better dinner; at least she got off the liquid diet. When she looked at her dinner tray her eyes opened with delight. I helped her eat, as necessary, and she put away cream of potato soup, Cornish game hen, fresh fruit, milk and coffee. Of course the Cornish game hen didn't come alone; it was accompanied by rice and veggies. The more I helped Nini, the hungrier I got, even though I'd already eaten at the cafeteria.

Again, I stayed at Maria's side that night until she tired, when I tucked her in, gave her a warm hug and some kisses, squeezed her soft hands, and left for home, to toss and turn another night.

Although I knew Maria was coming along very well, and even acting pretty chipper, still I was held prisoner by an edgy state of nerves and by deep-seated dark emotions, and when lying alone in bed, if I let the thought of that bitter operation creep into my thoughts, my eyes brimmed over and wet the pillow.

After leaving Maria in bed at the hospital the evening before her operation, I had gotten down on my knees beside our king-size bed at home to pray for the second time in my life. I prayed with deep fervor that the small lump in Maria's breast would be only a benign cyst. But like so many people's prayers, mine went unheeded. After our terrible disappointment, I nourished a bitterness within my heart toward whatever Being may be in charge of things, if indeed there is such a Being, and I prayed for divine aid thereafter only when it was vital to Maria's well-being.

Once again I realized it was up to us to make our own way through this life on earth. We weren't going to get any help from above. I wondered why I should pray, "Our Father, which art in heaven . . . " for surely no loving father could visit upon his children all of the sickness, accidents and unbelievable atrocities, both man-made and natural, which men and Mankind are constantly obliged to endure.

CHAPTER 6

Saturday I was beside my loved one's bed at the hospital when they brought her a good breakfast. She gave me one piece of toast, and I tasted her scrambled eggs, sort of like the Officer-of-the-Deck aboard a U.S. Navy ship checks the crew's meal to insure that everything is palatable.

After she'd eaten, Nini looked quite happy, relaxing against her pillow in an almost upright position. Her IV line had been disconnected, so her left arm was now free. She had learned to operate her electrified bed, and was adeptly running the TV with the automatic control.

With another decent meal under her belt, and the drinking of plenty of liquids, Nini had the color returning to her face; and with a few external things coming under her control, she began to look and sound much like her normal self. She even went to the bathroom alone. It is an understatement to say I was greatly relieved. (No pun intended.) If she continued to improve so well, I hoped to have her home with me by Monday evening. Of course, the final decision was up to her. The doctor and I saw how she looked, but only Maria knew how she felt.

The *St. Petersburg Times* published a comparison of local hospital rates, and the Pines of Ponderosa was about in the middle-range for its different services. Considering the great convenience we gained from such a nearby hospital, the costs were not out of line, though lord knows they were anything but cheap. At check-in time, the lady gave us a special kit which explained about the hospital. In it was a booklet with

51

the week's TV programs and plenty of ads, and a sheet of Prayers For Different Occasions, such as Before An Operation, After An Operation and a Prayer When Worried. In my emotional condition, I could have ticked off that last one over and over, like a Nepalese lama, for I was *always* worried.

Of special interest was a full sheet of information covering a patient's Medicare rights. In order to reduce the costs of hospital stays, Medicare had established a schedule of charges, based on average lengths of stay for different conditions and types of operations. If a hospital kept a patient in bed for extra days beyond the 'scheduled' number of days, it got no extra money for those days. On the other hand, if the schedule called for a five-day stay, and the hospital sent the patient home after four days, it still received full payment. That was one reason some hospitals had so many empty beds. The new rules kept them from holding onto patients for excess days.

The problem with the new rules, however, was that a hospital might try to send a patient home before that patient should be discharged. But money-grubbing had to take a back seat to proper medical care. The special page in Maria's folder pointed out all the recourses she had should the hospital attempt to discharge her too early. The underlined sentence said, "Your discharge date should be determined solely by your medical needs, not by . . . Medicare payments." I was happy to see how things *should* work; and in Maria's case there were no problems in that area whatsoever.

Thank God I didn't have to worry about some money-hungry HMO kicking my wife out of the hospital as soon as some bookkeeper felt she was ready, without regard for what she and her doctor might feel!

The substitute doctor came by again, looked at the chart, asked Maria how she felt and checked her blood pressure. "I don't think it will be necessary for me to come by any more, especially since your surgeon is seeing you every day," he said. He was most pleasant and charming, and we both thanked him for filling in for Maria's regular physician. I wasn't so pleased with him later on when I got his bill: $100 for his hospital visits, plus a 'first consultation' fee billed at $125, total, $225. That was larcenous!

In our area, many doctors charge an extra fee for a new patient's first visit, billing it as a first consultation. But that usually includes a limited physical check-up, a question and answer session and the preparation of a new file. We sure as hell hadn't had all that. In my mind, 100 bucks for the brief hospital visits seemed more than enough. To throw on another $125 was just rubbing salt in Maria's wound!

The food served in the cafeteria was excellent, and also reasonably priced, so I didn't cook at home much those few days. I just availed myself of the cafeteria's services, which gave me more free time to spend with Nini.

At lunch time I again helped her with her glasses and crockery, and when Maria began to show signs of sleepiness after lunch, I tucked her in for a nap, went down to the cafeteria to eat, and returned to the condo.

Maria had almost no visitors while in the hospital because her friends were not aware of her operation. That's the way she wanted it.

"Honey, don't you want me to put a note on the building bulletin board that you are here?" I asked.

"No, Daddy, please don't do that. I don't want people coming to see me like this," she insisted.

"But you may hurt their feelings," I pointed out.

"No, I think they will understand," she had a slight edge in her voice.

"Okay, I won't put up a note, so don't worry, *querida*," I gave in.

"Thank you," she said, and I knew she figured she had won out over publicity.

Bobby called the hospital and talked to his mother while

I was home. That small act helped to cheer up Maria, as it gave her a chance to thank him for the beautiful fruit basket. "He said they sent fruit rather than flowers, because he knew that I'm allergic to some flowers within a closed space, and besides, we couldn't *eat* the flowers," Nini said when she told me about his pleasant call.

Robbie called to say they were driving down to see Maria, and would arrive about 11:00. I suggested they go directly to the hospital, and I'd be waiting for them. So I was back in the hospital again by 10:30. The phone rang about 11:00, and it was the volunteer receptionist in the lobby, informing me the kids had arrived. I went down and met them in the main waiting room, where Larry was carrying a huge bouquet of mixed flowers, absolutely beautiful. Maxine and the girls were with them, and Sis had brought a pretty get-well card.

Robbie my namesake niece was a slender little thing, cuter than a Barbie doll at about 5'5" and not over 108 pounds, if that. Her happy face was punctuated with a darling pointed nose, and she had more energy than a barrel of "C" batteries. And most appealing, she was very thoughtful and loving.

Her husband, Larry, was a good 6'2" and somewhere around 175 pounds, with a shock of neatly trimmed wavy hair atop a usually red face, for he was very fair and was out in the Florida sun much of the time checking homes under construction as job superintendent.

He was a marvelous balance between toughness and understanding, between strict attention to details on the job, and easy-going relaxation at night, viewing a rental movie in the den at home. Sarah, age 9, was a tall girl with a lovely figure, a sweet face with blue eyes and dimples, a soft voice, and scads of glorious blond hair.

Laura, age 7, was a slight little thing, sharp as an icepick, with dark eyes and dark hair. She was vivacious and cocky, and although quite different from her older sister, was equally attractive and fascinating.

Both girls were quite smart, and very thoughtful, especially of Maria and me. They would make, rather than buy, the cards they gave us on various occasions, and they were always pretty and clever.

My sister Maxine, then 64, was widowed when Robbie was in the primary grades, so the two of them had struggled to survive together. Max was slender and blond, with a bit of gray mixed in. She was a pistol as a girl, but she had smoked all of her life, and now her lungs were almost shot.

She had helped to care for Maria when Bobby was born in San Diego while my ship was at the Battle of Okinawa. Her bright blue eyes stood out even more now, because her hair was thinner than normal.

There wasn't space in the room for more than three visitors, so I went up with Robbie and Larry, and Sis stayed in the lobby with the girls. Then Larry went back down, and Maxine came up to spend a few minutes with Maria and Robbie together. The children were not supposed to visit people in their rooms, but when Robbie and Larry descended, I went with them and took Sarah and Laura by the hand to the second floor.

In the central corridor, I was stopped at the nurses' station. "No children are allowed to visit in the rooms on this floor!" the duty nurse stated flatly.

"I know," I agreed with her, "But our two little grandnieces came all the way from Hudson to see Maria," I said. "They are gooder than little angels, so I'm sure we can bend the rules just a bit so they can say hello to their Great-aunt Maria, can't we?" If ever those two girls wore the looks of angels it was right at that moment—their halos were showing. The nurse looked at their seraphic faces, and saw nothing but Peace on 2nd Floor, Goodwill toward Maria. She didn't look that happy, but she relented. "All right, Robin, for a few minutes."

She now called me by my first name, a very common

custom in medical circles in the St. Pete area. While a 75-year old man is waiting in a doctors office, a slip of a young girl will walk into the waiting room, look at him and say, "The doctor will see you now, Walter."

The girls gave Maria big hugs, and kisses on her cheek, and then told her a bit about school, and hoped she would be well soon, and as the conversation petered out, Maxine took one in each hand, and prepared to leave.

"I'm going to take everybody to lunch, Mama," I said. "If your lunch comes before I get back, can you manage alone?"

"Of course, Daddy. Just wind my bed up a little higher, so I can use my table when lunch comes." I fixed the bed, kissed and hugged my darling, and descended with Sis and the girls. Larry followed me in their car, and we went to the Olde World Cheese Shop located on Pasadena Avenue just outside the main entrance to Bay Island. Everything there was served with flair—but too little flavor at times. We all ordered burgers, the girls dividing one between them, for they were always light eaters in a restaurant.

We left the Sheese House, as Maria called it, and drove on into the complex, to stop in our condo where I reviewed for them what we knew to date, but I couldn't tell them any more about the future than they already knew, because I myself had no idea what it would be like having Nini home again.

"I don't think it will be too tough," I said. "We'll get used to everything within a couple of weeks, I'm sure. I only hope that I can keep from being too nervous and tense. You know how I am."

"Sure, Uncle Bobby," Sarah piped up, "Mama says Uncle Bobby is always go, go, go!"

"Well, I'll have to practice sitting still, still, still for a while," I said, and laughed. "Strangely enough, we'd been thinking of going to Rio to visit Nivaldo and Ducle. They've been begging us to fly down. We were hoping to scrape up the money by May. But it doesn't look like we'll make it this year. Maria needs plenty of time to recuperate, especially emotionally."

"Yes, you're going to have to be very patient with her for a long time, Bobby," Maxine cautioned.

"I know. Believe it or not, since the word got around the compound here about Maria's operation, I've learned of several women in the complex who had mastectomies, even the lady who lives in the apartment right above ours!"

"No kidding!" Robbie was surprised.

"That's the truth; and there's at least three other women in this building that I know of. That's four out of thirty-two units . . . twelve percent of our group."

They all knew I was anxious to get back to Maria's side, so after a brief visit together, and quick trips to the bathroom, our guests gave me big hugs, tender kisses and warm handshakes. I walked to their car with them and waved as they departed. Then I headed back to the hospital, where Maria was finishing a lunch of tossed salad, swiss steak with 'taters and veggies, and a fruit cup. I helped her to a second cup of coffee, poured a dab for myself in a plastic cup, and we talked about how nice it was of Robbie, Larry and Sis to drive almost 40 miles through murderous city traffic just to bring Nini flowers and their best wishes.

"They're sure good youngsters," I said. And they really were. No drinking, no smoking, no chasing around, very kind and thoughtful to others, and with the sweetest little kids anyone could ask for, even if they were little imps once in a while when their enthusiasm bubbled over. As I told Maxine, "I look upon Robbie and Larry more like son and daughter than nephew and niece, and their girls like grandkids." In fact, a couple of times, I even introduced the girls as "my granddaughters, Sarah and Laura," and then blushed as Maria straightened me out!

Kathy called Nini at the hospital on Sunday, and had a

nice chat, for on an earlier call Maria had been able to talk for only a minute or two before she began to tire. But after a Saturday night dinner of broccoli soup, baked ham, and citrus sections dessert, plus a Sunday breakfast of orange juice, cereal, poached eggs and toast my partner was coming along very well.

She'd slept the last two nights with the little 'pillow' beneath her right arm, and now she felt quiet a lot better. She was back on her feed, and it looked to me as though she'd soon be back on her feet as well.

I spent most of Saturday afternoon and evening with her, had supper in the cafeteria Saturday night, made my own breakfast Sunday and spent most of the morning at her side. Lunch time came, and when the big rack full of food trays sat in the outer hall for 15 minutes and nobody made a move to distribute the trays, I went and found the tray with Maria's number on it, and helped her eat her lunch. All that chow sat in the hallway for another quarter of an hour before they finally carried the trays to the various rooms! Don't ask me why! Perhaps to be sure the food was not too hot when served.

Lunch was lentil soup, beef barbecue with veggies, strawberry mousse and hot chocolate to drink. It wasn't exactly gourmet, but it was very good food for a hospital to serve. And everything tasted delicious, according to Maria—and per the occasional sample I tested.

When Maria began to show signs of sleepiness after lunch, I tucked her in for a nap, had lunch in the cafeteria, and returned to the condo, where I read the Sunday paper and did a crossword puzzle. By that time it was 4:00 p.m., and I went back to Maria.

While we were visiting together, one of Maria's bridge-playing group, Lottie, arrived, carrying a pretty potted plant as a gift. Maria was delighted with her visit, and they had a good chat for half an hour, when Lottie said she'd better go so Maria could relax. I walked her to the elevator, while thanking the dear lady (who was well into her 80s) for coming to visit Maria. How she knew about Maria I don't know. But she was a sharp little gal, and if anyone would know, she would!

When the supper trays appeared from the kitchen, I pulled Maria's tray from the rack and started her on dinner; peach and cottage cheese salad, southern fried chicken with rice and carrots, and pear halves. I either watched, or helped as needed, while Maria did justice to her tray of comestibles.

"Don't expect to be fed like this when you get home!" I warned her, "unless I can buy take-out from the hospital!"

"Don't worry, Daddy, I'll fix our meals when I get home," my gallant spouse said.

"I know that. I was just teasing," I teased her some more.

Doctor Coe came by on his rounds, and asked Maria when she thought she'd want to go home.

"Tomorrow," Nini replied, which surprised him.

He examined her bare chest, for the heavy bandages had been removed. "Well, young lady," he said, "you are healing very, very well. I think we can let you go home tomorrow afternoon. Of course you'll still have the stitches in you. But you can come to my office to remove them in a few days. Nurse will set up the appointment for you."

By now, I'd caught a glimpse of Maria's right side, and like he said, there was no big round scar as I had so foolishly feared. The scar *did* look like a railroad track running across her chest from her left breast back to a spot beyond her right armpit. The 'track' consisted of a lot of narrow, ribbon-like adhesive tapes about two inches long, spaced half an inch apart across her chest, the tapes stuck on at right angles across the incision. The ends of some of those 'railroad ties' were coming loose, and I pointed them out to the doctor.

"Maria has already had a light shower, and the water loosens the tapes," he said. "You can continue to take warm showers at home, Maria. Just remember not to rub those little tapes too hard. But don't be worried if some of them fall off. That's kind of how we're going to let them go . . . as they please, like leaves on a tree in autumn fall when they're ready. If a few hang on until you come to take out the stitches, then we'll remove them. Just remember not to scrub your incision too hard. It's well healed, but we don't want to irritate it, do we?"

He seemed like a wonderful doctor, with a marvelous bedside manner, and his nurse was a veritable angel. She gave a lot of comfort and peace of mind to Maria. I was thankful they both were so nice to her.

Loyal little Kathy called, brightening Maria's evening. Kathy knew how to be both sympathetic and reassuring at the same time, which gave Maria both pleasure and courage. They had a long chat, until Maria began to tire, when they hung up.

We received get-well cards from some of Maria's friends, and from Kathy and gang. Even after Maria left the hospital, they forwarded a few of such cards. Maria had told no one about her coming operation; it simply leaked out when I was leaving for the hospital one afternoon and a neighbor in the next building was getting into his car with his wife.

They asked about Maria. "We've seen *you* coming and going the past few days, but we haven't seen Maria," the wife said.

So I told them about Maria's operation. They offered their sympathies, and I feel they mentioned Nini to others, and after some delay, Nini got cards from most of her friends.

Again I stayed with Nini until around 8:30 in the evening, with time out for a bite of supper downstairs. My angel had been sitting in her easy chair alongside the bed a good deal of the time, rather than lying in the sack all day, so there was no question in my mind but that she was coming along wonderfully. The surgeon had performed a fine operation, and except for a couple of instances, the care had been excellent as well. What I had greatly feared—after reading the many horror stories about people being infected while in the hospital—was that Nini might pick up staphylococcus in Sick Bay. But she healed quickly and properly, and happily enough, felt practically no pain during the process. They gave her Tylenol-3 the evening of the operation. Then the following morning the nurse gave her the pills, and Maria refused them at first, saying she felt no pain. But then she decided to take the pain-killer that morning, for she'd heard it was better to avoid pain than to let it start first and then take the medicine. But that evening she refused the medication, and never took a pain-killer again. She certainly didn't get into a drug habit!

Monday morning I was back at Maria's side to watch her consume orange juice, banana, French toast and coffee. Her appetite was hearty, which gave me further reassurance that she was recovering properly. To me, Nini had endured a monstrous operation, and I was relieved to see her over the roughest part.

I breakfasted in the cafeteria again, and then sat with Nini for an hour before returning to the condo, where I spent the rest of the morning vacuuming the carpet, scrubbing the kitchen floor, dusting, changing the bed linen so it would be fresh for Maria's return and running the dirty linen through the washer and dryer.

Back at the hospital, I helped Maria with lunch, then went to the cafeteria to eat, and by the time I returned, the discharge paperwork had been completed, and we could check out. I helped Maria dress, which included considerable preoccupation on her part as to what she should wear.

"I don't want people to know that I only have one breast," she spoke hesitantly, timidly.

"Honey, you mustn't worry about what other people see or think," I said. "But if you wish, we can pin the little pillow inside your bra, and you can wear your robe over that."

"But I'm afraid that might put pressure on my incision," she was reticent.

"That's why I think the best thing you could do is not to use a bra at all. Wear your dress and your robe, and I'll put the rest of your things in your suitcase. Remember, you will leave here in a wheelchair, so you'll be sitting down. No one will notice anything."

So that was how she dressed. A volunteer arrived with the wheelchair, Maria sat in it, and he rolled her to the elevator, and, once down in the lobby, on into the cashier's office. The volunteer left, and I paid for TV and telephone charges. "What about the extra charge for the private room?" I asked.

"We'll bill you for that later," the pleasant lady replied. "We'll send the bill to Medicare, and after they pay their share, we'll send the statement to you for the difference. If you have other insurance, you can then send the unpaid portion on to them. Medicare will send you a statement showing the part they paid to us, so you and the insurer know what remains unpaid." That dear lady had just begun my education regarding the processing of medical bills. I was glad she did, because keeping track of who had paid what, and how much we still owed to whom was enough to give a CPA the heebie-jeebies! I still had much to learn.

Now that we were free to leave, I pushed Maria outside under the portico, left her there, got the car, gently helped her in, returned the wheelchair to the lobby and drove home.

"Oh, Daddy, the water looks so beautiful today!" Maria said, as we crossed the inlet on the way home, and I realized the broad view of the bay just had to cheer her up after her days in that cubbyhole of a room.

"You're right, the bay is especially pretty today," I said. "I know you'll be happy to be back where you can look out the front windows and see the water and the birds. The blue heron was there this morning, a snowy egret was next door, and several pelicans were squatting or paddling around on the seawall."

We reached our carport, I helped Nini out of the car, and

we walked into our apartment—Maria holding my arm, and carefully covering herself so as to conceal the effect of her operation. To her utter relief, there wasn't a soul around.

"Boy! The place is really clean!" Maria cried as we moved through the apartment to the master bedroom.

"Well of course!" I replied. "What did you expect to find, a condo looking like a sow's bed?"

"Well, not exactly. But I didn't expect to find things so neat... everything dusted, the bed made and turned down, the carpet vacuumed, the kitchen sparkling, and no dirty dishes in the sink. I'm really proud of you, Daddy."

"No, *querida*, I'm the one who is really proud of *you*," I said, and gathered her gently in my arms for a warm hug and a kiss in her sugar bowl. God, it was nice to have my little chickabiddy home again! I helped her stretch out in bed to rest for an hour, after which she snuggled down into her easy chair in the living room.

"You can't imagine how good it feels to be back in my own little home," Maria observed as she peeked out the window at the egret moving about outside the door, and she squiggled down deeper into her lounge chair—much the way a mother robin settles down over the four pale-blue eggs in her cozy nest.

CHAPTER 7

Slowly we picked up our lives where they'd been so unhappily interrupted. It was still too incredible to believe. Maria had gone for a routine physical examination; and now, a mere 13 days later, she was back home after enduring a total mastectomy! Events had swirled past so swiftly that I don't believe either of us had truly grasped their import.

My precious wife, whose beautiful bosom had been one of the great joys of my life, was now sitting beside me with one of those breasts cruelly removed because of that vicious attacker. How thankful we were, though, that Maria had found the tiny lump the very morning of her annual physical—for there was every possibility her doctor might not have noticed it during his routine examination. Conceivably, that could have delayed discovery for at least another year.

The only good news to date was the pathologist's report concerning the excised lymph nodes. They were cancer-free. That seemed to indicate the insidious growth had not spread to any other part of Nini's body, or 'metastasized', as they put it in medical jargon.

Cancer's tend to send out scouting parties via the bloodstream, and sometimes one of those explorers will latch onto cells in another area, and produce another cancer. The process is much like the way European nations sent out colonists to take hold in the New World after Columbus discovered it—colonists who quickly preempted chunks of territory for their own.

Kathy called again that evening, and talked with her dear

mama at home for a change, and again her words were cheerful but caring as she bolstered her mother's spirits with her happy voice and consoling words. Always she told her mother not to worry, and not to be overly preoccupied with her appearance. "You're going to be just fine, Mama," she said. "I know Daddy is going to take good care of you, and you will soon be playing tennis!"

"Playing tennis?" Maria cried. "I've never played tennis in ny life!"

"Well, I had to think of *something* ridiculous in a hurry!" Kathy chuckled, and Maria laughed at her preposterous remark.

The doctor gave us a page of instructions, and Maria followed them sedulously. When she sponged off and some of her 'railroad ties' peeled off on the shower floor, she knew that was okay. She towelled off carefully, with me doing her back so she didn't have to strain. She babied her incision, which at first was a raw red streak across her chest. Then as she healed, the ugly crimson slash faded to pink, and finally turned white.

When the bills came drifting in I was overwhelmed. The charges came to over $6,300 dollars, just for the hospital. To that had to be added $670 for the anesthesiologist, $265 for the visits of the substitute doctor for two evenings, $330 for the pathologist, $1,600 for the surgeon, and $330 for his assistant. Without counting preliminary x-rays and tests, the bills came to just over $9,500, a startling figure. How lucky we were that Medicare would cover a substantial portion of the amount, and our Prudential insurance would pick up a lot of the remainder. But we would still spend hundreds of dollars for that life-saving surgery and hospital stay.

The evening after Maria came home, we called Nivaldo to tell him all had gone well. It was a relief to Maria to be able to discuss her operation with her doctor brother, who was extremely sympathetic, and offered a few additional words of caution as she progressed in her recuperation.

We spoke with Dulce, too, who now showed her true colors. "Oh, Nini, you should come to Rio and stay with us while you recuperate. We can look after you, and make you very comfortable here in our apartment. And we can go up to our mountain home in Nova Friburgo for a few days at a time, where the air is so healthful. Please come down right away!" I had never heard kinder words in all my life.

Of course we begged off—for there were too many things to do and to consider. The surgeon wanted to see Maria every week for a while. And when he said it was time, my darling had to buy a prosthesis to wear. That had to be done before she would feel like traveling overseas. And of course there was the money for our tickets, which we didn't have. So we thanked Dulce from the bottoms of our hearts, and agreed to visit them at the earliest possible moment.

"Are you sure you don't want to go to Rio as soon as possible?" I asked Maria after we'd hung up.

"Not for a while," Nini said. "I have to get used to having only one breast, and I will have many visits to the doctor before I'm healed. All that has to happen before I can think of visiting anybody."

A few days later I did my best to encourage her to go out, and begin to move her life ahead. "Would you like to go for a little ride, honey?" I asked.

"Not for a while," Nini said. "Remember, I am a shicken with only one wing now . . . and I have to get used to that strange and unbelievable fact before I can think of going out." Maria's words struck me like a knife, but they revealed what a courageous woman she was, and the stab of pain which hit within my heart was washed away by her laugh.

"You are the bravest person I've ever known," I said, as I hugged and kissed her after her surprising quip. Even her cute mispronunciation of 'chicken' sent a flood of warmth through my whole being.

"We do what we have to do, *querido*," she smiled softly.

"I can't believe how bravely you managed through those few days *before* your operation, really I can't."

"I wasn't so brave," she confessed. "Every once in a while when I was alone in the kitchen a heavy wave of worry and remorse would boil up inside me . . . and I'd rattle hell out of the pots and pans to keep from breaking into tears. No, I'm not very brave," she finished. But of course she was.

I remembered the lines of a quatrain I'd written years and years before:

> When bitter thoughts assail my mind,
> And sadness floods my heart with pain;
> I put those bitter thoughts behind,
> And fill my heart with joy again.

Maria now provided a paraphrase for a couple of those lines:

> When bitter thoughts within me well,
> I rattle pots and pans like hell.

Nini returned to the surgeon's office on the 28th to remove the stitches from her incision. Most of the railroad ties had fallen off by then, so the cross-stitching of her scar was more visible. Maria had been worried about removing the stitches; so on our way back to the car I asked if it hurt.

"Only a couple of times, like pin-pricks," she said, "but mostly I didn't feel a thing, just painless little tugs."

"I'm sure glad to hear that," I said. "That half a yard of incision had too doggone many stitches! Doctor Coe must have sewn on your for half an hour!"

That red-headed man had stolen Maria's heart, I believe,

for she always left his office in the blithest of spirits. He was kindly, attentive and apparently capable and skillful. And his staff—including the nurse who accompanied him on his rounds—was comprised of an exceptional group of lovely women and girls. Again, how fortunate it was that we had such a capable doctor just across the strip of bay, so close to home and so convenient to the hospital. After that visit Maria was doubly delighted, because the doc said she could now take regular showers instead of light 'sponge-bath' showers.

Mother's Day arrived, and I gave Maria a card and some flowers. After I coaxed her a bit, she pinned the little pillow in her bra, and we went to dinner at a seafood restaurant. That was her first outing, except to the doctor's office. Nini had ventured forth to confront the world just three weeks after her surgery. Things were coming along just fine.

My sweetheart was almost back to living a normal life, except that every now and then I would catch her with a pensive look as she sat in her easy chair, and I knew what she was thinking. She worried too much about her appearance, magnifying in her mind a blemish which most people would ignore. Even worse, she never could drive from her mind the pale apparition of cancer which I knew haunted her perpetually—the same as it worried me.

Maria returned for another check-up with her surgeon, who said she was healing beautifully. He suggested that Maria have a plastic surgeon do a reduction operation on her left breast. That would enable her to use a smaller prosthesis on the right side.

Maria rejected the suggestion outright.

Again I took Maria to her surgeon for a check-up, and again he was convinced that everything was fine and dandy, and that healing was progressing very well, though Maria complained of an occasional sharp pain, under the scar, near her breastbone.

"Those are just healing pangs, to be expected," the doctor said. "They'll go away eventually." I was with Nini when the doctor checked her this time because I was preoccupied with those 'pangs'. Now I felt better.

Our upstairs neighbors had talked with us on more than one occasion after Maria returned home. That lady had also had a mastectomy, and she did her best to cheer up Maria and to dispel her misgivings. And I remember the words of her chunky husband.

"All it really takes is a lot of love and understanding, and everything will be all right," he said, and he gave Maria a warm embrace. So did his charming wife, and we thanked them for the consolation they gave us. I say 'us' because I believe I suffered almost as much, emotionally, as my dear wife.

First of all, I was deeply affected by her stoicism in the face of that operation and the subsequent worries which surely festered deep within her subconscious; and second, I had to make certain that Nini understood, completely, that on my part, she was just as beautiful and as deeply loved as she'd ever been; and third, I had to control my conversation sedulously, so as not to say something, inadvertently, that in any way might cause her to think I was insensitive to her feelings.

As I mentioned before, there were many people involved in Maria's operation—people we didn't know, and some we never saw. We had supposed that all the expenses involved would be handled through Medicare first, and then we'd take care of the balance.

But that turned out to be a misconception—nobody used the same system of billing, and I had to puzzle out which program each care provider was using, and try to fit my actions to it. That particular problem began to resolve itself later on, and billings from virtually all caregivers began to flow 1) to MediCare, 2) to the insurance company, and 3) to me for the remaining unpaid balance.

The anesthesiologist's fee was separate from that of the hospital, even though the hospital had charged us quite a bit for the drugs and equipment he used for the anesthesia. When I got his bill for $672, I had no way of paying it, so I wrote to him:

> Dear Doctor Y; Thank you for offering to submit this claim to Medicare for us after we paid you. Actually, we had the impression that you would submit your bill first to Medicare, and then to us for any balance due. Our separate group insurance with Prudential will only pay us after Medicare has paid their share. So we ask that you please submit your bill to Medicare, and then we can take care of any balance, although we assume that you charge at the rate Medicare authorizes for such operations. (He did not. He overcharged—greatly!)
>
> Since you made no mention of the fact that you intended to bill us directly when we talked in the hospital the evening before the operation, I think we had the right to assume you would follow the program the surgeons and the hospital are following.
>
> Thank you very much for your cooperation in this matter, for we just don't have the money right now to pay this bill.

The man did as I requested, and Medicare paid him $342, and he sent us a bill for the balance in July, and I sent our check for the remaining $330, which took care of the anesthesiologist. By the end of July, Prudential had reimbursed us for 80% of that remaining cost which I had paid.

Poor Maria's troubles seemed to come in batches now, for just a week after her operation, she had a lot of pain in one foot. It was a Saturday, so I took her to a clinic where a doctor examined her and said she had gout. He prescribed some pills for her, telling her she'd have to take the drug for the rest of her life. She later went to a podiatrist, who said she should have a bunion removed and a big toe straightened out, but then referred her to a doctor who specialized in arthritis, for it was his opinion that she didn't have gout, but arthritis.

When I took her to the arthritis expert, he took one look at her foot and said she didn't have arthritis *or* gout. We had promptly accepted the first doctor's diagnosis, because of the fact that Nivaldo suffered considerably with gout, and we thought perhaps it ran in the family. The only nice thing about that whole 'gout-arthritis' episode was that when the nurse asked the arthritis specialist how much to charge Maria for his quick examination, he told her, "Don't charge her anything; I didn't do anything for her!"

The only thing 'so rare as a day in June' is a visit to a doctor's office without paying.

That whole unusual situation came about because the pain in Maria's foot—possibly a result of the operation—got so bad that I took her to a medical clinic nearby, for it was the weekend, her regular doctor's office was closed and I didn't want her to suffer for several days before she saw a medic.

There were other things to think about besides my darling's traumatic operation, for life at home and in the world around us continued unabated. Like millions of other people who had suffered, or were suffering, physical set-backs, Maria would endure, and had already begun to take an interest in national and world events. One of those events involved the American medical profession, and was unbelievably terrifying.

But let me first add a word of background on that international debacle.

During World War II, while I was in Iceland on the *Melville*, a Navy Repair ship, and the Russians were driving the Germans back toward Poland, I kept a large map of Russia on which I entered the 'front line' from day to day as we got the news by radio about Russian gains or losses. I'd fixed on the city of Kiev as being of critical importance, and watched as the Russians fought their way to it.

Now the city of Kiev made the headlines once more, and again the news was critical. In the town of Pripyak some 60 miles from Kiev, on April 25, the world came the closest yet to a nuclear disaster—for at the Chernobyl plant there was an explosion in a nuclear reactor which blasted the roof off the plant, began an actual core meltdown—just as depicted in the movie 'China Syndrome'—and spewed radiation across Finnland and Sweden.

Freak winds carried the radiation northwest, rather than east, sparing most of the Soviet Union, but causing the Swedes to restrict their children from drinking milk, and doing inestimable damage to the great herds of reindeer in Lapland, where the fallout settled into the food on which the reindeer fed.

People had to be evacuated from the area by the thousands, apartment buildings became empty ghosts, and there was great fear that the nearby rivers would spread the atomic pollution even farther. American doctors flew to Russia to perform bone-marrow transplants in an attempt to save some who were hardest stricken. The Russians had a far worse mess on their hands than America had had with the Three Mile Island screw-up. I wondered whose reactor would be next to blow up and strew death and destruction around like a hell on earth?

I insert this item to bring out an interesting, but sad, point. American doctors rushed off to Russia to give *free* bone marrow transplants to 'burn' victims of an unfriendly country; while people in America who were suffering from cancer were dying from lack of a bone marrow transplant, partly because the costs were so exorbitant they couldn't afford one, and the fact that insurance companies, Medicaid and Medicare balked at the cost.

We called Kathy the evening of the 27th, just to keep *her* phone bill from becoming exorbitant. She was still laying her

72

plans to visit us in June, and although I was worried about the effect that a rambunctious two-year old might have on Maria's nerves and consequently on her recovery, I did nothing to discourage their visit. Since Maria would have two months to recuperate before they arrived, their visit probably wouldn't be too bad for her physically, and would surely cheer her up emotionally.

Because we were staying pretty close to home all this time, I had to keep busy at something to ease my worry over Maria. She was coming along fine, even fixing our light meals most of the time after a few days.

I'd been preparing a book of my collected poems which I planned to produce myself by setting up a publishing company. I had to register a name, rent a post office box and apply to the state for sales tax registration, all the miserable complexities which often combine to keep a potential small business man from ever entering business.

I called the County Clerk's office and asked, "Is the name 'Gulf Coast Publishing Company' available for use?" One purpose of registering a name is to keep others from using it, and if that name were already in use, I couldn't take it.

"No, that name has not been taken," the lady replied after checking.

"Thank you," I said.

I named Maria Moura as our General Manager, because by using Maria's maiden name, it kept the Gulf Coast Publishing Company from looking like a one-book, family operation, which it would probably turn out to be. I wrote to the newspaper:

> Enclosed is my check for $20.00 in payment for publication of a fictitious company name. I have checked the official records, and the name is not already in use.
>
> Please publish as per legal requirements, and send me the affidavit for same. Thank you.

73

Getting back into the swing of things, and trying to lead a life similar to what we had been enjoying before lightning struck, was a psychological tonic for both Maria and me. It got our minds off the horrible set-back Nini had sustained, and gave us something to look forward to day by day.

Bobby's 41st birthday arrived, but sadly, Bobby did not call, and for some reason we failed to call him. With all of the changes in our lives and routines, Bobby's birthday just eased on past once we'd mailed a card to him, and neither Maria nor I noticed our failure to call. Perhaps we felt less sorry for our lack of action because for years Bobby never called *us* on such occasions, nor sent either of us a card. Kathy would send a card, and a present, and would call, too! She compensated for Bobby's lack of filial grace and attention.

CHAPTER 8

The doctor who filled in for Maria's regular doctor those three evenings in the hospital sent his bill through Medicare, and they approved $164 of the $225 he'd billed us. Of the approved amount, Medicare paid only $129.89. I was irked, to put it mildly, because the doctor had the gall to charge an extra $125 for a 'first consultation' as he called it. And I was even more irritated that Medicare let the thing go through, though they chopped it to $1OO 'approved'. I made up my mind to complain about that charge, because I was certain the doctor would come after me for any balance Medicare didn't cover.

But when I called the doctor's office, a snotty young woman promptly responded in no uncertain terms: "Doctor doesn't discuss his bills with patients!"

How about that? I could discuss my phone bill with GTE, my water and sewer bill with the city, an item on my account with any department store, but I had no right to ask a doctor I didn't know—and hadn't asked for—why he was charging me for something he hadn't delivered!

Anybody and everybody else I'd ever done business with had always been happy to explain their charges, but not Doctor X. He had installed a wall between himself and his clients, and let some obnoxious woman in his bookkeeping department refuse to explain his ridiculous fees.

On our next visit to our own doctor, I complained to the office girl about Doctor X's charges. She amazed me when she said, "Doctor Jones does the same thing when he makes the rounds for Doctor X."

"And does he refuse to discuss his bill with the other doctor's client, too?"

"That is right," she replied.

"It may be correct," I said, "but it damned well isn't *right!*" And would you believe it? There beside me in the waiting room was a gentleman in his 80s who had come to question our doctor about that selfsame thing on *his* bill! He got the same run-around as we'd gotten with Doctor X. To me it was all quite clear. Doctors made those neat arrangements between themselves to rip off patients. When one needed a few extra dollars to meet the payment on the Porsche, he 'made the rounds' for another doctor and overcharged the patient, as Mr. Y had done to us. Later, he'd return the favor for the first doctor. I call that a reciprocating money-making engine, powered by avarice.

It made me wonder how doctors had grown so infernally greedy over the years. A doctor not only overcharged some of his patients, but he also refused to discuss those charges. It was the sort of thing that would make you want to put up a statue in his honor when he died—and rather hope you had to order it soon.

In the meantime, the pathologist had submitted his bill to Medicare in the amount of $334. But instead of paying him, Medicare sent us one of their machine print-out letters with some comment that "We are processing a claim for you and cannot complete this processing without the information requested below. Please answer each question and return to us in the enclosed envelope." It was all gobbledy-gook to me, for the question was, "Please provide employer plan's primary payment sheet for services rendered from Apr. 16 to Apr. 18, 1986." I hadn't the foggiest idea what that meant!

The form came to me amidst the shower of other bills, claim forms and filings, and not understanding what in the devil Medicare was asking, and thinking it was merely something they had sent me a copy of, as they did with their payments, I stuck it in the file. On the 19th, Medicare sent me a note saying they'd denied the pathologist's charges—the poor guy hadn't been paid a cent in all that time! Not knowing what was going on, I sent the bills to Prudential, along with the Medicare denial. They paid the doctor some $160 on the bill. Then I got a note from a lady working for Prudential:

> Dear Mr. Leatherman; I contacted Medicare and was told this claim was randomly selected to audit whether or not your wife had a *primary* group insurance plan. As she does not, all you need to do is write on the original Medicare Statement that Medicare is the primary carrier for Maria and that you want the claim reinstated.

With Medicare's payment, and Prudential's contribution made, I paid the balance and cleared the account at last. It was interesting that I never once got a call from the pathologist's office, whose payment was held up by an 'audit' checking on folks who were totally ignorant of the devious ways not only of doctors, but of the Medicare bureaucrats as well!

As to our anesthesiologist, it was my belief that he lurked around in the background, regularly charged his patients more than Medicare allowed, then made them pay the overage—a neat ploy which I believe became illegal later on—and, surprisingly, one which made anesthesiology one of the highest paying specialties in the medical profession.

As things returned somewhat to normal at the Leatherman residence, I began to catch up on other matters which had fallen behind while I spent my days with Maria at the hospital. I wrote to Nadine Hutson in Parkdale, Oregon:

Please excuse me for not writing sooner concerning the coming class reunion. But I had been waiting to have the Alma Mater *(which I had written)* set up in readable form so I could send you some copies.

Enclosed are four copies, words and music. Printers won't print just a few copies of sheet music, but the copies I enclose can be photocopied.

I'm sorry to say that my Maria underwent serious surgery two weeks ago, so as of now we don't know whether or not we'll be able to attend the 50th reunion. For that reason, I suggest you and Vince Orcutt ask someone else to be master of ceremonies.

Best wishes for a great reunion, and if we don't make it, give our regards and congratulations to all those present. Sincerely, Robin.

Parkdale was a tiny farm-town in the upper end of the Hood River Valley in Oregon, nestled against the base of snow-capped Mt. Hood. I'd gone to high school there as a freshman and sophomore. Then my family moved to the Lower Valley, and I finished the last two years at Hood River High. The city of Hood River, perched on the cliffs above the Columbia River, was the county seat, with a few thousand people. The two schools were about 20 miles apart. Over the years Maria and I attended reunions of both.

Among other things, the Hood River Valley is famous for its fine apples and superb pears. In the spring the orchards stretch for miles in a blaze of glory, the air is laden with the perfume of the blossoms and the total effect is everlasting on one's mind. The music I wrote Is like a hymn, of course. These are the lyrics which I sent Nadine, an ex-Hood River High classmate living in Parkdale:

Hood River High Alma Mater

Above Columbia's wind-swept fount
So proudly stands Hood River High;
Behind it, Oregon's famous mount
Thrusts snow-clad shoulders to the sky.
Around, in perfumed panoply
Across the Valley's verdant breast
The flow'ring fruit trees fill the eye
With glorious promise, heav'n blest.

How proud we are to sing thy praise,
Oh, school we hold so fondly dear;
How bitter-sweet will be those days
Which mark our sad departure here.
We've shared the joys of friends so true,
We've suffered also at their tears,
With such rich mem'ries we'll pursue
Our lives down thru the circling years.

For when at last we leave thy halls,
To face a world with perils fraught,
We'll dream of life within thy walls,
Of us who learned, and those who taught.
For tho' we travel foreign lands,
Or climb to heights that touch the sky,
We'll ne'er forget those guiding hands
That helped us at Hood River High.

That same day I took Maria to see her regular doctor, who, of course, followed up with Maria after her operation, since he had recommended the surgeon to her. According to Maria, he was most pleased with the results of Doctor Coe's work. That put our minds at ease, reenforcing the surgeon's opinion that my beloved was progressing quite nicely, and that the vicious little cancer had been completely excised.

The following day, May 3, the U.S. space program had its third foul-up in a row, when a Delta rocket was launched at Cape Canaveral, lost power on lift-off, went veering off course and had to be destroyed by ground control. Along with the rocket, a $57-million dollar weather satellite (badly needed in space) was blown to smithereens. If people heading up our space program hadn't been sweating before, surely they ought to be now, for their butts had to be in hot water.

The real problem with such disasters, however, is that there's so much bureaucracy involved it's virtually impossible to pinpoint the culprits and nail them to the mast.

My own ideas on the subject of such governmental blunders are very simple: if there's a screw-up, you fire the top man in the civilian agency involved, demote the top military leader who is directly in charge (other than flight crews), and demand the dismissal of the Chairman of the Board of any negligent contractor involved. If his company does not fire him, then sue the corporation for negligence. Within a short time, the whole operation will begin to function much more responsibly. But without individual accountability. as against corporate or bureaucratic responsibility, things will get no better fast. In fact, they are slowly getting worse.

It was time to order letterheads and envelopes for my Gulf Coast Publishing Company. Maria went with me when I ordered the stationery, for we stopped off at the surgeon's office for another check-up on the way. I'd reached the point now where I knew the exact number of tiles in the waiting room ceiling, and the number of layers of art paper in the unusual 'impression' of a desert scene which hung on one wall.

Bobby called us to thank us for the card for Melissa, and check for Tina's First Communion. He was most happy to hear that his mother was getting along great. But sadly, Judy did not get on the line—she was still nursing her wounded pride at having been 'kicked out of the house' after one visit they made, which of course she had not been. She merely flounced out of the house in a fit of pique—or as Nini said later, "On a peak of fits."

The next day, Maria came home from the beauty salon looking like a new woman. For on that day she had gone to her usual beautician for a color touch-up and a wash-and-set. Now she *really* felt better. Nothing can perk up a woman more than a pleasant visit to her beauty salon. Since it had been almost four weeks between appointments, that trip was especially refreshing for my pet.

Kathy called on the 10th, to bring us up to date on life in the Navy, and to hear that her mama was doing just great, as well as to say she was still planning to make the flight from Seattle to Tampa airport, and kept praying that Terry would be a good boy on the plane—for it would be a long trip for him.

The next day I took Maria to dinner at Doe-Al's Southern Cookin' restaurant. The small eatery was owned by two sumptuous black ladies who really knew how to fix southern dishes. We left completely stuffed—also satiated—on barbecued chicken, black-eyed peas, collard greens, yams, and trimmings, held down by huge slices of incredibly glorious sweet potato pie.

Following a sample form shown in the book I'd bought on 'how to publish a book', I made up my own Request for Quotation form to send to several printers, inserting the specifications for the book, with a covering letter to several of them. Rose Printing Company, of Tallahassee, Florida was conveniently near, and Maria and I had met their salesman at a meeting of self-publishers in Tampa. We were delighted when their bid was lowest.

I'd received a special form from the Florida Freelance Writers Association, requesting information to be inserted in their new Florida Directory. Actually, I believe I was the only freelance writer in Florida with a broken spear! I sent the form back, showing that I had been published in the *St. Petersburg Times* and in several private house organs; and that I spoke Portuguese and would take assignments in Brazil. Had I been worried about being snowed under by a storm of jobs, my fears were soon laid to rest. I never got a single inquiry.

The next thing I wrote would be a letter to another old friend out in Oregon, also about a class reunion, but without an Alma Mater. Parkdale High had about 75 students in all four classes.

Chapter 9

In Brazil, the people sometimes say, "This is the day the month meows," referring to the 15th of the month which is payday for many. On the day that May meowed, we got a phone call from Kathy to check up on her mother and fill us in on her coming trip to our place; and we got another call from Nivaldo and Dulce in Rio, also checking on Maria's progress, and again urging us to fly down there and allow Nini to recuperate at their place.

That same day, I wrote to Melvin Monroe regarding the class reunion of Parkdale high. It was interesting that Mel, who arranged the Parkdale reunion, lived in Portland; and Nadine, who arranged the Hood River reunion, lived in Parkdale. I wrote to Mel:

> Please forgive me for being so dilatory in replying to your letter of January 20. We are still unsure whether we'll be able to attend the 50th reunion of our Parkdale High class. We both wanted so much to be there. But Maria underwent serious surgery not too long ago, and we are not certain she'll be up to making that 3,000-mile trip. In the event we don't make it, please express our love and best wishes to all that wonderful old gang. The days in Parkdale High were about the happiest days of my life. I'll never forget those times, nor you folks.

83

Another event on 'meow' day was that we got the final bill from Pines of Ponderosa Hospital, and I mailed them our check for over $400 dollars to cover the portion not covered by medicare or insurance, clearing their $6,300 charges.

To break the monotony of sitting around the apartment, I took Maria to lunch at the Columbia Restaurant in Ybor City on Friday. By then she had grown less uncomfortable about her operation. We drove across the bay to Tampa and on to Ybor City. Lunch was excellent, and afterward we visited the building which had once housed a cigar manufacturing company, to stroll through the gift shops located inside.

In the Red Horse, a place specializing in out-of-print items, I dug through the old postcards in a box labelled 'Oregon', and came across two interesting old cards which I bought for $2.50.

One card was a scene of Castle Rock on the edge of the Columbia River—the rock which Maria and I had once climbed, and which Lewis and Clark described in their expedition Journal. The card showed only the Washington State side of the river, but the caption read, 'Banks of the Columbia River, Oregon'. It was mailed by a man living in Portland to a lady in Washington, D.C. on Feb. 12, 1907, eleven years before I was born, and had a 1-cent postage stamp with a view of B. Franklin.

The second postcard had been mailed by a tourist lady in Portland to a friend in Champaign, Illinois, in August, 1937, shortly after I joined the Navy. It bore a picture of the old tunnel under Mitchell's Point near Hood River—as the highway used to be before the Interstate was built; before they blasted away that section of the sharp cliff's base, leaving no trace of the picturesque tunnel with its five arched windows affording views of the Columbia River.

How could I not buy such a treasure from the days of my youth in Oregon? That was the second time I'd located a picture of the old Mitchell Point tunnel.

Perhaps it was from the trip to Ybor City, perhaps not, but the next day Maria awoke with a sore throat. The following day, which was Saturday, she obviously needed medical attention so I took her once more to the nearby clinic. There the doctor made a smear test, said she had a strep throat, and gave us a prescription for pills to fight the infection. Sunday she was feeling much better. But for a while she suffered simultaneously from 1) her operation, 2) high blood pressure, 3) fake gout and 4) strep throat! In her case, when it rained it didn't just pour, it deluged! That clinic visit was exactly one month after her operation.

I was still rankled by that extra $125 charge the substitute doctor had tacked onto his bill for visiting Maria on his rounds. And the more I thought about it, the more it bothered me. When at last we got a check from Medicare relative to his services, I wrote to him:

> Enclosed is our check for $129.89 the amount Medicare reimbursed us for your services.
>
> We cannot understand your charge of $125 for a first consultation. It was our understanding that Doctor Jones asked you to take his place while he was out of town. *(It turned out that Doctor Jones never left town. We met him in the corridor and asked about the trip and he said he didn't go!)* We have no question regarding your fee for the three hospital visits and the reading of Maria's EKG. However, we feel that your $125 fee for a first consultation is unfair.
>
> Since a 'first consultation' normally includes an office visit, and extra time with the new patient, and usually a more complete check-up, we do not feel your fee is proper, and have already expressed our feelings on this matter with Doctor Jones. *(We already knew that Doctor Jones did the same thing when he took Doctor X's place—which made one wonder, did they use*

*that ploy regularly just to pick up an extra $125 to help
each other out with the BMW repairs?)*
I trust that Medicare's payment will cover your fee,
which still gives you $29.89 extra for filling out a card
for your file and mailing us your bill.

The response to my letter was a stinging telephone call
from the doctor's collections expert, who, with a voice
charged with acid, etched my eardrum in no uncertain terms,
saying they demanded full payment for their bill as submitted, or they'd turn the matter over to a collection agency or
sue us, whichever!

One nice thing about the clinic on St. Pete Beach—we
didn't have to pay a cent the day I took Maria there to check
her sore throat. They sent their bill directly to Medicare, and
after Medicare paid them $30.69, I paid them the balance of
$7.31. That was in sharp contrast to our substitute doc, both
as to the treatment of the billing and of the patient—as well
as to the amount of the charges.

A story came out in the paper on May 25 concerning the
manner in which deposed President Ferdinand Marcos of the
Philippines had earned millions of dollars selling illegal logging rights through friends and relatives. The article by Gregg
Jones stated that when Marcos took office in 1965, the islands had nearly 35-million acres of forested land. By the
time Marcos left office, only 5.5-million acres were still standing. The new regime of President Corazon Aquino said that
if the illegal logging wasn't stopped, the Philippines would
be denuded in 15 years. Marcos had operated his scam by
granting 100s of illegal logging concessions to friends and
relatives, including his sister, his closest palace adviser, loyal
political leaders and even Muslim guerrillas who had surren-
dered. He set up a series of 'paper loggers' who could earn
'royalty fees' up to $50,000 a month. Gregg said the Japa-

nese government refused to help the new Philippine government trace the flow of logs smuggled to Japan.

Georgia-Pacific (for whom I had worked in Brazil) was exporting lauan veneer, a type of Philippine mahogany, from their operation at Lianga, on the island of Mindanao. I wondered if they, too, had to pay the 'paper loggers' for the right to export their product. They might well be paying for the rights without actually knowing they were, because of Marcos' convoluted licensing procedures.

What Marcos did to the Philippine forests, was the same thing that was being done in Brazil's Amazon country when Maria and I were there—the ruinous exploitation of the rich jungle by selectively hewing down the greatest trees, destroying the so-called 'lungs of the world' and leaving the marvelous Amazon country, and its myriad species of plants and animals, in such a state of ruin they would take centuries to recover, *if* they ever did. In Brazil's case, the depredations of the gold miners, especially in the north, were wreaking destruction even on the ground itself—in addition to the atrocious deforestation.

Maria and I had lived in the jungle several years at Portel, up the Amazon about 200 miles from Belem, the capital of the huge state of Para. I was controller of a Georgia-Pacific subsidiary employing some 1,200 men and women turning the great forest giants into veneer, plywood and lumber, mostly for export.

After I read the article to Maria she looked at me and shook her head. "I know you made a good salary in Portel, but in a way I am sorry we took part in destroying the *matto grosso.* She used her native language term for 'dense jungle'.

'You're right, honey," I said. "Every time I watched a huge lathe bite into a magnificent *muiritinga* log several feet in diameter and convert it into a long, thin strip of veneer, I felt a twinge of remorse. I think it was because we flew over so many such trees when we traveled back and forth between

Belem and Portel, and I felt a kinship with them. They rose so commandingly over the other trees around them ... regal specimens standing guard over their subordinates. I always hated the idea of chopping them down and cutting them up!"

Our stay of nearly five years in the G-P encampment at Portel, and our concurrent trips through other parts of Brazil are set forth in a volume of my Memoirs.

Kathy called on the 26th, and she and her mother had a fine visit, which cheered up my little chickabiddy immensely. Those two always had much to talk about, and now more than ever, with Kathy planning her flight to Florida, and Maria recovering from her operation and plagued by a host of minor physical ailments.

On the 28th, Maria went to check a sore throat again, the doctor taking a throat culture to see if it was streptococcus, which it was not. Her 'gout' was having a resurgence, so the doctor put her back on Indosin and told her not to take aspirin, to take Tylenol instead, for aspirin irritated gout. The so-called gout didn't disappear overnight however, and during the last few days of May my darling suffered intensely from the pain in her foot.

We finally came to believe that the pain was brought on by the elastic stockings which the hospital had advised Maria to keep using at home for a while. She saw her regular doctor on the 30th, but he gave her no help with her problem, for he offered no opinion regarding the tight stockings. Thinking they might be the problem, Maria stopped wearing them, disregarding the hospital's suggestion. We decided they definitely *were* the cause of her pain, however, when a short time after discontinuing their use, Maria's gout went away and never returned! That was not only a case of improper 'over-nursing', but one which added a $25 pair of stockings to an already shocking bill.

An article in Friday's paper caught my eye, for it said the American Institute of Architects had placed a house designed by Frank Lloyd Wright at the top of the list of the 10 most interesting buildings in the U.S.. The item had a picture of Wright's fabulous 'Falling Waters' residence located on Bear Run in Pennsylvania.

In Pennsylvania, a 'run' is a 'creek', and the house was cantilevered from the low cliff out over that small stream.

"Look here, honey," I said, handing the paper to Maria. "Remember when we went to see this house in Pennsylvania during the Claim Conference?"

"I remember it well," Nini replied. "It's very unusual and interesting, but with that rock sticking up in the living room right in front of the fireplace, and so many ups and downs, I wouldn't want to live in it!" We both laughed, for that was exactly what she had said to the tour guide as we explored the home built over a small waterfall.

"Of course it's famous because of the way Mr. Wright built it by blending it into the rocky landscape, and even making the creek a part of the house, as well as the native rock in the floor."

"Exactly!" Maria said. "Who needs a creek running through the house? What if it floods? It could ruin the carpets!"

Of the 10 buildings listed in the paper, Maria and I had seen six, including MOMA in New York, also designed by Wright. We reviewed our impressions of the buildings we had seen, and for a few moments we relived many of the happy days of the past, offering some surcease from the bitterness of our more recent days.

CHAPTER 10

Maria's surgeon had not yet sent us his bill. I suppose he waited until he'd made the routine follow-up checks. Finally, the last day of May, he submitted a bill for $1,600, along with that of the assistant surgeon, another $330, a total of $1,930. I sent the bills off to Medicare, and waited for their check. It was interesting that doctors who submitted their bills directly to Medicare over a computer were paid within a few days; but when we submitted a doctor's bill, it took weeks to hear from them, and they'd often demand more information.

That was all part of the stalling tactics which the Reagan administration had set up at Medicare so the government could hold onto the money as long as possible. Reagan denied this, but everybody knew it was true; just another of his administration's ways to juggle the books to make the government's finances look better than they really were, and to hell with the elderly sick.

It was just like his ploy on Social Security payments: always round every payment *downward* to the nearest dollar on the old people's checks.

June 1 was a Sunday, and we went out for lunch after Maria got out of church. The rest of the daylight hours slipped away as Nini read, I worked on my 'bio' and we watched the evening news.

But what occurred just after dark that day stands out vividly in my memory. I'd invited Maria to go for a stroll with me along the seawall, but she begged off, saying she was tired, so I walked alone down to the clubhouse and back,

---

stopping to chat with a neighbor and his wife who were sitting on their patio. As we talked, I was looking to the east across 100 yards of saltwater toward the group of three-story buildings of Bay Island known as The Village while I admired the stars coming into bloom overhead.

Suddenly a bright light appeared in the northeast. It was low on the horizon, a blinding, ball-like mass of light, moving southward across the night sky trailing a comet-like tail.

"What the devil is that?" I cried, the hair on my body bristling. I was truly uncertain what the fiery object could be.

"It's not making any noise, so it can't be a helicopter," Rich said, as we stood transfixed by the vivid light moving slowly across the sky above the tops of the condos opposite us. Helicopters might fly over at night flashing searchlights, to look for drug smugglers on Boca Ciega Bay—but this wasn't one of them.

"I've never seen any type of plane with that kind of light!" I added. "It's very peculiar. Maybe it's a giant meteorite. Let me call Maria." I dashed the few feet to our apartment and yelled for her, but by the time she came outside, the glowing ball of white fire, still heading southward had disappeared from view behind the 18-story Admiral Building.

"What is it?" Maria wanted to know. "You were calling pretty frantically."

I explained about the 'thing'. "I felt it might be a meteorite. But they always fall to the west . . . I think. But this was a huge ball of fire traveling south. All I can think of now is that it was part of something from outer space."

"For a moment I wondered if the Russians had launched a missile at us!" Rich's wife, Louise exclaimed.

"Maybe it was a flying saucer," Maria suggested. Her idea reminded me of the time she spotted a gleaming object in the sky above a natural arch in one of my pictures taken in Arches National Monument in Utah when she cried, "There's a flying soy sauce!" It was actually a tiny flat white cloud, all alone in an azure sky over a vermillion landscape, marvelously out of place.

It was two days before we knew what we'd seen, and it turned out Louise and I were both partially correct. An inside-page article in the paper was headlined, "Spent Soviet Rocket Lighted Up Florida Sky," and stated:

> Florida residents who witnessed a long-tailed fireball that whizzed down the length of the state thought they'd seen a meteor shower or a UFO, but a U.S. air command official says it was a Soviet rocket falling to earth. Residents from Jacksonville to Key West—a distance of more than 500 miles—reported seeing the spent rocket. A spokesman for the North American Aerospace Defense Command, near Colorado Springs, said, 'It was the rocket body used in the launch of a Soviet satellite . . . designated Cosmos 1746'. He said the rocket hit the atmosphere near Jacksonville and was last seen near Cuba, but he didn't know where it hit.

From its low level and general trajectory, I judged the fireball splashed into the Caribbean, perhaps halfway to Panama. One thing was certain, it was a hell of a frightening sight!

Working on my 'bio' I was now at a point where I needed to check several points of information about the past. I organized the things I needed to clear up, and the following day got off a batch of letters. I spent much of Monday on them, but interrupted my work long enough to take Maria to her surgeon for another check-up.

Again, he was convinced that all was fine and dandy, and healing was progressing very well, though Maria still complained of an occasional pain under her scar, near her breastbone.

"The doctor says it's just healing pangs, to be expected, and that they'll go away eventually," Maria informed me. When we asked about the chest pains. Doctor Coe could have run off his response on a copier, like a hand-out, for it was always the same: 'Healing pangs'.

After returning from the doctor's office, I wrote one of the more difficult letters I had written for some time. It was to Nivaldo and Dulce in Rio concerning Maria's mastectomy, which was a painful subject for me, to begin with, plus I had to write in Portuguese. I now translate it back into English:

> Dear brothers (in Portuguese, to refer to brothers and sisters together, one uses the masculine plural). It has been some time since I have written you a letter, but finally here I am, sending you some of the news about Maria.
>
> She had her operation on March 17th, stayed in the hospital for four days afterward and returned home, where I took care of her for a few days until she could take care of herself. We are going to visit the surgeon this afternoon so he can check his work, which seems to be healing very well.
>
> Kathy arrives here on the 17th with her two children, to spend three weeks with us while her husband is on an aircraft carrier in the Mediterranean. Thanks to the Lord, the 'gout' in Maria's left foot is getting better, because we want to show Kathy a few things in this area that she hasn't seen yet.
>
> I'm very sorry that we couldn't visit you as we planned, but perhaps we can get together later in the year. We are most eager to see Margareth's (Nivaldo's daughter) little girls, and to meet her husband, a person we have yet to know. And naturally we have a great desire to see you folks there in Rio, I mean Dulce, Beth (their older daughter) and you.

93

We will communicate our thoughts about such a visit after Kathy returns to Oak Harbor and my precious wife has healed from the operation which she endured with such great courage. You have never seen a person as strong as your dear sister, Nivaldo. She's as brave as a tiger.

Now I have a couple of questions about life in Brazil which you can answer for me. First, what was the name of those small buses that used to run like crazy along the streets from your old apartment into center city in 1958 when we visited you? And second, what are the dates of the life of Francisco Alves, the famous singer? We visited his grave when we were there in 1958, near that of Carmen Miranda *(in the cemetery of St. John the Baptist, where Maria's father is buried)*, and I'd like to know when he was born and when he died, in order to place him in perspective with some of our own singers.

Well, that's about all for this time. Please excuse any errors in this letter—I'm out of practice writing in your lovely language. Strong hugs for all of you, from the sister and brother who love you very much and think of you always. Maria & Robin.

Doctor Coe had already told Maria she could begin using a prosthesis whenever she wished, but she kept postponing the sad day. Then one day she spoke quietly.

"I worry so much about wearing a prosthesis, Daddy," she finally confessed to me, "not because of my own feelings, but because of yours."

"Because of *mine?*" my voice showed my surprise. I wasn't sure I'd heard her right. "What do you mean, because of *my* feelings?"

"I'm afraid you will be ashamed of me, wearing an artificial breast," she said, her eyes downcast.

94

I was shocked. But I quickly set Nini straight. "Quite the contrary, honey. I won't be ashamed of you; I will be extremely proud of you, just as I have always been since the day we met"

"Honestly, *querido?*"

"Absolutely, *meu amor.*" (My love.) And I rose and lifted her to her feet to give her a long, strong embrace, with kisses on her lips and in her sugar bowl before I released her.

She smiled as she swept me with those marvelous eyes. "Then I guess I'm ready to go shopping," she said, and her face glowed like a little girl reaching for an ice cream cone—simply radiant!

And so on a bright, humid day in June we went shopping for an item which would help restore Maria's body to its normal appearance; or put her life back in balance, so to speak.

She already had some help in her shopping, for the young lady who called on her in the hospital gave her a list of places which sold prostheses. We were surprised to learn the major department stores had women specially trained to fit and sell them. That helpful list even supplied the *names* of the ladies. It was less embarrassing for Maria to enter the lingerie department when she could ask for a clerk by name.

The 'specialist' took Maria's measurements, determined which size prosthesis she needed, went into the fitting room with her and helped her try on several, each time placing the device into the bra and fastening the bra as Maria held the prosthesis in place.

Wearing a prosthesis and her blouse, Maria came shyly from the dressing room to show me. "What do you think, Daddy?" she asked apprehensively, as the fitter hovered in the background.

I was surprised and delighted. "You look *great*, honey" I cried, and rose to give her a gentle hug. "No one would know you've had an operation!" I was not lying to her. She did look completely natural. Just like the young lady who came to visit her in the hospital.

"I'm so glad!" she said, and began admiring herself in the mirrors, turning this way and that, inspecting her figure like a young girl going out on a date—or wearing a brassiere for the first time in her life. Maria turned to the saleslady. "I'd like to look in a couple more stores before deciding," she said very simply. "Do you mind?"

"Of course not, honey," the lady sympathized. "If this is the first place you've shopped, then by all means you should check in other stores," and she went with Maria to remove the prosthesis.

In the next store, Maria received the same friendly, understanding assistance. Again she let me see how she looked once she was fitted and dressed, and once again she told the fitter that she wanted to think about it for a day or two. I'm sure those ladies were accustomed to such hesitancy; for any woman who has suddenly lost a breast must be filled with a sense of apprehension and misgiving. She realizes she has to buy a prosthesis, but surely the thought of wearing it the rest of her life infuses her spirit with melancholy. It certainly is not the happiest purchase a woman ever makes, despite what it does for her. We returned home that afternoon, and let the matter incubate overnight.

The next day we returned to the mall, and Maria bought her figure-restorer at the first store we'd visited. It was soft and gelatinous, and came in a form-fitting box in which to keep it when not in use—at night, for example. She also bought three special bras which made the wearing of the prosthesis a little easier and helped to present a more natural appearance. Medicare would help to pay for the prosthesis and the special bras.

It was exactly eight weeks to the day after her mastectomy when Nini wore her new device home. She walked with a great deal of confidence, her face shining more brightly now that she was back in equilibrium. I was absolutely delighted, and oh, so greatly relieved—for my dear *Brasileira* had mentioned more than once over the past two months how she 'felt like a chicken with only one wing'. Surprisingly, though, she was already reconciled to the horrible misfortune which had befallen her, and when she made that comment now, she would give me a wry grin. She had courage enough to milk a jaguar!

Kathy called, for she thought we were going specialty shopping soon, and she was eager to know if we did, and how it went, and whether the quest had been successful. Maria gave her the details.

"Poor Daddy," Maria told her, "he has to help me put on my bra every morning. When I'm getting dressed, no matter what he is doing, I cry 'Help!' and he comes running to assist me in tucking everything into place and fastening the hooks, because I can't reach back that far."

"That's right," I said, for I was on the line. "I'm now as expert in fastening bras as I once was in unfastening them." It was several months before Maria grew adept at inserting the prosthesis in her bra, fastening the hooks, and sliding the whole assemblage around into proper position. But eventually she overcame all the difficulties.

When Maria returned to her surgeon for another checkup. Doctor Coe suggested she might wish to have reconstructive surgery on her right side.

But Maria replied negatively. "I'm in my sixties, and I'm not that vain. Besides, I hate operations. I don't wish to reduce my left breast, or create a new right breast; I'll use my prosthesis and be what I am," she said in all finality.

Doctor Coe again dismissed the occasional stabs of pain Nini felt near her breastbone. They were 'healing pangs', nothing to worry about. I suspected that was the case myself, so the doctor's comforting words reenforced my own belief, and made our Christmas a bit more relaxed, for we were approaching the end of what had been an unpleasant and far from happy year.

I knew Maria still had days when the trauma of her operation and the terrible effect it had on her profile would sneak into her thoughts, and she would suddenly be overwhelmed with remorse. I'd sense it clear across the room, and I'd promptly go to her and gather her into my arms for a silent embrace.

I easily knew how she felt, for at times when I was alone, I would suddenly think of the atrocious way fate had mistreated my sweetheart, and my throat would squeeze shut and grow painfully tight, and tears would well up and overflow, and it would take several minutes for me to grab hold of my emotions and fight off the burning ache which filled my head and heart. This happened every few weeks, after which it would be several hours before my spirits revived. If such emotions of pity, and fear of the future for my brave wife could well up and overcome *me*, how much worse it must have been for Maria herself!

Sometimes those attacks occurred because I was worried about the quick stabs of pain which Maria occasionally felt in her chest and ribs, causing her to catch her breath and grab herself. But I'd recall what the surgeon said, that he'd removed all the cancer, and that the pangs were healing pains. Then I would push my preoccupations to the back burner. Doctor Coe said he'd removed all of the cancer. It was gone forever. We could relax.

Maria and I had been busy kid-proofing the condo, as Kathy suggested, putting all the bric-a-brac out of Terri's reach. I switched my typing gear and manuscript to our master bedroom, got the sofa-bed ready for use, and set up the cot for Terry, assuming that Kathy would sleep with Cynthia.

Kathy called to give us final warning. "Remember, we'll be there tomorrow at eleven in the evening!" she cried. "I hope you did as I said, and moved all breakables out of Terry's reach."

"Everything's taken care of," I replied. "Mama and I have been going full bore all day, tearing the place apart just so Terry can't!"

"Don't worry," Nini said, "we'll be waiting when you come up the escalator. We can't wait to see you all."

"Well, I only hope you guys can endure Terry, for he's a regular cyclone," Kathy continued to caution us.

"Again, no problem," I said. "I managed with Bobby and you—I can manage with Terry. If he doesn't behave, I'll give him a darned good thrashing!"

"Oh, Daddy, you sound just like in the old days!" Kathy giggled, and with that we said goodby and hung up.

The stage was set, and the condo was ready for the guest appearance of Terry the Typhoon, live at Bay Island. The lights would dim (they really did) and the curtain would go up in a little over 24 hours.

Maria was as eager to see Kathy and Kids as was any young girl awaiting the arrival of her favorite rock and roll band. And I admit it: I was equally as nervous and anxious.

CHAPTER 11

By the time Kathy brought the grandkids home for their visit, Maria was already accustomed to her new prosthesis, or 'my rubber titty' as she once called it. They arrived at Tampa International Airport on June 17, exactly two months to the day from the date of Nini's operation.

Kathy was almost as tall as her pappy, and had a trim figure, topped with a mass of blond hair, and always dressed well. After college she went to officer Candidate School in Newport, Rhode Island, became an Ensign, then a JG, married Charlie, a tall Texan with a big grin, an easy manner, and the job of A-6 bomber pilot. They became lieutenants, and were married. While Charlie flew test runs with new weapons being developed at China Lake, California, Kathy was Legal Officer on the same base. When she became pregnant with Cynthia she resigned her commission to become a housewife. At the moment, Charlie was aboard a carrier on patrol in the Mediterranean, a ship which he had the temerity to call a 'boat'!

As her gang of three came up the escalator, Kathy had tears in her pretty eyes. Surely she'd been thinking of her mother's operation and its disfigurement, and was worried lest she was coming to visit too soon. But when she saw Maria at the head of the stairs waiting for her, and looking for all the world like the mama she'd always known, her gray eyes glowed and a big grin illuminated her face. "Oh, Mama, it's so good to see you!" she cried, handed me the stuff she was carrying and swept Maria into her arms to hug and kiss her voraciously.

With Charlie overseas on his cruise, that was probably the best grown-up hug Kathy'd had in some time. The two of them clung to each other like a pair of Florida love bugs as people fought their way around them to get off the escalator.

I managed to ease them aside so others could pass, and then turned to Kathy. "And what about your old Pappy? Isn't it good to see him?" I asked, in a wounded tone of voice.

"Of course it is, Daddy," she cried brightly, just like she used to talk when she was a young girl, "I've missed you, too, really!" and she threw her arms around me for more hugs and kisses, while I strove to hang onto the stuff she had foisted off on me.

Then it was time to hug Cynthia, and her little brother, Terry, blond, bright and vivacious, was clearly surprised by all the grappling and smooching going on with his mother. Cindy, tall for her age but cuter than a kitten's ear, with dark hair and eyes, was her usual cool—almost calculated—self, neither coldly aloof, nor too warmly receptive.

Terry on the other hand, quickly asked, "Do you want some sugar from my sugar bowl, Grandpa?" and I said 'sure', and bent down to put a kiss at the juncture of his throat and shoulder, while he giggled happily.

"I'm so glad you guys could come," Maria said with no small measure of joy showing through. "It's been a rough two months. To have you here with us will help a lot, honey," and she enfolded her pretty blond daughter in another embrace.

We were soon across the bridges and causeways to the condo, where the kids promptly fell in love with the slender egret outside our door and the pelicans a few feet down the seawall where a fellow was fishing. The birds were waiting to see which one got his catch when the fisherman pulled in some tiny fish six or eight inches long. Our visitors were even more thrilled when a pair of dolphins swam slowly past our 'front porch'.

Kathy's visit with the children had a most beneficial effect on Maria's recovery, but I will only mention here that we did some whirlwind tours of Florida which the children lapped up eagerly: to the St. Petersburg Pier with its inverted pyramid of gift shops, restaurants and aquarium; to Silver Springs to ride the glass-bottom boats; to Homosassa Springs to see the wild life, pet the animals in the petting zoo and watch the fish from inside the 'reverse' fishbowl; to Sarasota to see the Ringling circus stuff; to Flagler Beach, and to St. Augustine, where Kathy went to the little mission to thank *Nuestra Senora de la Leche* (Our Lady of the Milk, the only Madonna and Child I have ever seen where Mary is nursing Jesus) for giving her the son she had prayed for. During all these trips, the kids were balls of fire, filled with delight at all we saw, and at day's end, dog-tired and ready to hit the hay.

One incident I must mention was our visit to the Olde Worlde Cheese Shop just outside the gate to our condominium complex. We were having lunch, and Terry was absolutely, unbelievably tractable. He ate his sandwich and watched everything going on around him. He was so calm and well comported we paid him minimum attention until the lights faded and went out.

Kathy looked at Terry's chair, he wasn't in it, and she let out a gasp. There was Terry over by the desk of the receptionist. Anything mechanical fascinated him, and he had spotted the dimmer-switch and promptly operated it! The whole place went dark until Kathy rushed over and dialed the lights back up. The luncheon crowd gave Terry a round of applause and returned to their meals, and Kathy brought a proud Terry back to his chair for dessert.

An unfortunate, but not serious, incident occurred the first morning Terry got out of bed. I was in the bathroom when I heard the loud thump and immediately knew what had happened. Little Terry had come out of the guest room, saw a blue heron on the seawall outside, and dashed across the living room heading for the patio to get a better look. But the big, sliding glass door was still closed, and Terry ran smack into it. His speed bounced him back on his bottom on the carpet, but he didn't cry. Before we could pick him up, he rose and cautiously approached the glass window to see what the dickens had happened. When I did my pre-Terry child-proofing I'd forgotten to hang some ornaments on the *lower* part of the glass door to warn little Terry.

Although some of our trips were a bit tiring, Maria bore up under them well, and I knew that she was enjoying herself and the children enough to occasionally forget about her operation and her eternal fear that the cancer was lurking somewhere inside her, waiting secretly for the opportunity to spread its ugly tentacles again.

Kathy and crew took the plane for home on July 8, ending a pleasant interlude in our lives, filled with visits to fascinating places and lots of dining out, with plenty of seafood, which Kathy and Cynthia adored and Terry ate with some gusto as well. When they left, the condo echoed emptily for days thereafter as we suffered deep feelings of homesickness—not for having forsaken our home, but because of those who forsook it and left us behind.

We picked up our 'pre-kids' routine by seeing Drs. Coe and Jones, and Maria began taking 250 milligrams of Aldomet twice a day. Aldomet is a brand name for methyldopa, an antihypertension drug. She then went to 500 mgs of Slo-K twice a day, then three times a day, to replenish potassium loss, as Nini explained it.

My book of poetry, 'Rhymes of a Bluejacket', was finished by Rose Printing Company of Tallahassee in time for me to take a few copies of the thin volume with me to the *Maryland* reunion. Hopefully, some of my ex-shipmates would

invest $5.00 in such a fine volume—even if they hated po-
etry.

It was September 29 when we flew to Boston to join the
gang of ex-crewmen of the battleship *Maryland*. The get-
together featured a lot of side trips to see New Hampshire's
autumn foliage and eat fresh lobster in a quaint restaurant
near Haverhill; a trip to Pease Air Force Base (since closed);
a tour of Cape Cod; a visit to the *USS Constitution* and tons of
rich fellowship with the men I'd known on the *Mary* and others who had served on her before or after my three years on
board.

Maria was always very gregarious, and as she met my old
shipmates and their wives she blended with them like gin in
tonic. During the day's activities it was apparent she forgot
completely about the alien object filling one side of her bra.
I was thankful that she was so relaxed.

A number of men and wives bought a copy of my poetry
book. Some bought two, one to give to a friend—or perhaps
an enemy.

Maria and I took a private tour of Boston by taxi before
going to the airport to head home. The driver took us to all
the famous historical sights downtown, in the midst of which
we became entangled in the Boston Marathon and had to sit
for ten minutes going nowhere, with the meter running, until
all the would-be runners at the tail-end of the parade drug
past our check-point intersection and the cop got out of our
way.

We arrived home tired but happy; happy to have met so
many of my old shipmates, and in particular, those who once
worked with me in Big Mary's shipfitter shop.

For the next few months there were constant visits to
Nini's physician, her surgeon and her oncologist; while she
changed her drug treatments regularly. It was either take
more of something or take less of it, or discontinue it altogether, or begin using it again, or start using it for the first

time. This was particularly true of her blood pressure drugs, Aldomet and Lopressor through the end of the year. Lopressor is the brand name of metoprolol, a betablocker used in combination with hydrochlorothiazide to relieve hypertension—or high blood pressure. The use of that combination made it necessary for Maria to take Slo-K to keep her potassium level up where it belonged,

November 20, Maria and I went out for dinner to celebrate the 42nd anniversary of her arrival in America from Brazil. She was feeling quite well, and I luxuriated in knowing my sweetie was not only physically better, but the emotional trauma of her terrible ordeal was beginning to fade. Occasionally she joked with me about her prosthesis, the very pronunciation of which was a tough job for her, with its 'th' in the center—an alien sound not found in her native Portuguese.

Christmas 1986 was about the same as always; some small things swapped between Maria and me, boxes of cheeses and sausages to Bobby's and Kathy's and Robbie's houses, and an extra big one to Charlie at sea, so he could share with shipmates. We went out to dinner at a beach resort hotel, after which it was early to bed.

New Year's Eve we were content to go outside and blow our horns until the condo neighbors appeared on their balconies to see what was going on, when we wished them all a happy New Year, went inside to kill our bottle of champagne and went to bed.

New Year's Day was no more exciting, for the shock of Maria's surgery still cast a pall over our lives. We watched the Pasadena Rose Parade, went out for lunch, then followed some of the football games on TV. After all our harrowing experiences in 1986, we were happy to greet the New Year. I prayed it would be better for all concerned—and especially for my beloved Maria.

As we moved into January, I did my best to relax and quit

worrying, but somehow I could not forget about Maria's cancer, and in my own, unexpressed thoughts, I worried deeply about a recurrence. In fact, I feared the pains in her chest predicted that eventuality, for I could never force myself to believe those were 'healing pangs', as the doctors put it.

Because of my unvoiced fears, I determined to give Maria as much pleasure in life as I could on our tight budget. We went to a travel agency, read brochures, booked a flight to Guadalajara, Mexico and spent eight wonderful days there.

We visited marvelous old churches and cathedrals, museums, parks and the great indoor marketplace. We saw the academy for young people which teaches Mexican folklore ballet, the famous *Ballet Folclorico* school. There we watched kindergarden children training in their special areas, while older grade-schoolers and people in their teens and 20s practiced in different studios, or in the open air patios, all in one great building which had once served as an orphanage.

One cool evening we went to an outdoor performance of Ballet Folklorico at the 'orphanage' and were highly enchanted by the handsomeness and beauty of the dancers, and by the variety of the dances they presented in a kaleidoscopic melding of exciting musical rhythms, mesmerizing movements and colorful costumes.

We visited the artisan's colony suburb of Tlaquepaque, then a tequila distillery in the city of Tequila, and Lake Chapala, Mexico's largest fresh water lake, which is infested with Americans. The area from Guadalajara to Lake Chapala—including the fascinating town of Ajiji (pronounced A-hee-hee, with four dotted letters in a row)—contains one of the largest colonies of American ex-patriots in the world, said to be over a quarter-million strong.

By the time I was recalling some of my 'speaking' Spanish, it was time to head for home, but not before we visited the nearby park which had a commemorative plaque saying Guadalajara was the Sister City of our old home town, Portland, Oregon. It seemed impossible that our day to head for home had arrived so swiftly. "Where did a week go?" Nini asked.

Strange as it may seem, we both felt sad to be leaving Mexico. The people at the hotel had been most kind to us. The whole staff of the dining room lined up after our breakfast the day we left, and we shook hands with the entire 'receiving' line. The folks didn't line up because of big tips, but rather because we'd made friends with everybody, from the woman who made the tortillas in the buffet line at breakfast to the waiters and the maitre de. At breakfast we usually had the same waiter, and by the time we left, Maria knew his wife's name and the names and ages of all his children. *'She is almost back to her old self!'* I thought happily as I observed her conversations. We had done our best to speak Spanish with them, although most of them spoke some English. Dear Maria spoke 'Portanhol', a mixture of her native Portuguese and Espanhol, while I simply garbled my Spanish.

The 'limo' which was to take us to the airport was at the door right on the hour, and in no time we were on our way to Mexico City, where we'd change planes for Miami, and again for Tampa International Airport. When we arrived in Miami, the Customs agent asked if we'd brought any food with us from Mexico.

"No, sir," Maria said brightly, charming him with her dark eyes.

He reached over to an open-top sack of our things to pick up a sealed box of Mexican cookies resting there in plain sight. 'Isn't this food?" he asked.

"Oh, I thought you were talking about fresh *fruit* when you said 'food'. Those are just cookies, not food," she smiled.

"Only trying to keep you honest," the man said, and laughed at Maria's discomfiture. He scanned the small list of things we had bought in Guadalajara, and waived us on.

"Boy! He sure scared *me*," Maria whispered as we left.

We recalled how she had been stopped in Customs when she came from Brazil to Miami during the war in 1944. She refused to let go of a package of letters which I had written to her while we were apart. She was latched onto one end of the package, and the customs man was clamped onto the other. When I intervened, the agent said he wasn't trying to steal her letters, but all such correspondence had to be censored before it could come into the country.

When I showed him all the censorship stamps already on all of the envelopes he just shook his head. "There could be new material in some of these envelopes," he was adamant. "They all have to censored again. Give me a mailing address where we can ship them after we're done," We gave him my mothers address out in the state of Washington. When they were done re-censoring, the censors blithely shipped all of Maria's love letters—not out to my mother in Bremmerton, Washington—but back to Maria's mother in Bahia, Brazil!

Our first evening back home, as we sat in the living room eyeing the bay outside the door, Maria turned to me. "I truly enjoyed our little evenings at the hotel in Guadalajara," she said.

"Me, too, Nini," I said. "I felt totally relaxed and at home in that hotel."

"I miss the two young men who played the guitar and organ in the lobby bar," Maria continued. "And that young woman who brought us those little treats on the cute plates. She was so nice . . . and the food was so good . . . I really enjoyed the whole affair."

"And I had fun trying to speak Spanish with that dignified lady and her husband at the next table who were so friendly." "Oh, yes," Maria agreed, "I'm glad she showed me her silver beads, and told us where to buy them."

The beads were hollow balls about a half-inch in diameter, a trademark of Mexican silverwork. The day after meeting that warm Mexican couple, we went to the huge indoor market where Maria promptly spotted a stall which sold the unusual beads. A lovely Mexican girl was running the 'shop', and she and Maria bargained like little Trojans for ten minutes before Nini bought a 16-inch necklace for about $49.00.

The very pretty girl polished and wrapped the necklace carefully, and then reached into a 'back room'and came up with a charming pennant saying *Recuerdo de Guadalajara*, souvenir of Guadalajara, which she gave to a delighted Maria. They hugged and kissed cheeks before parting. I stayed far enough away from the sexy little beauty to avoid any such embrace, as delightful as I knew it would be.

Maria's operation had not removed any of her primal Brazilian jealousy streak!

CHAPTER 12

Spring slipped into summer without any unusual incidents. Nini continued to keep her various doctors happy, and they did nothing to spoil her happiness, and after Medicare and Prudential had ponied up their fair share, I paid off the difference.

To put Maria into even better spirits, I set up a tour of America, with Kathy's place in Oak Harbor on Whidbey Island in Puget Sound as our western objective. We had a new 32-foot Airstream trailer which we'd traded a small motor home for at an advantageous discount. We pulled it with a Chevrolet Suburban, a vehicle which could take the trailer up a 14-degree climb without a whimper. We got permission to bring the rig into the Bay Island condo grounds to load it up, and by the evening of July 2 had everything in it except the final refrigerator items.

Early in the morning of July 3, we were moving the final items from the condo refrigerator into the one on the trailer, working in semi-darkness, when Maria tripped over a cracked section of sidewalk, and, to break her fall, put out her right hand. That not only broke her fall, it also broke her wrist. It didn't *seem* broken, though, so we set off on our trip, with Maxine going along to visit her sons and grandkids in Vancouver.

After we'd gone 50 miles, Maria complained of pain in her wrist, which had begun to ache. When we reached Ocala we stopped and had an orthopedist check it. The x-rays showed the bone in which one's thumb-bone rests had a cracked socket. The doctor put a temporary splint on her arm to hold things in place until we got to Kathy's, where a permanent one could be applied. For the rest of our trip, poor old Pappy had to help Maxine cook, do dishes and keep house, while Princess Maria enjoyed life, using the wrapper off a loaf of bread to keep her splint dry when she showered! She got a permanent cast in Oak Harbor, and the wrist healed perfectly, so time took care of that unfortunate mishap.

We took Sis through Georgia, Tennessee, Kentucky, the tip of Illinois, Missouri and Kansas to Colorado, and she was amazed. It had been a moist spring and summer that year, the eastern end of Kansas was as green as Ireland; then as we crossed the western section of the state we found the great combines were already harvesting the golden wheat, following along behind one another in an adagio parade of mechanical monsters, each spewing a golden stream out its side into a suffocating truck.

"I've always thought of Kansas as a big, flat dry state, with wheat and little else," Maxine said. "I can't believe how bright and green it is, and how lovely the rolling hills are!"

"Oh, yes," Maria joined in, as we sat at a table in a charming roadside park to eat a picnic lunch, "Kansas is very pretty. The hills are like great ocean waves ... only done in dirt." She paused, then added, "And so is Nebraska, you know."

We reached Denver and turned north toward Wyoming to see Cheyenne and Laramie—my own, and Max's respective birthplaces. Just before we reached Cheyenne, we paused on a high hill overlooking the capital before descending to the city, and for good reason. An afternoon thundershower had just finished washing the sky, and had hung out a magnificent double rainbow to dry, spreading it above the scene before us. The twin arcs gleamed gloriously, their northern ends embracing the city of my birth. Surely two pots of gold were on the very steps of the capitol building itself! (Of course, if the pots really were there, the politicians and bureaucrats would spend the golden contents in a week.)

"I can't believe how beautiful it is!" Maxine cried with joy over the double arc, for it was indeed an awe-inspiring sight from our lofty viewpoint.

"I think the Lord had the rainbows spread just to welcome you home, Daddy," Maria said.

"It's a welcome for all of us," I replied. *'Maybe it's a sign from above that my darling Nini is going to be all right from now on,'* I found myself thinking, and prayed to heaven it was true.

When we pulled into the RV park I told the lady co-owner it seemed Cheyenne had grown considerably since my last visit.

'Oh, my yes," she was proudly emphatic, "this is the capital, you know. We're growing very fast. We have almost fifty thousand people now!" We adored her glowing enthusiasm.

The next day we went a bit out of the way to visit what was left of Foxpark, the tie-hack camp where Dad hewed jackpines into railroad ties, and where I lived as a small lad in the early 1920s. It was from there that Mother left to take the stage from Wood's Landing into Laramie to give birth to Emma Maxine Elizabeth Leatherman, on June 14, 1922, the day before her own 34th birthday. Mom always called Sis her birthday present.

We spent the next night in Green River, Wyoming, located on the Green River—just as Utah's town of Green River is located on the Green River, farther downstream. One of the Green's principal tributaries is the Yampa River, the same river which flowed past the log ranch house where I had lived with my brother Frank as a third grader in Colorado, south of Steamboat Springs.

Leaving Green River, it was all uphill into Utah through the Wasatch Mountains and down the long grade to reach Ogden. Sis passed up a visit to Yellowstone Park, she was so eager to see her sons and their wives and children in Vancouver.

We followed the course of the Old Oregon Trail, pulled our modern covered wagon westward for miles through Utah, Idaho and Oregon, and finally dropped Sis off with Dick and Jimmie in Vancouver. We went on up past Seattle to spend several days with Kathy in Oak Harbor, the Navy base where A-6 bomber pilots trained when not stationed on a carrier at sea.

Maria and I left Kathy's to tour Glacier National Park in Montana, one of the three national parks we had not yet visited. The park is now known as Waterton-Glacier International Peace Park, sharing part of the spectacular scenery with Canada, whose adjoining park was once called Waterton Park. Leave it to the politicians to make park names longer and more tedious.

We left the Airstream in the RV park in Kalispell, west of the park, drove around the south end of the park and up the eastern side to St. Mary, where we headed west through the park. We followed the Highway-to-the-Sun to climb up and over the Continental Divide at Logan Pass, 6,680 feet, then on around the incredible knife-edged mountain called Garden Wall. That long, sharp peak was formed when a glacier on each side of a mountain wore the mountain down to its current eerie, thin-bladed shape.

The drive was absolutely mind-boggling, the views filled with great peaks, that unbelievable 'wall' formation, tumbling waterfalls, large and small sapphire lakes, and glaciers which had once adjoined the road but were now melted far up the valleys they had helped to create. After a very long, delightful day we left the park at West Glacier and returned to Kalispell and our portable home.

The next day we headed for Vancouver, crossing Idaho and Eastern Washington in heavy heat. We soon said goodby to my nephews and their wives, the two daughters of Jimmie

113

and Dena, and the two sons and two daughters of Dick and Judy. Sis called that night to say she was afraid she couldn't leave with us the next day because a tooth was hurting her. I suggested she floss very carefully, then rinse her mouth two or three times with warm saltwater that night.

Next morning she called us at the RV park to say her tooth was okay, and she could go home with us. "Just how did you know about flossing and salt water?" she asked with admiration.

"I just figured you'd been eating some of those delicious wild blackberries that grow on the hill behind Dick's house, and maybe a seed was stuck under your gums. Flossing and a few good rinses might take care of it," I replied.

We picked her up, along with some extra gear she wanted to haul back to Florida, told everybody goodby, and started the 3,500 mile trek back to Tampa Bay. We reached Burns, in Central Oregon the first evening.

Next day we drove south into Nevada, to turn east for Winnemucca. There the slot machines at lunch gave Maria a pocketful of quarters while Sis lost $20 playing blackjack.

We spent that night in tiny Ely, Nevada, then headed south next morning and turned east across Utah to make the long, steep climb to a 10,000 foot mesa to view the colorfully eroded amphitheater of Cedar Breaks National Monument. From there we went on to see one end of Bryce Canyon National Park. We couldn't go far into the park because trailers were not allowed beyond a certain point, and we didn't want to unhitch. From Bryce we headed south to spend the night at a small RV park located beneath 2,000-foot towering vermillion cliffs, and the next morning made our way through the long tunnel and down the serpentine drive to the floor of Zion National Park, where incredible monoliths soar as much as 3,000 feet above the valley floor, all done up in reds, pinks, grays and whites.

From Zion we headed south, then east along the gorgeous Vermillion Cliffs to Navajo bridge over the Colorado River, and on around to Grand Canyon National Park in Arizona. This was about my fifth visit to the canyon, and was the only time it rained while I was there.

"I think you brought on this rain, Sis," I said, and she tried to push me off the cliff where we stood 7,000 feet above sea-level, and a mile above the Colorado River which chewed away at Arizona's foundations far below.

From there we made our way across the Southwest to El Paso, Texas. We visited a series of old missions on our way down the Rio Grande to McNary, where we turned our noses east across Texas. Near Sonora I stopped at a lonely little RV park operated on the 'honor system', and put $8.00 in the slot in the box before I tied up. We were the only guests in that small spot lost in the Texas vastness, and there was no one in the tiny 'offfice'. A big semi van without a tractor stood in eerie silence inside the park, and, except for us, there wasn't a human being in sight.

During the night Maxine awoke to voices, and peeking out from behind the trailer curtains saw four men unloading cartons or bales from the semi into a small truck. "I was scared stiff," Sis cried the next morning. "I think they are smuggling dope!"

To which Maria asked a succinct question. "Then why did you keep watching them from behind the curtain . . . did you want them to catch you spying on them, and come to kill all three of us?"

We stopped in San Antonio to take Sis through the Alamo, then continued toward home. After long hours (make that days) of driving across the Texas landscape we found a place to tie up overnight in Orange, the last city on I-10 before Louisiana. Next morning we crossed into the Pelican State and kept going. We reached and crossed Mississippi and Alabama, and found ourselves sort of 'home' as we neared and passed Pensacola. We drove until midnight before settling down in an RV park in Perry. Next day we had an easy drive home.

Arriving there from our tour of the Old West, we dropped Sis off, along with her suitcase, vacuum cleaner, 3-legged 'knitting keg' and pair of lamp tables. We dropped the trailer in storage, and were soon snugly ensconced in our condo.

That summer tour was filled with a great number of sights and experiences, but they are not too pertinent to Maria's battle with cancer, so I have touched on but a few highlights. I felt the trip did Maria a lot of good. She rarely mentioned the word 'cancer' during the whole expedition, but sat contentedly beside me on the high seat of the Suburban to be sure I stayed on course and didn't get gobbled up by a car-eating semi-trailer. We covered over 10,000 miles through 21 states on that marvelous highway trek.

The entire story of the tour—our long visits with Maxine's kids and with Kathy, visits to other national parks and monuments, fishing trips, sightseeing trips and jaunts back into American history are more thoroughly set forth in another volume of my Memoirs.

Home at last, we immediately went to a local orthopedist who x-rayed Maria's wrist and showed us the crack was healing well. In due time he freed Maria's arm. I watched apprehensively as he started his buzz-saw and dug into the cast, and cautioned him not to cut my darling's arm. He laughed at my fears as the circular saw threw plaster dust all over the place. With the cast off, and Maria unscathed, we all admired her very white arm. She was fair-skinned to begin with, and wearing the cast had bleached her forearm even lighter.

With the 'gout' no longer bothering her, and her broken wrist healed and the cast out of her way, Maria was at ease, and it was time to settle back into our old routine in the condo. For Nini that meant read, play bridge, get her hair done, go to church, watch TV and visit friends. For me it meant work on my memoirs, and, as an elected member of the Board of

Directors, help to guide the destiny of the 850 condominiums in our complex, watch TV and hike the seawall. For both of us, it meant dining out whenever the mood struck us. We shopped for food, I helped keep the condo presentable, and we lived the simple life. Maria was feeling so fit we almost forgot about her arch-enemy.

Until early September, that is.

Then suddenly she suffered a series of extra-sharp pains in her chest. "It's like something bited me!" Maria nervously explained. I listened with a troubled spirit, for I was becoming more and more convinced that deep inside my *Bahiana* all was not well; surely something within her was greatly amiss.

CHAPTER 13

It was September 18 when I took Maria to the hospital for a bone scan, a liver scan, a spleen scan and x-rays of her skull. As I waited for her to take the skull x-ray, I thought bitterly of the old gag, "They took an x-ray of his brain, but it didn't show a thing." I prayed hard that such would be the case with Nini's head x-ray that day.

Most of those scans, as I recall them, were what they dubbed CAT scans, medicalese for Computerized Axial Tomography. Tomography is a word from the Greek: *Tomos*, meaning slice or section, and *graphia*, meaning recording, so, slice-recording. Since the scan is done along an established axis, it's axial tomography, and since a computer controls the whole operation, it's Computerized Axial Tomography, or a CAT scan.

The scans were done in a huge machine with a tunnel-like opening, and the object being scanned was put on a moving table which passed the person through the opening in small fits and starts, taking cross-sectional x-rays of the body or part being scanned at each pause, until as much of the part as requested had been photographed. If one can visualize the machine in a deli slicing up bologna, the effect would be about the same, except that instead of actually cutting, the x-ray takes pictures in 'slices'.

Not unexpectedly, the chest scan clearly showed a lesion in the area to the left side of Maria's sternum, or breastbone. The other scans and x-rays apparently revealed no problems.

118

For some inexplicable reason, the results of the bone scan were not available to us until October 7th.

When Doctor Coe informed us the chest lesion 'appeared' to be cancerous, my darling almost came unwired. Once again I held her in my arms and fought from crying while trying to give some comfort or solace to my little sweetheart until she could pull herself together. As I wiped away her tears she grasped the doctor's hand. "Can you remove the lesion, Doctor Coe?" she asked weakly, a tremor in her voice.

"Absolutely," Doctor Coe replied, "we'll take care of that right away, Maria," and he gave her a reassuring squeeze.

Despite his earlier boasting, Doctor Coe most assuredly had *not* gotten all of the cancer when he removed Maria's breast. He should have gone all the way, doing a radical mastectomy and removing the tissue beneath the breast, too, for that ugly monster still skulked within Maria's chest wall. Better yet, they probably should have ordered either radiation or chemotherapy treatments immediately after her mastectomy, as a form of insurance.

Because Maria was so relieved when the doctors informed her further treatment was not needed right after she'd endured the mastectomy, neither of us questioned their decision.

Ten days after her visit with Doctor Coe, on a beautiful fall day, my darling returned to the hospital at 7:00 a.m. to have an operation to remove the cancerous chest lesion, proven to be such by a lab test of the material after it was excised. They didn't even have her stay in the hospital overnight, just let her rest a few hours in 'day care' and sent her home with me where she could go to bed and rest some more.

In contrast with her mastectomy operation, which had no hint of infection, the 3-inch incision appeared swollen when I looked at it just before Maria returned to Doctor Coe's office to remove the stitches. When we left Coe's office I asked

Maria, "Did the doctor say anything about the swelling along your incision?"

"No, he said everything is looking good, and I'm coming along great," she answered. "It didn't hurt the least bit when he took out the stitches, so I guess I'm healing okay."

But to me the incision appeared infected and was obviously swollen. At home in the bathroom, *less than two hours* after her surgeon removed the stitches, Nini barely touched the wound with the tip of her finger and it ruptured and squirted pus clear across the tiled floor!

It took me fifteen minutes to clean the bathroom.

It took several weeks to heal Maria's incision.

Surely her doctor recognized that deep infection as he pulled the stitches, but he obviously worked damned carefully so as not to rupture the swollen area in his office. He left it for Nini to break open.

At first, we had a visiting nurse who came every day to cleanse and dress the gaping wound. Within a few days, the 'hole' was the size of a penny on the surface of Maria's chest, but underneath, it opened out to an elongated quarter and was half an inch deep! I watched the nurse do the relatively simple treatment each day, removing the old dressing, sterilizing the surrounding area, swabbing out the wound, repacking it and covering it with a fresh dressing.

After a few days, I spoke with Doctor Coe and took over the daily treatment. I did that for three reasons. First, it cut down on the cost of a visiting nurse. Second, we eliminated the nuisance of waiting each day for the nurse's visit. She never came at a set time, which often ruined most of our day for other things. And finally, I did the job with greater care and tenderness.

"At first I was scared to have you do it, Daddy," Maria said, "but now I realize you are even gentler than the nurse was . . . I don't feel a bit of pain when you clean the wound."

"Not bad for an old Navy shipfitter and deep-sea diver,

huh?" I asked, pleased with my little chickabiddy's compliment.

I had learned to swab out the pit-like opening, gently pack small squares of sterile gauze into it and then cover it with sterile gauze held on by tape, always wearing fresh sterile rubber gloves as I worked. It took nearly two months for the 'chasm' to heal, with Maria going every week to see Doctor Coe. He never once mentioned the fact that the incision had been swollen and infected when he removed the stitches. Even when she told him how it burst and squirted pus across the bathroom two hours after he'd removed the stitches, he was unapologetic.

His failure to acknowledge his own laxity caused me to look upon Doctor Coe with a jaundiced eye thereafter. But to Maria he was a god who could do no wrong, and she continued to visit him regularly for examinations, even though such examinations were not his specialty: he was a surgeon, not an oncologist. Of course Doctor Coe was not going to dissuade her. Every visit she paid to his office was money in the bank.

At last Nini agreed to my suggestion, and sought out an oncologist whom I shall call Doctor Able. He was a small, worried man, thin and grayed. His office, located in what had once been an old residence, was anything but pretentious, despite its adjoining laboratory and a couple of pleasant nurses. He studied Maria's medical records and ordered tests in his own laboratory, run by a tall, overweight young man whom I assumed was a lab technician, or a paramedic with special training.

Shortly after Maria began to pay visits to Doctor Coe's office, he closed down his lab and let the technician go, telling us it was something about a state inspection or some new, odd-ball regulation. That meant Maria would now take all tests back in the medical building across from the hospital, which made them more costly. This latter factor may have been part of the reason why his lab was shut down. Each segment of the medical profession will fight like a pit bull to hang onto its turf and keep out anyone who tries to cut prices. And a labs makes more money than a 5th Avenue call girl.

After examining Nini thoroughly, Doctor Able gave us his opinion. "There doesn't appear to be any reason for chemotherapy or radiation treatments at this time, Mrs. Leatherman," he said knowingly. "We will just keep an eye on things with regular check-ups in my office and routine lab tests."

His cheering words quickly dispelled our fears that Maria would need further treatment. The surgery had been enough, even if it was screwed up a bit. Doctor Able was the most admired oncologist at the hospital where Nini had her operations, so we were eager to believe him and trust his judgment. His words as an oncologist also buttressed the opinion of Dr, Coe, so we naturally assumed that, finally, all was well with Maria.

But such was not the case.

Most unfortunately, the pain and inconvenience of the chest surgery, the infected incision, and the prolonged treatment of the wound had all been for naught, for my darling had not been cured of cancer. She began to feel, not just light stabs of pain in her chest, but prolonged periods of dull pain. After she complained to Doctor Able several times, he referred her to the lady doctor who ran the radiation unit at Pines of Ponderosa hospital.

Finally, months and months after her mastectomy, the three doctors got their heads together in conference, and decided that, yes, Maria should undergo radiation treatments.

That news almost broke Maria's heart. "I'm so upset, Daddy," she complained to me back in the condo. "Everyone told me I was cured, that the cancer was gone. Now they say I wasn't healed, and the cancer is still inside me," and she broke down and cried in my arms, her head resting on my chest, her body racked with sobs, her mind beset by new fears. I held her tightly, and almost silently, except for my own repressed sobs, until her weeping weakened and ceased.

It was almost criminal how we had been conned into believing Maria was overcoming the Big C, and then were let down so suddenly and so heartlessly. *"It just isn't fair,'* I thought, and grew so angry I wanted to attack someone barefisted.

Out on the inlet which formed our front yard, a pelican was fishing, pestered by an obnoxious seagull which kept trying to steal the fish from his very bill!

'*My poor Maria,'* I thought as I held my Bahiana close and stroked her back and kissed her coppery hair, *'just like that pelican, she is under attack by a worrisome, unrelenting enemy, and there isn't a damned thing I can do to help her. We are caught up in the web of modern-day medicine, and are virtually helpless in the hands of a crew of medical practitioners.'*

How I wished I'd been born rich, or had garnered wealth as I grew up in the Great Depression! Then we could have gone to a great cancer clinic, such as in Houston, and Maria could have had the professional care of a battery of experts, using all of the latest equipment and drugs for testing, treating and curing cancer, or putting it in remission, if there were no cure. But we weren't rich. We just had to make do.

CHAPTER 14

It was October 15 when, at the suggestion of Doctor Able, Maria went to see Doctor Brown, the lady in charge of the radiology unit at Pines of Ponderosa hospital. That pleasantly efficient lady, a tall, thin, intense brunette, said that before she could start any radiology treatments on Maria's chest, she needed more than a skull x-ray: she needed an MRI *brain* scan. Maria braved the special Magnetic Resonance Imaging machine—a form of magnetometer used to measure the magnetic field of certain body organs, including the brain—to take the scan the next day. To our knowledge, that scan did not reveal any type of abnormality.

Doctor Brown scheduled Maria for a pre-radiology examination on October 27. "We need to calculate how much radiation we have to use, where to focus it, the angle of approach and the duration of each treatment," she explained to us as we sat nervously in her small consultation room off the Radiology Unit. (Damn, how I hated even the *name* of that unit!) The preliminary part of the procedure was critically important, because if they used too much radiation, or directed it to the wrong area, or for too long, Maria could suffer either external or internal injury, or both.

"I'm so scared of radiation, Daddy!" Nini said, almost in tears. "Nivaldo does a lot of radiology work, and he says it is very rough on people and sometimes makes them very sick."

Before I could answer, Doctor Brown tried to ease her fears. "We have very advanced equipment now, Maria, and we can determine almost precisely how to attack any cancer

---

which may remain in your chest. You may feel a sort of 'morning sickness' after a treatment. But it shouldn't last long."

"What has to be done has to be done, so let's get started right away," Maria said resignedly, What a stout-hearted woman I had selected from among all that bevy of beauties back in Bahia!

I had one request to make before starting treatment. "May we see the machine which you use to give the treatments, Doctor?" I asked. I felt that becoming acquainted with the device before she had to lie on its table and be treated by it might make the first treatment less frightening for Maria.

"Of course," the doctor said, and called a young man who was a technical specialist trained in the field. He was over six feet tall, husky, but not fat. In his early 30s, he had a warm smile, and turned out to be a very kind and caring individual. Most certainly he helped make Maria's treatments a bit more bearable, looking after her with tenderness and patience. For example, he never had a nurse 'call' her, but always came out to walk her from the waiting room to the radiology room with his arm around her. By the time her treatments were completed Maria adored him almost as much as her red-headed surgeon.

We were soon in the insulated room where the large, sleek machine stood in mid-floor. It really didn't look too ominous as it sat there alone, waiting to go to work. The young man showed how a patient would lie immobile on the table, and demonstrated how the 'head' of the device could be programmed to reach any part of one's body, from any angle, with its curative rays. He showed us the screen-like material of mesh which he would place on her chest to contain the range of the radiation within the proper area. The mesh resembled the chain-mail of a knight of old.

We didn't know the radiation was Beta rays until we talked to Bobby on the phone that night and he told us. "Oh, sure, Mama, I know the machine. It's a Beta-ray generator, and is quite simple. It should be able to help you. And don't worry about it, Mom . . . the machine is a regular pussycat." Bobby had majored in physics at Drexel Institute of Technology in Philadelphia, so I figured he knew Beta rays, and many other rays as well.

"I'm not too sure about that," Nini replied. "Anything that can zap you with any kind of rays is something to fear. I don't even stay in the kitchen when the microwave is on!"

We went to Radiology on the 27th, where they used what I believe was an x-ray or a special scanning device with which to plot out the angles of attack, and did the math to determine the strength and duration of radiation for the treatment next day. Maria's chest was covered with purple lines when she came back from that session. "I have to take care not to erase the lines," she said, "they are guides to tell the technician where to set the machine to work."

"So they drew up a plot plan for your treatments, huh?" I asked, trying to ease the force of the headache I had suddenly taken on. I rarely ever had a headache, but lately I'd found myself taking more aspirin in a week than I'd taken in all my life before. The worry was just too much for me, and I'd build up an awful pressure in my thick skull. That was one reason I took Maria on our Mexico trip via air, and our U.S. tour via Airstream—to get *my* mind, as well as hers, off her medical problems. To have her break her wrist the day we left with the Airstream dampened the relief I'd expected, but still I had no headaches during either of those trips.

The radiology unit had its own parking lot, segregated from the rest of the hoi-poloi, with special windshield passes for the patients. We were in it just before 8:45 on October 29 for Maria's first radiation treatment. That was not a very happy way to start our day, or to finish the month of October, for Nini had another treatment on the 30th.

We had the weekend off, but Monday, November 2, we were back in Radiology, sitting among a number of patients who were there for the same reason. Luckily, we were able to schedule Maria as the first patient every morning. Or perhaps not so fortunately: for the man who previously had that appointment time had just passed away. I knew that, but Maria didn't.

The radiation treatments continued through November 25, when we had a day off for Thanksgiving, and the current 'series' ended a day later. By that time, Maria's poor chest was bright red and 'burned' worse than if she'd spent days at the beach sunbathing. Because of the effect on her skin, and inner flesh, I suppose, Doctor Brown held off for a few days, before beginning the next series of treatments.

My little Bahiana remained so much in command of her will and her body that Wednesday evening we drove south to Marco Island to visit Robbie and gang and Maxine for Thanksgiving. At dinner next day, Robbie invited me to ask the blessing.

I gave thanks that Maria had come through her operations, and asked for support for her in standing up to the fearsome radiation blasts. Then I asked the Lord to bless Maxine and the Taylor family, thanked Him for His care of them during the past year, and they all said 'Amen'.

We were ready to tackle the turkey, dig into the dressing, put away the potatoes and cram down the cranberry sauce.

Robbie and Sis and girls had prepared a magnificent dinner, and Nini and I gorged ourselves. Other than that, it was not a happy holiday for us. As we dined, a lot of the conversation was about Maria's radiation treatments, the novelty of which evoked considerable curiosity among their family.

"At least my hair didn't fall out!" Nini exclaimed with a show of pride. "I was so afraid I'd have to go around in a wig, like a circus clown."

"Well, we're all glad you still have your coppery hair, Aunt Maria," Robbie said. My sister's pretty daughter had been named Robin after me. She was slender, smart and perennialy cheerful. Their two girls, Sarah and Laura, were equally bright and energetic. Their blithe spirits soon rubbed off on the two of us, and we drove home that Thanksgiving evening in the happiest mood we'd been in for some time. The sack full of turkey and stuff Robbie had fixed for us which rode in the trunk may have helped a bit. There was still the dampening effect of the radiation sessions yet to come, but one bright thought cheered us up: in two more weeks Nini's radiology treatments would end.

The day after Thanksgiving, Maria got the final radiation treatment of that first 'series', as Doctor Brown called it.

During those treatments, Maria sometimes felt weak or sensed some dizziness, but they never upset her stomach nor made her truly ill. *'It's as though she has the blood of Vikings in her,'* I thought. But in fact the Portuguese blood of the Mouras and the Andrades flowed in her veins. She was descended of the race which gave the world the dauntless explorers who dared to sail around the southern tip of Africa to fight their way to India and the Spice Islands; men with the nerve to push their tiny caravels westward across the unknown Atlantic in 1500 to discover the continent of South America, particularly what is now Brazil.

Unquestionably, Maria had the blood of brave, strong people coursing through her body, and she stood up to those radiation treatments with Portuguese courage and stoicism.

In actuality, Maria *was* 'burned' as she endured her weeks of daily treatment in the radiation unit. The skin on the center of, and right side of, her lower breastbone dried out, and turned red and scaly-rough. Regardless of where they programmed the machine to move and zap, most of the time the rays entered her chest within a small radius. And that small area began to resemble the surface of a piece of seared beefsteak.

Fearing for Maria's health, I had to inject myself into the process in the middle of the series. "Isn't Maria's chest getting terribly burned?" I ask Doctor Brown as we met after one treatment.

"Yes, it is, Robin, but I want it to get that way. It's part of the proof that I am reaching the points inside Maria which we have to treat. But don't you worry . . . either of you . . . for I keep a constant control over the radiation, day by day," and she gave Nini a squeeze, her slender frame pressed close to Maria's ampler one.

It was not simply a program of radiation, of course. For it was necessary for Maria to have special x-rays and blood tests taken regularly in order for Doctor Brown, the radiologist, Doctor Able, the oncologist, Doctor Coe, the surgeon and Doctor Jones, her regular physician, to assess the results of the treatments as they progressed. Medicare, Prudential and the Leathermans were helping to support not just the radiology unit at the hospital, but four doctors as well, each of whom wished to keep abreast of Maria's progress or lack thereof.

The bills which poured in as Maria's treatments went along were anything but trivial. The hospital charges to cover the radiation were $826, $475, $1,060, $833, $2,203, $3,682 and finally, $631. Those bills included the radiation therapy, plus drugs, lab tests, scans, x-rays—perhaps even janitorial services. Added to those charges was the steady flow of bills from the doctors involved; plus charges for interpreting x-rays and CT and MRI scans, pathology expenses and the cost of oral medications.

Doctor Brown picked up Maria's treatments from December 1st through the 8th. She followed that for another week, up to the 16th with what she called 'booster' radiation, which I believe was of lesser intensity, or shorter duration or both.

To what benefit Maria had endured all that microwaving nobody knew. Neither Maria nor I, nor the surgeon, nor the oncologist nor the radiologist knew. Drs. Coe, Able and Brown, plus the X-ray technicians and radiology technicians hadn't the vaguest idea whether or not that long series of radiological intrusions had effected any progress in curing Maria's cancer. If all, or any, of those medical specialists and their technical assistants *did* know, they never communicated such information to Maria and me. For us, it was a bitter case of 'pray for the best, and wait and see'.

Before the year was over, then, the doctors ended Maria's series of radiation treatments, procedures which Maria and I both recognized now should have been done right after her mastectomy, despite Doctor Coe's reassurance that he had removed all of the cancer during his surgery. Nowadays, I believe most doctors suggest that either chemotherapy or radiation be pursued immediately after a lumpectomy or mastectomy brought on by breast cancer. But in my beloved Maria's case that was not done.

One other problem arose in December when a test of Maria's stool revealed occult blood. Doctor Smith, a proctologist, examined her in his office and found three or four polyps in her colon. They called me in to review the findings and discuss the laser surgery involved. "About what will that cost?" I asked, to get some idea of the effect on our already stretched-to-the-limit budget.

"A bit over eight hundred dollars," he informed us. That was a lot of money, but less than I had expected.

"Well, we have to take care of Maria as soon as possible," I said. Maria said she would like to get it over with quickly, they promptly arranged to do the job the 16th, at Pines of Ponderosa.

"I am so worried about polyps I don't know what to do," Maria sighed as we drove home. "I'm afraid they are caused by the spread of that breast cancer."

"No, honey, I don't think they are necessarily connected. Anyway, Doctor Smith will take care of them when he operates. The laser will burn them out and seal the wounds, like he said."

Perhaps a few words concerning my 'cost' worries are
in order. I am not a mercenary man, and money does
not control my life; if it did, I'd have a lot more of it.
But it was my impression that asking what some medical procedure cost *before* proceeding with it made
sense, what with our tight budget. We don't buy cars
or houses without asking what they cost, so why should
we buy operations without inquiring?

With Maria's health, perhaps even her life, at stake,
we would proceed regardless of the cost, but asking
beforehand seemed prudent. Look how that substitute doctor shafted us!

I will also give recaps of some costs from time to time
as I go along, but again that is to show how medical
costs have sky-rocketed, and to engender a little
shame in our health care providers, if such is possible!.

On the 16th we went early to the out-patient unit at the
hospital, they prepared Nini for surgery and before noon
Doctor Smith had used special hospital gear to peer far into
her colon, and burn out and seal off several polyps. Nini had
a liquid lunch at the hospital while recuperating, and after a
two-hour rest she was ready to go home with me.

When we got the bill from the hospital it was for $826;
and that of Doctor Jones was $834. We had asked the good
doctor what the surgery would cost, and he had quoted only
his fee, not the hospital costs. No wonder it had seemed cheap,
for it was double his figure when all the bills were in. Happily, Maria was never bothered again by polyps of the colon,
so it was certainly worth the money, even if the doctor had
not been that forthcoming.

The year 1987 finally ended after a sea of troubles; a
year filled with doctor visits, a plethora of medicines, several
catscans and x-rays for Nini, scores of blood tests which left

Maria's poor arms filled with needle marks, a visit from Kathy and kids, a trip to Mexico by air, another to Kathy's house by Airstream, and ending with Maria's tiring series of radiation treatments and her 'embarrassing' colon surgery, as she referred to it.

Over it all, for me, had been the constant worry that my darling Maria's cancer was not yet under control, despite the surgeries and drugs and tests and scans and radiation. Deep down in my heart, suppressed from truly coming to the surface, lay the nagging fear that we'd never whip that bastard of a cancer.

When at times I caught Maria with a far-away look in her eyes and with her lips slightly compressed, I knew that in her, too, the same horrible thoughts persistently oozed to the surface of her consciousness—like prehistoric fossils pushing up from the depths of the La Brea tar pits—to harass her mentally and emotionally, and never permit her any true peace of mind.

CHAPTER 15

During the first weeks of 1988 our lives together were a bit less hectic, insofar as doctors, hospitals and treatments for Maria were concerned. "I'm so thankful that Doctor Smith took care of those polyp things," Nini said as we moved into the second half of a rather chilly January.

"I know, *querida*," I agreed. "I'm glad he had them checked by the pathologist. It's such a relief to know they were not malignant." I knew what she was thinking, and I tried to add to her peace of mind on the subject.

"*Gracas a Deus!*" Maria said, with a sigh. Thank the Lord.

We lived our lives in the same basic routines or ruts: Maria's bridge and church, my work on my bio, watching TV in the evening, and dining out regularly, varying from seafood places to steak houses to Wendy's to Chinese or Mexican food. When we got an urge for Greek food, we'd drive up along the coastal barrier islands north to Tarpon Springs and dine at Papas Restaurant, where I loved their huge Greek salads with a scoop of potato salad buried in the middle and the anchovies on top. Or we'd have gyros at the Lighthouse Restaurant.

We'd stroll the sponge docks and gift shops and maybe ride the 'tourist' sponge boat out into the Anclote River to watch the sponge-diving exhibition. Because I'd been a hardhat diver in the Navy, I enjoyed swapping stories with the sponge diver, who at least feigned an interest in my Navy diving anecdotes.

The first week in April Maria returned for a chest x-ray

133

and another mammogram (*At half-price now?*, I mused bitterly, though I doubt that it was), and with nothing reported as out of line, we relaxed again.

Maria continued to take Nolvadex, the brand name for tamoxifen, an anti-cancer drug used in the treatment of advanced breast cancer. She didn't seem to suffer any ill effects from the drug, which works against cancers whose growth is stimulated by female sex hormones called estrogens. Tamoxifen latches onto the cells that recognize those hormones and thus slows the growth of the tumor and even shrinks it.

At least that's how it was supposed to work. It wasn't until late August of 1999 that word hit the papers and airwaves that prolonged usage of tamoxifen can actually abet breast cancer, rather than hinder it. I don't know just how long a period the experts meant when they said 'prolonged' usage, but I'm sure it varies by expert. And I have an idea Maria was on the drug long enough to qualify!

After blood tests, EKG and x-rays again on May 1 revealed no problems, and with Nini feeling chipper, I suggested another trip out west. Nini was ready, but she put a condition on her acceptance. "I want you to trade the Airstream trailer for a small motor home, Daddy. I don't like to watch you strain to hook the trailer to the Suburban. It's not good for you at your age."

"If you insist," I gave in easily. We drove to a large dealership in Tampa and traded the Airstream and a few dollars for a brand new Winnebago motor home, which, as I recall was 26 feet long. In a few days it arrived from the factory, and we pulled the Airstream to the dealership and completed the trade.

"It's very well laid out," Maria observed as we transferred our gear from the Airstream to the Winnie, being careful not to break anything—especially on Maria, such as wrists, arms or legs. "I think we will enjoy it a lot," she said, settling into her co-pilot's seat to test it for size and comfort. We headed back across the bridge to a storage place we'd found on Park Boulevard, with me driving the Winnie and Nini following in the Suburban.

June 24th we wrestled the Winnie into Bay Island and put the food and such in it for the trip. We had picked up a TV set, and an excellent small microwave-broiler-toaster combination to use on the trip, for the Winnie was not so equipped.

The next morning, Saturday, Maria went to early Mass—to compensate for not going Sunday—and we left the complex at 9:50 to begin our trip. I was especially happy as we headed up the highway, with Maria apparently feeling almost 100%—and with no doctors to see for a couple of months. We drove to Forsythe, Georgia, and stopped overnight in a KOA campground.

Sunday we continued on to Nashville. I had taken the demo tapes of two songs I'd written lyrics and music for, and Monday I visited two music companies, for my songs were closer to country than anything else. I was speedily informed by each company that they had their own song writers and didn't buy from outsiders: take that, along with forty lashes!

But then one secretary at Roy Acuff's outfit listened to the tapes, telephoned someone somewhere, and after hanging up turned to me. "If you wish, I'll send your tapes over to the Hee Haw show. They may have an interest in them. But it will take a while, because Roy Clark [singer, guitar player *par excellence* and Hee Haw emcee] is in Europe."

"That's great, thanks a lot," I said, and my co-conspirators bestowed pretty smiles on me as I left the office. At least that was something to look forward to. The Hee Maw show, despite its country corn, performed some excellent music and had top-flight musicians. If they used one of my songs, it would be a real break for me. I'd written several songs over the years without ever doing anything with them. Now at least I had tried.

1020-LEAT

Space does not permit my detailing the many adventures we had on what turned out to be a fantastic tour of the West and South, But I will include a few details, starting with our visit to what was then the Country-Western Music Capital of the World. Maria enjoyed Nashville and the music immensely, and since she was the inspiration for some of my songs, she'd have been highly pleased if I could finally get one published and perhaps on the air. Besides, she loved people, and we met a number of most interesting folks all along our trip.

We took a night tour of Nashville, visiting a club owned by the Statler Brothers (I think it was), where they served us a great dinner and put on a fine show. From there we took in the show put on by Boots Randolph and his famous 'Yackety Sax' style music. He and his band were great, and he had a young man who was a virtuoso guitar player, at least in my opinion.

Boots had a great idea to increase sales. Our tour included his show, plus a drink. When Nini spied the glass boots with his name on them she was delighted. "I want to drink my beer from a boot!" she cried.

"You can even take the boot home with you for a dollar extra," our pretty server was pleased to point out. So that's what we did. To keep the tab down, I drank my beer from a plain glass or mug.

On the way out after the show, Boots was in the lobby with a goodly stash of records, and I bought one, which he very happily autographed. The reason he was happy was because Maria had asked him for his autograph but didn't buy a record.

"So what should I sign?" he laughed.

"My purse, so all my friends will see your autograph!" she laid her big brown eyes on him, and he laughed and complied.

The purse was made of material resembling parachute cloth, and his husky signature stood out brilliantly.

If Maria ever thought about breast cancer, which did not cause her any pain or inconvenience during our trip, it wasn't revealed by her words or actions for the next few weeks as we made our sweeping tour by motor home.

That trip carried us through 20 states including Florida, and lasted from June 26 until August 27, two months and a day.

Major events included a motor home breakdown in the Idaho desert 80 miles from nowhere when we visited the first atomic reactor in the world to produce electricity, and a Montana restaurant and saloon with 10,000 silver dollars glued in the walls and tables.

Then a special tour which began with granddaughter Cynthia accompanying us to a reunion with my classmates of Parkdale High in Oregon; then a trip encompassing Central Oregon and Eastern Washington. We returned her to Oak Harbor, and soon left for home, driving the length of the rugged Oregon coast south to California, where we called on Mt. Shasta to view the scenes of her great eruption back in May of 1915, three years before I was born.

We made visits to several Indian tribes in New Mexico, including the Hopi, the Zuni, and the Acoma atop their 357-foot high mesa in the middle of the desert. We toured the El Morro cliffs where pioneers stopped for water when crossing that diabolical stretch of desert known as the *mal pais*—badlands.

We visited the old haunts of Geronimo, and hit Tombstone just in time for their annual festival of the days of Wyatt Earp and the O.K Corral—and of Judge Bean, who, in olden times, was the law west of the Pecos, and the saloon he ran, where spitting on the floor and cursing were not allowed.

I must recount the incidents in Tombstone, where in the space of two hours there were several shoot-outs between vicious gunmen, and some between gunmen and marshals. After one of those noisy scenes, a 'marshal' wearing a star

137

and twin holsters, sidled up alongside Maria. "Are you the woman who's been causin' all the trouble in that saloon across the street?" he asked in a gruff voice. Before she could sputter an answer, he continued, "You look mighty suspicious to me. I think I'd just better lock you up." He took her by the arm and headed into the street.

"Help me, Roberto!" Nini cried, not really sure if the cop was playing with her or was maybe serious.

So I cut in to save my darlin'. "Unhand that lady, marshal! She's ma woman, and she ain't done nothin' wrong in this yere town since we got in this mawnin'." The marshal released his prisoner and in two seconds Nini was back clinging to my arm like a leech to a wader's leg. Maria was no more than free, when the marshal was suddenly mixed up in a battle with some shifty-eyed gunslinger trying to make a name fer hisself. Happily, the marshal kilt him, provin' the Lord is on the good guys' side.

From El Paso, we made a tour of the old missions down the western border of Texas along the Rio Grande to Brownsville, with short visits across the border to the 'sister cities' in old Mexico; a tour of Big Bend National Park, via tiny Presidio on the Rio Grande, where in one place the Winnie had to climb a 17-degree stretch of narrow road poised over a canyon chewed out by the muddy river below.

We had the chance to watch a herd of pronghorn antelope grazing south of Alpine; and had stays in Corpus Christi, San Antonio, Galveston and Houston, which meant that almost every important city in Texas was now entered in our travel log.

To end the trek, we made a dash along the Gulf across Louisiana, Mississippi and Alabama on our way home. As a last treat in our tour, we stayed overnight in the isolated village of Steinhatchee located on the Florida Gulf Coast not far from where the Florida panhandle begins. Steinhatchee was famous for its seafood and laid-back atmosphere, and was said to catch and import a fair amount of 'square grouper', which was not fish, of course.

This was back in the days that smugglers dropped bales of marijuana into the gulf from airplanes, and fishermen in small boats retrieved the pot and hauled it ashore.

It was perhaps some kind of miracle that Maria never had a twinge or an ache caused by anything inside her. She bounced along beside me in her co-pilot's chair as happy as a schoolgirl with a new beau; and whatever there was to do, she was ready and able to do it, although we refrained from hikes and climbs such as we'd made in our younger days.

When the rest of 1988 passed without incident, cancerwise, I felt sure Nini had bested her attacker, that her cancer was in remission and we were home free. She made regular check-up visits to Doctor Jones and Doctor Able, and from all appearances she was doing exceptionally well. She had no complaints, and was happy in her life in the condominium. Christmas and New Years came and went, with a nighttime boat parade outside our front door as yachtsman from the surrounding communities decorated their boats with colorful lights and fancy motifs and passed in a long procession around the inlets of Boca Ciega Bay, including our front yard.

I have no record of treatments or special medications for Maria during all of 1989 except for the Nolvadex, or tamoxifen, pills which she continued to take on a daily basis. She took a Tylenol from time to time, as well as Ativan, but no 'special' drugs for cancer or any other ailment. It was like being in heaven to have her at my side living a normal life. There was a time for about five days in January when Maria had some pain in her left arm, but it went away with a bit of help from Tylenol.

We celebrated our 45th wedding anniversary on January 20 with dinner at a steak house; and on January 27 we visited

139

the dinosaur museum in St. Pete, and saw the 'Junkosaurus' statue, created from scrap metal and trash, which adorned the corner of the parking lot outside.

The new year was going along well, until on February 10 I accidentally mashed my finger in the car door when it slammed on me while I was stowing groceries in the back seat. We went into an Italian restaurant for lunch, and they put adhesive strips on the cut to stop the bleeding so we could dine on linguine with white clam sauce. The finger healed in a few days, and that was that—though I was still teed off with the car door.

In early March we shopped for a smaller car after finding a buyer at a good price for the Suburban. Our final choice was a new Dodge Shadow, which rode softly and ran like a jeweled watch. It was much easier for Maria to maneuver in a parking lot or on the street, as compared to the big Suburban.

Maria visited Doctor Brown on April 17, her dermatologist on the 18th, and had a mammogram on the 19th, taking care of her appointments for the month. Again, nobody informed us of any problems, and when Maria called the offices of the medics, the girls told her everything was normal, she was in fine shape. All of our doctors had the same habit of sending Maria for tests, and never reporting back. "Oh, if there's nothing wrong we don't bother," one nurse said blithely.

Day by day, the month of May drifted off into eternity, and all the while, Maria was feeling great. In June her dermatologist removed a mole under her left arm, and she visited Doctor Brown on the 23rd for a simple consultation so doctor could verify how she was doing. July was equally suave. Maria's dermatologist removed three 'molls', as Maria showed them on her calendar, and that took care of her physical condition and medical check-ups.

We were both greatly relieved as the weeks passed and Maria's visits to the doctors revealed no new problems or any resurgences of old ones.

Eventually I suggested another trip in the motor home. "You enjoyed the reunion of the battleship Maryland sailors in Boston, didn't you?" I asked Maria one evening.

"I really did," she replied. "They're such a great bunch of people, and the tours we took were a lot of fun."

"Then we should drive up to Bobby's place for a visit with his gang, and from there head out to Denver and the Big Mary reunion. Does that sound okay to you?"

"It sounds wonderful," she said, "Perhaps we can thaw some of the ice out of Judy's relationship with us. If not, we can still enjoy Bobby and the girls."

"Right on!" I said. "But it's inconvenient to have to go everywhere with the motorhome when we're traveling. If we want to go to a movie, we have to unhook the RV and drive to the theater, and sometimes have trouble finding a parking space that's big enough. Then after the show, it's drive the RV back to the park and hook up the water, electricity and sewer again. I'm thinking of getting a simple, two-wheel trailer to tow behind the Winnie, with the Dodge's front wheels on it. [The Shadow had a front-wheel drive.] Then when we take a side trip to see a canyon or some Indian ruins, we can leave the RV behind, and just take the Dodge. It might save us some gas, too," "That sounds like a good idea," Maria agreed, "if it's not hard to put the car on the trailer and take it off."

"Actually, it takes about five minutes for each, and it's easy. When we're driving, the Shadow will not be a problem. It will follow along behind like a dog at our heels." Maria was ready and willing, so I found a shop to supply the trailer at 30% off list, and to install the tow-bar on the Winnie. In a few days we set off on another high adventure.

We didn't know it, but that would be our last marvelous trip together; so I beg the reader's indulgence as I take a few pages to describe briefly some highlights of our tour—which turned out to be an interlude of peace and calm just before the storm.

141

CHAPTER 16

It was August 14th when we stuffed the last of our gear in the Winnebago and hooked up the Kar Kaddy trailer with the Shadow resting its front wheels comfortably on the wee rig and rarin' to go. We headed out at 9:40 a.m.. Seven miles up the road, I stopped to give the Shadow and its carrier the once-over to insure that all was well in the towing department. The retaining straps around the front wheels were as snug as two lovers in the rumble seat of a 1932 Chevy coupe. I didn't expect any towing problems, and there were none. A glance in my rear-view mirror showed the Dodge trailing the motor home like a whale calf following its mother.

We dropped anchor that night in a delightful RV park known as the Oaks Plantation, on the outskirts of Charleston, South Carolina. The next day, we took the Shadow and toured the city: the streets of lovely homes; the Citadel; the great Farmers' Market, where we bought Benne Seed Wafers (sesame seed, that is) to take to Bobby's gang and to nibble as we toured, and a cute basket hand-woven from marsh grass; then coffee and creampuffs. We finished off with the Sight and Sound Show, and an Adventure Sightseeing tour, both fascinating.

The next day we were back in the city to walk the parks and the Battery, and take a boat to visit Fort Sumpter, where the first shots of the Civil War were fired. The number, types and sizes of guns and cannon at the fort amazed me, and we soaked up history by the gallon before the boat took us back to town.

The Captain was a fine guide, and proudly pointed out one feature which was surprising. "Y'all should know that Charleston is located at the mouths of three rivers, the Cooper, the Wando and the Ashley which converge here to form the Atlantic Ocean."

The next day we were off for Rochester, through Columbia, capital of South Carolina, and on to Charlotte, following I-77 through Virginia and over the Appalachians into West Virginia. We traveled 500 miles that day, through enough greenclad mountains to keep even an old Coloradoan happy.

The next day we drove I-81 to Harrisburg, cutting across western Maryland. We fought our way north through Pennsylvania and New York to find an RV park in the tiny community of Le Roy, a suburb of Rochester just off I-490. The beautiful park was in what had once been an apple orchard nestled in a pretty vale.

Bobby's entire menage came out to see us. He looked great at 220 pounds after losing some weight. Judy, too, had lost a few pounds, but not her grudge. The girls were their usual slender, ebullient selves, relating adventures, and going about the park playground doing dance routines, for Sheila, Tina and Melissa had all taken dancing lessons since age three.

Next day we cleaned the motorhome and had it serviced, and washed clothes in the park laundry where we met a man and wife who were circus performers. They had four cylindrical bags of clothes at least two feet in diameter and four feet tall. "I'm so happy when our schedule allows us an afternoon off so I can catch up with our laundry," the lady told Maria. "We haven't been able to wash clothes for almost two weeks, and we're about out of anything clean to wear!"

"Now that's very interesting," Maria said amiably, "I had never thought about that. When I see a circus I think of lots of animals and excitement . . . but it never occurred to me that you folks may have a hard time keeping your laundry caught up. It's tough enough for me, even with a washer and dryer in my condo!"

That night at Bobby's we dined on turkey sausages and buns.

Later we toured the Rochester Zoo with Bobby, Tina and Mellisa, eating hotdogs for lunch. Then in the afternoon we went with them to a shopping mall where the girls performed dance routines for the busy shoppers. Sheila was fine in a duet with a girl from her dancing class, and Tina was in a small group which did well. But little Melissa did a solo that radiated more energy than the nuclear pile of a generating plant. For supper Bobby got 'fancy' pizzas from a place where he and the owner were well acquainted, and added hot Buffalo wings for dessert.

The next day, Bobby took us on a tour of old Fort Niagara with Tina and Melissa, where Maria bought a white rabbit skin for a dollar. We then picked up Judy and Sheila to dine on 'red hots' and 'white hots' (sausages), specialties of the Rochester area, and, to Maria and me, *muitos gostosos*, very tasty. They dropped us off at the Winnie, and stayed long enough for Sheila to eat most of the Rice Krispy and peanut squares Maria made for our trip.

We bid Bobby's gang goodby the evening of the 28th, and the next morning at 8:30 we were on the road, heading for Denver. We drove as far as Sunbury, near Columbus, Ohio before bedding down for the night. That we had decided to head west via that capital was most fortunate, for the next morning we learned that the 'Son of Heaven' exhibit from China was running in Columbus. We spent several hours visiting the historic display, which included many of the terra cotta soldiers which had been unearthed in China, along with a team of clay horses from that same archeological site, plus a reconstructed wooden cart. Of course there was a gift shop filled with beautiful Chinese objects, none of which we could afford.

That special exhibit would be shown in Columbus and Seattle, and perhaps Topeka, Kansas. The rest of America missed a golden opportunity by not hosting the show, although it cost Columbus a small fortune to set up the great hall exactly as the Chinese insisted it be done. The show was a masterpiece of display and lighting. Nini and I tingled with excitement as we moved from one enclosed section to another.

After the exhibit, we went west on I-70 through Indianapolis and on to Effingham, Illinois, where we spent the night. The next day we drove to St. Louis, passed through the two Kansas Cities and camped for the night in Salinas after 530 miles on the road.

The following day we drove through heavy gusts of wind and spates of torrential rainfall. Then in the afternoon the sky gave up its dark and threatening manner and became an aquamarine dome with an undercoating of buttermilk clouds reminding us of Wedgewood. It was a fascinating day of driving, even though at times the wind shook the Winnie and her trailing puppy like toys. When we reached Denver the heavy weather had abated, and the sky was clear when we pulled into an RV park in Loveland, near Fort Collins.

Although the reunion was in Denver, we chose a Loveland RV park so we might see Maria's grandniece, Cristina, and her husband Hugh, both of whom were engineers at Hewlett-Packard nearby. Cristina was the daughter of Maria's brother's son, Agildo. She spoke several languages and ended up managing a research project at H-P, after graduating summa cum laud in electrical engineering at the University of Miami and earning a doctorate in same at Cornell.

We went by their apartment and left a note on the door, and that evening they came to visit us in the Winnie. The next day we took the Shadow and toured Estes Park and crossed over the Divide through Rocky Mountain National Park to Grand Lake and Granby. We had lunch in that city

145

where my step-dad's brother had once owned a small hotel back in the 1920s. Then it was south to Tabernash and Frazer, and more south, to I-70 and east to Denver and home.

"I will always remember the first time we crossed through these mountains," Nini said, as we followed Trail Ridge Road through the glorious peaks and areas of green tundra over the Continental Divide. "I was awfully scared of the twists and turns, but Bobby and Kathy were filled with excitement. And when we reached Loveland for lunch, Bobby had a hamburger, and when the waitress asked what we all wanted for dessert, Bobby said he'd like another hamburger! That was so cute. Especially when the waitress looked at us, and asked, 'Is that okay?' and you said, 'Give the laddie what he wants', just like Marshal Field's store always tries to 'Give the lady what she wants'!"

September 5 we went into Denver to the Regency Hotel, registered for the *Maryland* reunion, left copies of my poetry book with the 'registrars' and visited with some ex-swabbies who had already matriculated. Ed Davis appeared to be in good health, though cancer had caused the recent removal of two feet of his colon. Another shipmate, the third member of our 1930's Shipfitter Shop trio, Tony Belotti, had died of lung cancer since the Boston reunion. We also learned about a man we met in Boston whose aneurism ruptured on his way home from the reunion, resulting in his death.

The following day we drove into Denver and found a beauty salon to do Maria's hair, then made a tour of the downtown area, including the capitol and its lovely grounds. I went to a bank and drew $800 against a Visa card, replenishing our supply of walking-around money.

The next day we went to the Regency to visit with old shipmates, and from there took tour busses to visit the Coors brewery in Golden. The trip was fabulous. The brewery is huge. It employed over 10,000 people, and gave business to over 1,700 farmers in Wyoming, Montana and Idaho. Coors had their own can factory, and even grew the flowers on display in the plant. They told us it was the largest brewery in the U.S., and 70% of the output was shipped in cans. It went in refrigerated trucks and railroad cars to every state in the union except Indiana, which demanded that all beer shipped into it be pasteurized.

After our plant tour, we saw a film on Sports Bloopers, and then enjoyed a buffet supper in the offices of the plant. That free supper was special for we veterans, and was an excellent repast. As a memento they gave me a miniature Coors beer can containing two golfballs.

The next morning we had a simple business meeting, and then took off in busses to visit the grave of William Cody, or Buffalo Bill, located high on Lookout Mountain, where he is interred, as is his wife, Louisa. Buffalo Bill lived to age 71, and died in 1917, less than a year before I was born. There was a connection between us, for I was born in Cheyenne, and Buffalo Bill killed the Cheyenne chief called Yellow Hand. Buffalo Bill was famous for killing 4,280 buffaloes in 17 months, helping to drive that species almost to extinction. He was also known for his Wild West show which toured America and Europe, featuring Chief Sitting Bull and the lady sharpshooter known as Annie Oakley.

Back home at last, we cleaned up for the dinner-dance that night at the Regency. "You veterans can't get in the hall unless you wear some part of your old Navy uniform," Ed Davis put out the word. All I had was my blue jacket with eight decorations from campaigns in the Atlantic and the Pacific. Apparently it had shrunk, for it would no longer button. I wore it open in the front.

The dinner was mediocre, and the sound system awful, but we danced a few times to a live band which played many of the Big Band songs of the 1930s and '40s. We were home and in bed by 11:00, just as a lightning storm struck our area. It featured gigantic, dazzling shots of forked lightning, sheet

147

lightning and chain lightning, plus peals of heavy thunder which made the Winnie quiver like a go-go girl's bottom in full swing.

It was interesting that the shipfitter who had reached the highest rank in the Navy was 'Scoop' Johnson. He was not our brightest man, but he had reached the rank of Commander, or the equivalent of Lieutenant Colonel in the Army. He did 30 years of active duty before retiring. That told me where I might have ended up had I stayed in the Navy when the war ended. But I sacrificed over 9 years of service and the rank of Chief Warrant Officer in order to be home with my wife and children, which meant more to me than a Navy career.

On the 9th, Maria and I went our separate ways for the tours. She took in the Air Force Academy, and I toured NORAD, and went under Cheyenne Mountain in the tunnels to see the heart of our Distant Early Warning System, or DEW line, our guard against Soviet missile attack. We didn't tour all of the underground set-up, but it was obvious the taxpayers had forked over a lot of money in order to carve enough room out of solid granite to build a virtual city underground.

We broke camp on September 10, and drove over several passes as we headed west on a mixture of old US Route 40 and Interstate 70. We stopped for lunch in Breckenridge, where the sky spit snowflakes at us for several minutes. "Do you think we should take a chance driving over the passes in a snowstorm?" Nini asked, trepidation filling her voice, face and eyes.

"I don't think this will amount to much, *querida*. I think we can go on." As I thought, the snowfall petered out within the hour. We continued west over the passes, and beyond Vail crossed the Colorado River on state route 131 to head over the hills and down into the Yampa Valley, past Yampa and Oak Creek (tiny towns where I'd lived as a youngster) and on to Steamboat Springs.

We arrived at 5:00 p.m., so we went to test the waters of the Yampa River before dinner. But now the river was completely changed. There was a limit of *two* trout, and a large section was fenced off as a private fishing club! Signs said, 'Leased Land' and 'For Members Only'. When I saw that, I couldn't believe my eyes. "We can't fish in the river from here upstream almost to Phippsburg," I complained as I tried without luck to get a strike in the 'open' part of the river using a variety of flies.

"That's just like in Canada!" Maria exclaimed. "You buy a fishing license and still have to pay to fish in the public streams because the rights are owned by individuals. It just doesn't seem right!" she ended.

"Well, one thing is certain, I sure as hell won't come back here again to go fishing!" I griped. After a final fruitless cast, I retrieved my line, stowed my gear and climbed into the Shadow.

All of my aunts and uncles who once lived in the Oak Creek area were dead now, so I had no relatives to console me, and the next morning we took off for Craig, located in the northwest corner of the state. The town was much bigger than when we Leathermans stopped our little Model-T coupe there on the first night of our migration from Colorado to Oregon in 1928. From Craig we headed south to Meeker, and in both places I checked the records for information about my half-brother, Frank, whom we had not seen for ages. He had worked on ranches in those areas. We could find no notice of his death or of a marriage or a divorce, so I gave up, and we continued our march to the south.

I don't know whether Frank is dead or alive, and if dead, where he's buried. I have a hunch he is dead, for he was older than I, and had become an alcoholic after he quit working for Bing Crosby on Bing's ranch in Elko, Nevada where he supervised Bing's sons when they were not in school.

We reached the Colorado River at Rifle, and turned west,

to head downriver past Grand Junction and pick up Utah route 128 and follow south through the beautiful 'beginning' of the grand canyon country along the Colorado to Moab. When we found a space in an RV park, it was overflowing with German tourists to our surprise! It had been a gorgeous day and a magnificent drive, though we had driven but 311 inspiring miles.

CHAPTER 17

We rose late the next morning to overcast skies, and the park owner said we'd probably have rain before nightfall. After a quick breakfast we headed for Canyonlands National Park in the Shadow, to visit the Island in the Sky, an exotic peninsula formed by the junction of the Colorado River and the Green River. There was one spot in the narrow road where the cliff dropped thousands of feet into the canyon on our right, while the left side was a huge funnel with one side cut away, swirling down into the depths below and almost giving me vertigo. That narrow neck of stone we drove across could not have been over 40 feet wide!

Beyond that tight isthmus, which was all that connected that large section of the mesa to the 'mainland', we were on the Island in the Sky.

To us, that portion of the canyonlands of the Colorado River was more interesting in some ways than Grand Canyon itself, because we actually drove out above the various canyons, and gazed down into their multicolored depths. The upper level of the canyon is gouged out in great breadth. Then, halfway down, there are broad benches on either side, topped with a spotty coating of white stone across their surfaces. Then carved into that bench is a second, narrower 'canyon within a canyon', with the river gnawing away at it's floor far below. It is a sight of such grandeur as never to be forgotten.

Sadly, the sky remained overcast, and the colors were not as bright as they should have been, so my pictures would

---

151

not be very good. Still, we stopped at several overlooks, made our way back along the tedious road, crossed the skimpy isthmus to the main body of the mesa, and leaving the park, drove back into Moab for a quick lunch.

After that, we drove up along the great Moab fault to enter Arches National Monument. We moved right along, enjoying the many formations and the incredible arches until we ran out of road. Then I walked on a trail about a mile farther to see Landscape Arch while Maria stayed in the car to read.

Landscape Arch is a 291-foot span of stone so thin I wondered what kept it up as it stretched perilously across a wide vale like one of those footbridges which dangle across defiles in the Peruvian Andes. It was getting dark, and my film-winder was acting up, but I got a few shots of that incredible stone span, but 9 feet shorter than a football field.

The 13th we rose early, bought film, and took off to see some sights to the south. We were overpowered by the majesty of Wilson Arch, which stands beside what is now US 191, for it is one of the huskiest and most openly available of all the arches. Maria bought a little necklace from a Navajo girl who was selling trinkets and jewelry at a tiny stand beside the highway there.

We soon headed west on the Needles Overlook road to view the canyon from that vicinity, then returned to Moab for lunch. It was a clear, bright day, so we decided to take the Island in the Sky tour once again, and I re-shot many of the pictures I had taken the day before. On our way back, we went to see Dead Horse Point, where tremendous cliffs overlook the Oxbow Bends of the Colorado River at a point before it unites with the Green River—a spectacular view of a serpentine canyon carved into multi-colored stone by the ceaseless attack of the river. We had skipped that off-the-trail vista the day before because of the rain.

Leaving Canyonlands, we crossed the highway and entered Arches once more, to soak up the beauty of great walls, balanced rocks, multiple arches and delicate spires. It seemed we never tired of the beauty and grandeur of Arches, for we had gone there several times already. I did not realize it at the time, but one of my shots was of some heavy rock formations, with a slender spire between them, and it was not the same as before. Back home, when we compared the new shots of Arches with some of my earlier views, we saw that sometime in between our visits, a balanced rock, which had once been atop a slender spire, had fallen.

If the mountains and the stones are not eternal, how much less so are the lives of we human beings?

The following day we took a side road to see a spot in a cliff where, under an eyebrow overhang, the Indians in days of yore had carved petrogliphs on a flat surface of stone. Indian trails between the south and the north passed through that area for ages, and the travelers carved their marks on the big blackboard, their designs protected from the rains by the overhang.

We returned to the main highway and drove on south to Blanding and had lunch after which we went to visit the Mule Canyon Indian Ruins. We then toured the nearby area of natural bridges which traverse a narrow canyon. They were extremely interesting.

The arches of Arches National Monument were carved by wind and rain and heat and frost and snow; but the bridges of Natural Bridges National Monument were carved by water, and thus are true 'bridges', and not 'arches'. We visited the museum in Blanding and toured the Edge of Cedars Ruins there. We dined out that evening, and were in bed early, after driving a mere 111 miles.

On the mid-day of September, we drove to see more Indian ruins near Blanding, then crossed a section of empty desert to visit Hovenweep National Monument. What a lonely outpost for the Ranger who tended the tiny park! But what

153

an amazing sight. There in one of the most isolated sites we'd ever visited were several Indian ruins, among which was an incredible tower of stone built by unknown hands centuries ago. We walked the trail which took us past the various ruins, and then headed 'home'. That was a round-trip drive of about 50 miles.

Back in Blanding we put the Shadow on its trailer, and took off on US 191 to Bluff, and on south into Arizona to see Canyon de Chelley (pronounced de Shay). We camped for free at the Navajo campground, and ate our meals in their restaurant in recompense. Fair is fair.

We took the Shadow that afternoon and toured the near side of the canyon rim, peering down into a canyon which was broad, had a level floor, and, with water available, was being farmed by the Navajos. Along the sides of the canyon, up on narrow ledges, were the vestiges of old cliff dwellings. As we moved along the canyon lip, and peered down some 800 feet to the canyon floor, we came upon a spot where a tall spire had survived the erosion of the ages, to rise in regal splendor from the bottom of the canyon. From our vantage point, the shadow of that spire on the canyon floor far below looked for all the world like a tall nun standing alone, reading a bible.

Oddly enough, the Indians call it Spider Rock.

After breakfast next morning we toured the North Rim of the canyon, then headed south and east to US 666 to reach Gallup, New Mexico, where we stayed the night. We got into town around 2:40, and took the opportunity to wash clothes and bedding and relax.

One set of Indian ruins which I had always wanted to visit was the Chaco Canyon Ruins, more formally known as the Chaco Culture National Historical Park. They were some 90 miles north and east of Gallup, and the last 20 miles consisted of rough, dirt road, with ruts, rocks and occasional stone outcroppings to traverse. Normally dry, dusty and irritating, those final miles were often impassible when it rained, and notices were posted to that effect. Once before, we had meant to visit the ruins from the north, but that road had even more miles of dust and dirt and stone ledges to cross, and the sky was threatening rain, as well. But now the day was bright and fair, no rain was expected and we put the Shadow to the test.

Despite its importance in the history of Indian culture in the west, Chaco had only a handful of visitors when we pulled into park headquarters, three carloads of us. It was just too far off the beaten path for most tourists. There in solitude, almost forgotten, along a narrow valley beneath the great cliffs, lies an amazing collection of stone buildings erected by Indians, meticulously put together without mortar. We attended a half-hour movie, then walked among the many ruins to take pictures and study the craftsmanship displayed by a long lost civilization—a community of 'savages' who had developed canals to carry water, and put together a city there in the desert.

Most interestingly, the Anasazi—or 'Ancient Ones' in the Navajo language—existed over 2,000 years ago, and were precursors to the Hopi, Zuni and Acoma tribes as well as other branches of pueblo Indians. Their ancient culture had set up a 'sun dial' fitted to the solstice and the 19-year cycle of the moon—an item which was now a thousand years old!

After spending much of the day touring the various sites, and walking through most of them, we took the cowpath back to modern civilization, and in Gallup bathed and scraped the sweaty dust off our bodies and went out to dinner.

During all of the past days of driving, walking and exploring, Maria had felt not a symptom of cancer: no pains, no uneasiness, no worry. The drives through such beautiful country, the relaxation in the evenings, and the quietude of many of the historical spots we visited had combined to cast a soothing aura of peace and happiness over our little two-piece family. That peace would be ruptured soon—but only by a sudden toothache which struck as we headed farther south.

Our tour now led us east on I-40 to Albuquerque, and south on I-25 to Socorro, then east on US 380 to Roswell. On the way, we stopped in Lincoln, where Gen. Lew Wallace ended a range war in 1889, and wrote the famous novel, 'Ben Hur'. After lunch in a McDonald's, we took US 285 south to Artesia. We stopped in a small, but excellent RV park. The land we'd just driven through reminded us greatly of Nevada, except with a bit more vegetation.

During the afternoon, Maria began to have pain in her jaw. She took aspirin, rinsed with saltwater and applied some Ambusol we bought in Roswell, but she was sick all night, and didn't sleep well.

We rose at 7:15 and were under way at 8:55. We continued south to Carlsbad, where we finally spotted a dentist's office. Doctor Robert Murray quickly fit Maria into his busy schedule. They took full x-rays, and he cleaned out a small cavity in one tooth. He gave us prescriptions for pain and antibiotics, and we were on our way. It cost only $52 for that emergency visit to a fine dentist. In no time at all, the pain had vanished, and my dear Bahiana was back in the pink once more. We did not visit the marvelous Carlsbad Caverns, because we had toured them during an earlier visit.

We drove south into Texas, through Pecos to Fort Stockton, then took I-10 east to the Caverns of Sonora, which are a few miles west of the city of that name. We stayed in an RV park at the caverns, where a number of peacocks paraded about the grounds. The schedule called for one more tour of the caverns that evening, but Maria said she was too tired. She took a chair to read a book among the strolling peacocks, and I went with a chubby, but sweet, tour-guide girl about 16 years old.

Just the two of us made the arduous trek through the cavern, with many steps, narrow passageways, plenty of ups and downs, even ladders to climb. It was well that Maria had not started the tour with us, for we'd have been obliged to turn back almost immediately.

The mile and a half tour visited spaces with 'popcorn' ceilings, some with delicate formations of butterflies, soda straws and other fairytale shapes made of calcite. Even my little guide was pooped when we finally arrived back topside.

I found Maria fixing a supper of fried chicken, collard greens, sliced beets and Danish. She was feeling much better, and her appetite proved it. We had driven 315 miles that day, through mostly arid country, and had been very fortunate to find a dental office in Carlsbad which was owned by a doctor with a sense of pity.

On the 20th we left Sonora and drove south on US 277 to Del Rio, where we stopped overnight at the Sportsmans Corner Rv park, the same as on our previous visit. We toured the city, and Maria fell in love with it. I don't know just what it was, but it may have been the mixture of English and Spanish in the air, the cleanliness and charm of all the stores and shops we visited, and the downright friendliness of the folks who live there. Before I knew it, Maria had me in a realtor's office, and he had given us the location of three homes which were for sale. We soon learned that a nice brick home could be bought for $75,000, and the taxes on it would be about $1,000 a year.

We crossed the Rio Grande to take a quick tour of poverty-stricken Ciudad Acunha in Mexico, and then made our way back to camp, to relax for the rest of the day. In one store we had bought some cookie-like objects called *piedras*, and when we began to chew on them we knew why they were called 'rocks'. They were harder than bricks. But as we gnawed into them we discovered the flavor was great. Happily, Maria didn't upset her once-sore tooth during the experiment!

To this day, I cannot understand just what it was about

Del Rio which so caught Nini's fancy that she actually took me house-hunting there! She was ready to give up her water-front condo in St. Petersburg for a house in arid Del Rio—miles and miles and miles from any friend or relative!

The next morning we left Del Rio at 9:10 and drove east on US 90 through Uvalde and Hondo to San Antonio. We looked for an RV park called Mazda, couldn't find it, and tied up at 99-Mo RV Park, squeezing into a space which was very tight for our rig. Next day we discovered the Mazda park was just across the road!

We drove the Shadow into the city to take the Riverwalk boat tour through the center of town. It was a relaxing tour, drifting past businesses and hotels. We stopped for a luncheon of Mexican food in the Cafe del Rio, and were delighted with the food, the service and the lovely view of the river with its boats filled with tourists passing by below. We ate on the terrace, tossing crumbs to the pigeons and sparrows and to two varieties of fish in the river.

We took a trolley bus to Market Square. But the Square closed at 6:00 p.m., so we took the trolley bus back to the parking garage, ransomed the Shadow and headed for home. It was 7:35 when we ended that day filled with great scenery, friendly people and good eating. We were totally relaxed and extremely happy, and had driven but 142 miles.

There was no room in our heads for nagging worries about cancer that day!

It was the 22nd day of an inspiring September when we tied the Shadow to its wheels, hoisted anchor and pointed our bow toward home. We drove I-10 through Houston and Beaumont and into Louisiana. We stopped to have a Cajun dinner in a place called Breau Bridge, west of Henderson. "We'll eat crawfish at the Crayfish Kitchen," I told Maria.

"Well, which is it, crayfish or crawfish?" she demanded to know..

"Either one. Some parts of the country call them crawfish or crawdads, others say crayfish. In either case, when cleaned they're a shrimp-like, fresh-water creature, and very tasty."

Inside the modest cafe, we discussed the 'hotness' of various dishes with the waitress. Then an obese gentleman seated at a nearby table with a friend said, "They're all hot; but some are hotter than others. If you order the really hot ones, keep a glass of water handy to put out the blaze when the roof of your mouth catches fire!"

We quickly formed a friendship with the chubby owner, Monsieur Elmer, and his wife Michelle and their daughter-in-law. (She was so pretty I didn't dare to ask *her* name!) We tried some crayfish Boulets and a bisque, and a crayfish casserole. All of them were plenty hot and superb in flavor, and as we ate, Maria sipped a cola and I took on a Martini. After we'd whipped the hot stuff in one-on-one combat, we cooled our innards with Key lime pie. Maria was still on penicillin, but thankfully the Cajun dinner didn't upset her innards.

Before we left, we bought a music cassette titled 'The Best of Cajun', plus a praline the size of a saucer to take with us. The pretty daughter-in-law was our waitress and also the cashier, and it was she who suggested we take home some downright good, Cajun dance music. That was Cajun soft-sell, and it worked.

We departed with the folks in the cafe yelling at us in French accents to 'be sure to come back'. Following their directions, we found Frenchie's Wilderness Campground, and tied up for the night. We'd covered 464 miles that day.

The next morning we got back on I-10 and continued into New Orleans to stay at Parc d'Orleans. We shucked off the Winnie, and took the Shadow to drive down the delta of the Mississippi to the end of state route 23 at the city of Venice. I'd always had a yen to drive to the end of the delta, and now I did. The only 'town' any farther out on the low-lying land was Pilottown, with no roadway to get there. We

159

saw mountains of yellow sulphur, and drove on the levee for some distance to watch the ships on the river sailing along high above the surrounding delta land. Venice was a supply center for the oil rigs located out in the Gulf of Mexico, and was also a fine fishing community.

Back at the Parc, we tidied up for a night tour of New Orleans. The bus picked us up at 8:00 p.m. and took us to visit the French Quarter. We drove along the Esplanade, and down Royal, Canal and St. Louis Streets, and saw an above-ground cemetery. (If they bury a body below ground in New Orleans, the casket tends to work its way up to the surface again because the land is so low and damp—so burials are in above-ground tombs or crypts.)

We then toured Bourbon Street, where the fabulous beat of Dixieland (one of my favorite styles of jazz) streamed forth from dozens of clubs.

Our tour included stops at two such bistros. One had a real Can Can show, where the beautiful bare thighs must have put those of the Moulin Rouge to shame. Then some of the can-can dancers did strip-tease dances to the delight of the ladies in our group. At each stop we got a free drink, included in the tour price, and of course we were allowed to buy more of them if so inclined. Maria and I purchased no extra drinks at the can csn show, to avoid becoming inclined.

Our next stop as we strolled the narrow street was at the James Dee Jazz Unlimited Club, where the music was unbeatable. There I saw and heard the head man play a trumpet, a trombone and a clarinet, all with total control. Considering the different embouchures—or positions and tensions of the lips—required of a musician for each instrument, I knew we had witnessed something extraordinary in the field of Dixieland music—or *any* kind of music for that matter. I not only bought us another drink, I also put a couple of bucks in the fishbowl for the band.

It was almost midnight when we left Bourbon Street to

go to the Cafe du Monde for *cafe au lait* and the specialty of the house, the incomparable squarish doughnuts covered with powdered sugar and called *beneighs*. The waiter brought Maria and me a basket at least 9-inches square heaped four inches deep with the gourmet treats. We looked at the basket and shuddered, then waded in with a will and cleaned out the lot. I thought I was in heaven, they were that delicate and savory. How many calories that binge contained we didn't want to know!

By one a.m. we were back at the Parc and soon in our soogens. We'd had a magnificent time, and were more than pleased that the tour cost only $60 for the two of us, including the food we ate, the shows we saw and the drinks we enjoyed along with that fabulous spate of Dixieland music.

September 24 we left New Orleans to head east on I-10 through Mississippi and Alabama into the western end of Florida, to the edge of Pensacola, where we found a campground. We drove the Shadow into downtown Pensacola, recalling our visits there when Kathy's gang lived in nearby Milton while Charlie was giving advanced training to new pilot graduates from the Navy flight school in Pensacola.

There was an art fair *and* a seafood fair in town. We enjoyed both, and took on Vietnamese dinners and funnel cakes, a fine combination after our night on the town in Creole country.

We didn't get under way until 10:00 next day. We stopped for lunch near the town of Mariane, then made it all the way to the Big Boy restaurant a few blocks from our condo complex in South Pasadena. Manager Jim Dorsch said we could park the Winnie in the rear of their parking area, free, which we did, and drove the Shadow on home.

We were both tired, but we took the stuff from the Winnie's refrigerator to our condo cooler, along with leftover food, our clothes and toilet gear. The air-conditioner soon had the condo cooled to a comfortable degree, and we unpacked and stowed most of our gear. Then we showered, watched the 11:00 o'clock news and a Johnny Carson monologue rerun and hit the hay.

"I loved our trip," Maria said, before we kissed goodnight, "but I'm glad to be back in my own comfy bed."

"Me, too, honey . . . especially with you," and I squeezed her hand 'goodnight'.

Our journey had covered 5,891 miles, plus the extra miles we drove the Shadow, which we both failed to record! We had seen exciting parts of many fabulous cities and towns, scads of interesting natural features and 'enough Indian ruins to last us for years', as Nini so aptly put it.

Before dropping off to sleep I whispered a 'thank you', to any God in general who might be listening, in gratitude for the joys and pleasures we had experienced together those past weeks.

I didn't know how our lives would move along in the future, but I couldn't shake off the eerie premonition that my beloved Maria and I had enjoyed our last memorable tour together.

> *I hope this brief description of our tour will lead some of my readers to visit a few of the sights and scenes which I have briefly limned; for any one of the places we visited merits almost anyone's time.*

CHAPTER 19

An optimist might think that to have one person in the house enduring an atrocious affliction should be enough medical problems for one family. But such was not the case in our tiny *menage*.

After one of my ex-shipmates from the *Maryland* died of a ruptured aneurism on his way home from the reunion in Boston, and another died from the same cause on his way home from the get-together in Denver, I grew leery of the aortic aneurism which nursed itself within my own bosom. With Maria already worried about her own medical difficulties, I didn't want that damned aneurism to rupture, for if it occurred in her presence, she'd have a nervous breakdown for sure.

There was no doubt in my mind that a rupture of the wall of my aorta would kill me. My life's blood would flood my abdominal cavity, and within minutes I'd conk out like a car with a plugged fuel filter.

We had kept an eye on my aneurism now for three years after my doctor discovered it while palpating my abdomen. When I took my annual physicals, the sonograms revealed that it had grown slightly each year. The aneurism was a sac, or balloon, pooched out on the wall of my aorta, the main distribution line for blood to the lower body. It may have occurred of its own volition, or it may have been brought about when the wall of my aorta was weakened, as by the strain of heavy lifting some time in the past. For example, from when I was 16, weighed 135 pounds, and worked in an

163

Oregon sawmill, where I had to shove around railroad ties weighing several times as much.

That was followed by more heavy work when I became a shipfitter in the Navy, and perhaps was aggravated by my being a hard-hat diver, often working under pressure during those shipfitter years.

Whatever its cause, that aneurism, which I could feel with my fingers, like a large oval grape, was a threat to my life. Having two friends hauled off to the cemetery early because their aneurisms ruptured, made me even more apprehensive. I most assuredly was not eager to join them, since they were ex-sailors and I didn't know which way they went.

Our local hospital had an expert heart surgeon on its staff, and doctor Gottcha went over my file with me, and agreed that an AAA was just the thing for me—reduction of the Abdominal Aortic Aneurism which lay a few inches south of my breastbone, as readily operable as any aneurism could be. Our rather brief little get-together in his office cost me $135; but when I left, he had me scheduled for surgery and had explained to me all about the operation, or so I thought.

I entered Pines of Ponderosa hospital around noon May 1, and began the 'prep work' required to put me in proper form for surgery next morning. As I was eating my dinner, Doctor Gottcha came by my room. "Well, I see you are all set for tomorrow," he said, a setup which, among other things, included the insertion of tubes in my bodily orifices, much to my dismay and disgust.

"Yes, I guess I'm ready . . . physically, anyway. I'm not sure about emotionally!" I sighed.

He looked at me for a few seconds, then spoke again. "At your age, I doubt that it would make any difference to you . . . " he said, hesitantly, almost as though talking to himself.

"What won't make any difference to me, doctor?" I asked,

my curiosity piqued, having no idea what the hell he was driving at.

"Well, to reduce your particular aneurism, I have to make an incision from your breastbone practically to your penis," he said, and paused. *I quickly envisioned the beautiful 23-inch cut-throat trout I'd caught in the Shoshone River in Yellowstone National Park, a fish which I'd slit open from anus to gills to clean. Did this man plan to treat me that way, for God's sake?*

Before I could frame a reply, Doctor Gottcha continued. "When I make that incision, I have to cut a tiny nerve which controls ejaculation during intercourse." Before I could scream, he went on. "You can still have an erection and ejaculation, but after the operation it will be retrogressive . . . that is, you will ejaculate back into your bladder rather than out through the urethra and penis."

I was stunned by his words. And I was pissed off (an apt phrase) that he had waited until I'd incurred hundreds of dollars in preparatory expenses before he revealed this unhappy news. I recovered quickly, and asked, "When I paid you a hundred and thirty-five bucks for a consultation regarding this surgery, how come you didn't mention this to me at that time?" He made no reply, so I went on, "It's too late for me to back out of the operation now. But that knowledge might have affected my decision as to whether or not I should proceed with it!" I shot out.

But Doctor Gottcha was unperturbed by my question, and deigned not to reply to it directly. "Another thing," he continued his revelations, "there is a 20% chance you may die on the operating table." Before I could absorb that great news, he made it even better. "And patients who survive the operation may lose one or both legs, if a blocked artery occurs in them. We turn off all the blood circulation to the lower part of your body for about half an hour, and that sometimes leads to a blockage when we turn the blood back on."

Turning off my major artery like a damned water faucet! I

165

thought to myself, *except water doesn't clot.* "Doctor, I have the strange feeling you have not acted in a very professional manner with me, not to have told me these things during our visit three days ago. I have a wife who had, and may still have, breast cancer, and she needs my care and comfort. Had you offered these bits of info earlier, I might have forgone this operation, at least until the aneurism got too far out of hand, or Maria is well." [I almost said, 'or until Maria is dead', and the ugliness of that thought sent a horrible chill through me!] "Now it's too late, so I'll go ahead with the surgery . . . but you'd better do the best job you've ever done in your life, sir."

"Oh, I will, Mr. Leatherman, I will!" he expostulated. And that was a natural expostulation, not a retrogressive one.

But the truth of the matter is, he didn't.

That night was a dark flood of mixed morbid fears and sleeplessness as the doctor's words percolated through the labyrinths of my disoriented mind. The anesthesiologist came by early next morning and gave me a shot, and I didn't know a thing after that until I awoke in the Intensive Care Unit, with Maria sitting beside my bed. Now that I knew I hadn't died on the operating table, my next check was to wiggle my toes. If they moved, I had not lost any legs yet, either. They all wiggled.

"Hi, *querida*," I spoke with some difficulty to my little wife, and her tears welled up as she bent over to kiss my parched lips between the tubes in my nose and throat.

"Hi, Daddy," she smiled at me, and took my hand in hers, in a passionate squeeze. "*Gracas a Deus tu estas bem!*" Thank God thou art all right, she used the charming Portuguese second person verb.

It was the next day when Nini informed me that another man from our own condo complex recently had a similar aneurism operation, and they'd had to amputate one of his legs because of a blood clot. Both he and his wife were engulfed in tears not too far away in the same Intensive Care Unit.

That very evening, the nurses made me lift myself to turn over without their help, all of which was extremely difficult because they had placed one of those knobby, foam-rubber mattresses on top of the regular mattress on my bed. For what reason they did that I have no idea, except that when I left for a regular room, someone drug along that monstrosity in a big roll, and left it at the foot of my bed. Obviously it wasn't needed, but they charged me triple the price for it on their statement. What a racket!

"Don't you want your special mattress on your bed?" the nurse asked when she came in. "It belongs to you, you know, so you can take it home with you."

"I hate that damned thing!" I spat. "I couldn't turn over because of it, and the ICU nurses refused to help me. Now my incision is torn open. See?" I asked, and tossed aside the sheet and placed my hands on my abdomen with eight fingers inserted two inches deep into the incision, *which had come apart!* I could lie there and feel all of my innards, with nothing between them and my fingers except a layer of skin and the peritoneum, the thin membranous sac which holds one's innards in place. My abdominal muscles were totally separated, split open north and south!

"Please, don't do that, Mister Leatherman," the poor nurse shuddered, and left the room.

When Doctor Gottcha came in while I was still in Intensive Care, I complained to him about the ICU nurses refusing to help me move around in bed, and about the infernal sponge rubber mattress which made turning over extremely difficult.

His reply was very professional. "That is good nursing practice, Mister Leatherman. You have to move around a bit to recover properly." I invited him to put his fingers into my midriff arroyo, my personal hidden Grand Canyon, which he did most unconcernedly.

"What do you think, doctor," I asked after trying to catch some indication in his face that he, or his cohort, had done a piss-poor job of sewing me up; but his demeanor never changed.

"It happens that way sometimes," he said laconically.

For years I have not been able to exercise my abdomen in any manner, for fear of coming completely apart. My stomach sagged, and my lower bowels ballooned out like I was pregnant. I finally had to have remedial surgery, to re-sew the muscles, and add mesh patches to reinforce them, like fixing up an old inner tube. That was a worse operation, pain-wise and discomfort-wise, than the original AAA set-to. And it did nothing to restore my body to its former, rather decent appearance! The muscles of my legs, arms and shoulders are hard and firm, although covered with a thin layer of baby fat. But my abdomen sags like a tired old hammock with a fat man in it.

Despite all the problems which arose after that operation, and the misery and discomfort I would feel later on, I left the hospital the sixth day and went home. Considering the condition into which Doctor Gottcha and the nurses in the Intensive Care Unit had put me, I didn't know how either of them slept nights!

My beloved Nini stayed constantly at my side, and was much relieved when she saw me up and walking in the hospital, and moving about the condo quite naturally when I got home.

My incision was an ugly red line drawn down the center of my body, barely bypassing my navel. But unlike the centerline of a ship, it ran, not from stem to stern, but from sternum to stem.

Within days our lives were back to normal in our condo. Nini continued to take her medications, play bridge with her partners at the clubhouse, and go out to lunch or dinner with me occasionally; I went back to work on my bio and walked the seawall almost daily. Slowly my midriff scar faded from red to pink to yellow; and in due time I discovered that retrogressive ejaculation is better than no ejaculation, but still not as satisfying as a plain, old-fashioned orgasm.

Nature knew what she was doing when she hooked up Man's sexual apparatus. Gottcha also knew what he was doing when he altered my personal pelvic controls and left my stick-shift permanently in reverse.

When, in 1999, news reporters revealed the results of a nationwide survey, they showed that over 50% of our doctors do not give complete explanations to their patients regarding their medical condition or the treatment thereof, I understood fully, and ruefully, what their lack of explanation signifies for us long-suffering patients.

And people have the temerity to criticize the witch doctors of Africa and the voodoo experts of the Caribbean or the *maes de santos*, (mothers of saints) in Brazil, who are no more secretive than our own medicos, and at times are just as effective in treating their patients! No Brazilian *mae de santos* would ever leave a poor fellow in the utter confusion of a retrogressive ejaculation!

169

CHAPTER 20

As we move onward through the balance of this story, I fear the reader may come to feel that some of the time the material reads almost like a diary. And such is partly the case; for as the days and weeks passed in mostly unhappy procession, the lives of Maria and me became slaves to the calendar and to the machinations of the very devil himself.

We came to have almost no free time, and what we had was collated between appointments with doctors, labs, and special machines, as well as tests, dosages, infusions and injections.

And as time progressed, we engaged in less and less outside activity other than dining out. Many times we ate out just to eliminate the nuisance of planning, fixing, and cleaning up after a meal. We ate breakfast at home most of the time, for cereal and fruit and toast required little time and almost no cleanup afterward.

But this rather carefully delineated schedule of Nini's medical appointments and changes of medicines, will give the reader a sense of the progression of Maria's war with cancer; from the rare problems in the early months, to the occasional ones in the ensuing months, to frequent attacks in the later years, and finally to where she waged a continuous daily battle against the enemy.

The description of the many drugs Nini took, and the changes in their usage or discontinuance, and my brief sketches of what they were supposed to do, and the continuing fright which each new medicine gave me, reveal the bitterness with which I accepted them, and the effort I deliberately made not to alarm my beloved wife with explanations about them or any of their purposes if I could avoid it.

The years 1991 and 1992 were miserable years for my darling, and consequently for me, and I believe that showing things exactly as they transpired will give the reader a truer insight into how really rough Maria's fight finally became.

In late May Maria ended the first course of methyldopa and began a second one. Her prosthesis looked a bit worse for the wear, and I went with her to a specialty shop to order a new one. She came to me in the den in mid-July. "They just called to say my new titty has come in. Will you take me to pick it up?"

"Naturally," I teased. "I sure don't want you taking one of the other men at Bay Island to pick it up!" We headed for the store where Nini tried on her new 'plastic boob' as she sometimes referred to it scornfully. The new model was totally satisfactory—if even the finest of artificial breasts can *be* satisfactory.

Summer came and went, but we did little of either. We traveled very little, and we dined out less than had been our normal practice. In early September Maria completed the current course of Aldomat, or methyldopa, she'd been taking.

We went to see Doctor Able on the 12th, and found Maria's blood pressure high at 158 over 102. While we were there, we discussed another lump which had appeared on Maria's chest. The infernal things just refused to stop coming! In two days we had spent $260 for office visits to Doctor Able. As the weeks rolled by, we would be in and out of his office more often than a mother wren goes in and out of the nest to feed her multitudinous offspring.

On our visit of the 14th, Doctor Coe stopped the megace dosages, and increased the level of Aldomat dosages, which carried Maria through until her appointment to go back on the operating table on September 24, when Doctor Coe re-

171

moved the chest lump in a one-day surgery visit. Then it was back to Coe's office on the 26th to change the dressing.

The many succeeding office visits with Doctor Able were a mere $40 each, but they slowly grew closer together than Concord grapes in the bunch, and were a steady outpouring of assets. The bitterly sad part was that I was never sure we got our money's worth. Thankfully, Medicare and Prudential picked up most of the tab, but still we spent thousands of dollars as the months passed.

I pity the young couple whose lives are struck by breast cancer and have little or no insurance protection. Not only does the young lady suffer the physical and emotional pain, but the atrocious drain on their finances must be frightening, and at times insupportable.

"I've contacted the cancer center in Houston, Texas, for their opinion and advice on Maria's next protocol," Doctor Able informed me on one visit. Such remarks in private to me, out of Nini's earshot, did little to instill confidence in the man, although he may have been a genius of an oncologist. But I could see his side of things, too. Naturally he was happy with our contributions to his quality of life; on the other hand, it must have been emotionally disturbing to treat large numbers of patients with all types of cancers, knowing that most of them would succumb to their insidious attackers to die an earlier-than-natural death, regardless of what protocol he used in counterattacking the besiegers.

In early October, Naria stopped taking Aldomat, and began taking Cytoxin, the brand name of cyclophosphamide. Cytoxin is an anticancer drug known as an analkylating agent. It interferes with the growth of cancer cells, which are later destroyed by the body's immune system. Cytoxin causes nausea, vomiting and loss of hair. It often reduces blood cell production leading to abnormal bleeding and the increased risk of infection. To combat the risk of infection, Maria was given Betapen-VE, a synthetic penicillin form of antibiotic for a wide range of infections. Taken with food, the drug is more effective than oral penicillins.

Maria began taking that medicine on the 19th of October. After her office visit, including a blood test that day, Doctor Able prescribed the use of neosporine on the incision temporarily. Maria was scheduled to go to the hospital for chemotherapy, but the nurse called to say she was not permitted to take a treatment that day.

"I can't understand why Doctor Able can't make up his mind whether I should have chemotherapy or not!" Maria complained. "It seems to me that either I can, or I can't, and if I can't, he shouldn't schedule me for it. That is such a nuisance." Her brown eyes flashed fire for a moment after she hung up.

"It's probably that he cannot know for sure whether you should take a treatment or not until he gets your blood test from the day before. If your blood isn't in proper condition, whatever *that* is, he has to cancel your appointment. I don't think he does it just to annoy, *querida*." "Maybe not, but it is very upsetting. I get my courage all together, ready for the treatment, and then it's cancelled. Now I'll have to build up my nervous all over again!" In her natural irritation, she misused the word 'nerve', turning it into something to reflect her disgust, rather than her courage.

I still didn't have a clue as to what was going on with all the blood tests, the scheduling of chemotherapy and the frequent cancellations of same, but I felt certain there had to be a reason for the apparent indecision.

In fact, the composition of Maria's very lifeblood was undergoing almost constant change, what with the attacking cancer and the campaign of drugs against it. But I was not aware of the complex chemistry involved within her bloodstream as the drug-saturated liquid coursed through her body on its perpetual rounds of pick-up and delivery for the billions of normal cells which constituted her physical makeup, not to mention feeding or fighting off the avaricious invasion of the cancer cells.

It was early in November when I broached the subject of our motorhome to Maria. "I think maybe we should put the Winnebago up for sale, Nini. What do you think?" I asked one evening. I doubted that we would be making any more idyllic treks with the home, and it represented a lot of money sitting idle, money we could use. Of course I didn't reveal my exact inner thoughts to my little Brasileira. I refused to set her mind out to sea on an ebb tide of appalling thoughts.

"You're probably right, Daddy," she agreed. "The way I feel lately, I doubt if I could enjoy another vacation in it. Besides, I think it will be better for me if we stay close to home until my cancer is cured." I adored her faith in God and in her doctor. My darling certainly planned to whip the Big C if it could be done. She wasn't about to lay down her oars and let her bark of life go drifting onto the reefs. She would keep rowing as long as she had the strength.

We took the motorhome to a dealer in Clearwater and put it on consignment. That beat advertising it, and having to answer the telephone during a period when a doctor or a nurse might wish to get in touch with us. I drove the Winnie to the dealer, with Maria following in the car. Then we drove home together, stopping for dinner at the Pasadena Steak House.

From time to time, the drugs she was taking would cause Maria to vomit, and I'd go to the bathroom with her and hold her forehead in the palm of my right hand while my left arm encircled her waist to lend strength and reassurance as she bent over the commode and retched. But in between those occasional attacks, Maria still enjoyed a good meal, for which I was very thankful. Most of the time I prepared the food, set the table, cleared it and did the dishes. To stop at the Steak House for dinner was not only a gustatorial treat, it relieved me of a lot of homework!

The last day of November, Nivaldo arrived in Miami with his daughter Margareth and her husband Edwardo, both of whom were doctors serving in the Medical Corps of the Brazilian Navy. They came to America, not so much for vacation and sightseeing, as for shopping. They would return to Rio with baggage and boxes bulging with their purchases in American stores. So many things here were cheaper or better made than their counterparts in Brazil; and besides, Margareth was in hog heaven when turned loose in a mall!

They stayed one day and night with Agildo, who was the son of Nivaldo's brother, Antonio. Agildo had entered the foreign service after college, and had served in Chile, Germany and France, as well as in Brazilia, the capital of the country, high on the plateau in Central Brazil, far from all the fun places along the Brazilian coast. Agildo was a true polyglot, and was currently serving as Consul General of the Brazilian Consulate in Miami, one of their busiest consulates because the Big Wheels from Brazil arrived by Varig Airlines in Miami in a steady stream, and Agildo catered to their needs and whims to start their US visit off on the right foot.

Our visitors arrived at the condo on December 4, which, fortunately, was after Maria's visit to Doctor Able that day. Nivaldo was also a medical doctor who had specialized in both dermatology and radiology; my niece Margareth was more of a general practitioner, and Edwardo was moving into the field of oncology, assimilating everything he could from the literature and at conferences.

Nivaldo was a man of my own height and weight, with a stern, closed face, not too often lit with a smile. He was nine months my junior. He was studying medicine when I met Maria in Bahia, and was living at home. Perhaps my being a minor naval officer influenced his decision, for after graduation he joined the Braziliian Navy Medical Corp, and when he retired was a full Admiral.

Margareth was a wisp of a woman, but full of energy,

quite pretty and very smart. I'd asked her once, "Maggie, are you anorexic?" and she had looked me in the eye and replied simply, "*Sim, Tio Hawb, eu sou.*" Yes, Uncle Rob, I am."

Margareth's husband, Ed, was a husky young man filled with humor and bonhomie, quick to laugh, and always ready to eat. He went through medical school with Maggie, they graduated together, married and they, too, entered the Brazilian Navy's Medical Corps. The amazing thing was that Ed's father was also a retired Admiral of that Medical Corps!

"I'm so glad you could come, Nivaldo," Nini said, "but I'm sorry Dulce couldn't come with you. I miss seeing her. She's so pleasant to visit with and talk to."

"Someone had to stay home and look after our girls," Maggie said (of which, like Bobby, they had three), "and *mamae* said she was happy to have a vacation herself, even if she stayed in Rio to enjoy it."

"Your *sogra* (mother-in-law) is a saint, Edwardo," Nini observed, and went to give him and Maggie warm hugs.

The conversation that evening slowly drifted ashore on the island of Maria's cancer, and the three visiting doctors looked at the sheaf of notes I'd kept regarding her treatments, and said they thought Doctor Able was quite professional in his approach to treating their beloved sister and aunt. And when Maria let them see the scar from her mastectomy, they were quick to aver that Doctor Coe was most certainly an adept surgeon. So I didn't tell them about the bursting pus container that followed one of his operations.

Our visitors favored us with a stay of barely a week, then left for Miami with their rental automobile loaded to the gunwales with the fruits of their shopping spree. For the next few days, the condo rang with emptiness, but soon we had adjusted to being 'alone' again.

Maria was scheduled for chemotherapy on December 29, but after Doctor Able got the results of her last blood test his nurse called to say, "No infusions tomorrow, Maria." That ended blood tests and therapies for the year 1990.

We sent cards and gifts of fruit to our kids, and to my niece and her family on Marco Island, then sat back and let both Christmas and New Year's Day come and go with but very nominal celebrations of either one.

It was over four years now since Nini's frightening discovery of the lump in her breast, and we hugged and kissed with great warmth and tenderness as we greeted the two major holidays.

"I pray to the Virgin Mary that I will be completely cured of cancer in 1991, Maria said as we kissed our first goodnight of the new year.

"May the good Lord so bless us, sweetheart," I said; and after a tiny hand had slipped across the sheet between us, to gather my hand within its tender clasp, we soon welcomed the intrusion of Morpheus and his blessed gift of sleep.

Thank God we could not foresee the travails to come during the new year as the world proceeded on its inevitable, circling course while the foe within Maria's breast just as inexorably enlarged its domain, like some vicious conqueror of the Dark Ages trampling on the serfs and peons of the adjacent fiefdoms.

CHAPTER 21

The year had scarcely begun when I celebrated my 73rd birthday on Epiphany, which fell on Sunday that year. Kathy called to wish me a happy one, as did Nivaldo and Dulce and Ed and Margareth from Rio de Janiero. Up in Tarpon Springs the St. Nicholas Greek Orthodox Church celebrated the day with their usual ceremony: tossing a crucifix into the waters of Spring Bayou in order to bring good luck for the coming year to the fishermen and sponge divers working out of that community.

Shivering young men dive into the depths and compete to retrieve the cross and bring it back to the Bishop. The happy young man who succeeds is said to be blessed with good luck all the rest of the year. However, on one occasion in later years, the lucky diver was soon in the hands of the police for some misdeed he'd committed. Apparently triumphing in the shivery crucifix rite does not provide sanctuary for lawbreakers.

Two days later, Nini was back taking methyldopa three times a day.

Nine days later, on January 17, the allies launched a devastating aerial attack, starting the war in the Persian Gulf against Iraq, which had invaded Kuwait in August of 1990. It had taken all the intervening time for the U.S. to put together a coalition in favor of driving the Iraqis out of Kuwait, and to mass the forces needed for the job in Saudi Arabia.

Charlie, our son-in-law, was on the aircraft carrier *Independence* when she steamed boldly into the Persian Gulf, the first carrier ever to venture into those constrained waters. Maria and I took on an added worry then, for Charlie would fly radar-jamming missions in his EA-6 during the Navy's bombing attacks on Iraq and the Iraqi tanks and troops. "I'm so worried something might happen to Charlie," Maria cried out in anguish when the story of our Navy's daring Gulf entry broke on the evening news and in the papers.

I had run with the great carriers in the last months of the war in the Pacific, and had battled against the Japanese bombing attack which set fire to the carrier *Franklin* off Japan during our raids on that waning country just before the Battle of Okinawa. So I knew the damage a well-placed bomb or torpedo could do. A huge carrier has a tough task maneuvering on the open seas during an aerial attack; how much more dangerous it could be if she were attacked within the confines of a narrow gulf.

But I spoke comfortingly to Nini. "Don't you worry, Mama. Charlie and his ship will come though this affair with flying colors and great honor."

"But he is so close to Iraq and Iran. Who knows what either country will do?"

"Well, Iraq has bitten off a lot more than Sadam can chew; and I doubt if the religious zealots running Iran want any part of tangling with the United States for fear of losing their hold over the unhappy people of that sad nation," I tried to soothe her fears, even though I shared them to a considerable extent.

The ground war, conducted mostly with tanks, did not begin until February 24, at which time Iraq suffered horrible losses in men and equipment, to such an extent that President George Bush ended the war unilaterally after 100 hours of battle. The Iraqis had predicted 'the mother of all tank battles', but the mother miscarried, and the bulk of their tanks and crews were destroyed. Bush's top man in the field, General Norman Schwarzkopf, was completely abashed when a wishy-washy Bush and his top military advisor, Colin Powell, who was even more wishy-washy, overruled his objections and called for a cease fire.

Sadly, that left Saddam Hussein still running Iraq; a man who had used chemical weapons of mass destruction against his own people. Bush's shortsightedness cost, and is still costing, American taxpayers millions of dollars per month as the years roll by, because America has to slap down Hussein every now and then, while maintaining continuous aerial surveillance over Iraq. And the petty tyrant always stirs things up at an inconvenient time for the United States. He may be a sadist, but he's no dummy.

It will always be my belief that Bush thought the '100-hour War' would set a 'cute' record, and make his name go down in history. After all, the Jews required six whole days back in 1967 to beat the Egyptians and Jordanians et al!

It was during this period of Middle East hubbub that Doctor Able had Maria use a heating pad on her chest every day for two weeks. It was never clear to us why he did this, but a week later, he ordered her to begin taking Nizoral, a brand name for ketoconazole, basically an anti-fungal drug. Investigations were under way into the use of ketoconazole for treatment of prostate cancer and adrenal gland disorders. Was Doctor Able running his own test to determine if the drug would help to cure breast cancer?

Unfortunately, there seems to be no law to prevent a doctor from launching any new medical procedure he may desire, providing his patient doesn't insist on an explanation. But how many people know enough about complex medical treatments to realize when they are being used as guinea pigs? Especially when the procedures are for the treatment of cancer, for which every week brings some new drug, or fad or hope, or even worse, the proof that some loudly heralded 'fabulous' new drug was a failure or had an unhappy side effect.

Every day the news touts some new hope for a breast cancer cure, and every other day the result of some study conducted somewhere by someone belittles the very cure which was being pushed earlier. Who these people are who engage in all these 'studies', and what particular part of the drug and medical industry they are serving, and how slanted the results are, or what special grant from the government is supporting their work, and who and how many will profit from any new drug added to the lengthy list of 'anticancer drugs' I cannot say, for that type of information is rarely revealed in the brief news items.

One thing I do know, there was a time when over one-and-a-half *billion* dollars per year was spent on AIDS research, from which only a few hundred deaths occurred annually, and for which most of those who had the disease were afflicted through their own carelessness; while only a few *million* dollars were being granted for research into breast cancer, with over 40,000 women dying from it each year, not one of whom had done anything to bring on the atrocious attack! What poorly set priorities!

I personally felt the logic behind such a foolish allocation of funds was simple: a cure for breast cancer would stop the flow of billions of dollars per year into the medical industry, while research on AIDS could be another income-producing program for years to come, so why not give it a jump start? Of course I had no objection to spending whatever was necessary to find a cure, or better yet, a preventative for AIDS, but surely breast cancer research needed to be stepped up as well.

On the 19th, Maria went in for a CAT scan and a chest x-ray, and six days later the doctor ordered her to stop taking Nizoral. That was probably because the following day at 1:00 p.m. Maria began new chemotherapy treatments. She received 100 milligrams of Methotrexate, along with 1,000 mgs of Flourouracil, plus 30cc of NS, or normal saline solution. We would never have known what drugs Doctor Able was giving Maria intravenously had I not examined every plastic 'bottle' as the nurses needled its contents into Nini's bloodstream, and taken down the name of the medication and the amount given.

Methotrexate is an anticancer drug sometimes given to treat cancer of the breast, and can, and did, cause nausea, vomiting and diarrhea. It can also lead to disorders in blood clotting and even to ulcers of the mouth. Methotrexate is often given along with other anticancer drugs, and in Maria's case the helper was flourouracil. Flourouracil is an anticancer drug which interferes with tumor cell growth. It can affect *healthy* cells as well as cancerous ones when given by injection, as Maria took hers. The drug reduces the production of blood cells and causes hair loss.

Poor Maria had a tough time wrestling with *that* protocol series, and lost her hair in the process!

"Come in here, Daddy," she called shortly after she had begun the new series of injections.

"Do you need some help, honey?" I asked as I reached the bathroom door.

"i sure do!" Maria almost cried as she responded. "Look at my poor hair!" and she held up her brush so I could see it was full of long hairs. "I'm shedding all over the place," Nini cried, and showed me strands of hair on the floor, in the sink, and especially on her brush. "I noticed a few hairs in my brush the last couple of days, but today I'm overdoing it. *Com certezxa vou perder todos os meus cabelos!*" In total disgust she reverted to Portuguese: It's certain I'm going to lose all of my hair!

"Maybe you'll only lose part of it, *querida*, I'll keep my fingers crossed for you and say a little prayer." But neither fingers nor prayers were to any avail. In a very brief period of time all of Nini's hair was gone!

She continued in a lighter vein, "I've been a shicken with

only one wing for ages it seems; now I'll be a *plucked* shicken with only one wing," and she sat down on the toilet to contemplate her hairy hairbrush.

I had to shop for a turban for her to wear when she left the condo, for all of her hair did fall out, just as expected. As her hair disappeared, I remembered how beautifully it had gleamed in the Brazilian sun when first I met her, a bright crown of rich brown hair with a coppery cast to it, set perkily atop her cute little face. Despite my effort to suppress it, a sigh escaped me. I found it hard not to dwell on that unhappy loss of Maria's hair, for she, herself, was so disgusted with her lack of hirsute adornment. No hair on her head, no hair on her arms and legs, no hair anywhere.

After a lengthy search, I finally found turbans in an unlikely corner of a K-Mart store, and bought four, two white ones, and one each in pastel pink and blue. As the 'protocol' of those treatments continued, Maria's body began to gain control over the nausea and diarrhea. So we went to a wig store in downtown St. Pete to buy a more attractive cover for her cute bald pate.

The shop belonged to a diminutive Chinese lady, who showed us wigs in various colors and styles, flitting about with such animation she reminded me of a hummingbird. Maria picked a wig in a dark brown which resembled the hair she once possessed, but without its seductive coppery glint.

When she felt up to it, Nini would don her wig on Sunday and I'd take her to worship in the charming Catholic church just across the intra-coastal waterway *in* St. Pete Beach (the town), or *on* St. Pete Beach (the beach). It was only a short distance to St. John's, but the intra-coastal waterway lay between us, and it could take extra time if the bridge opened for a boat to pass through. That stopped all traffic on and off the beach, and hundreds of cars chaffed at the accelerator while some individual tediously idled his dinky boat with its stick of a mast through the opening.

Maria customarily wore neat, solid-color slacks topped with a pretty blouse to church. She had at least a dozen pairs of such slacks, and 30 or 40 blouses to mix or match, plus sweaters and light jackets for cold days. There were only a half-dozen dresses in her wardrobe, two of them formals. She always looked neat and trim in slacks with blouse or sweater despite her tendency toward obesity.

For several months, then, my Brazilian darling wore a turban around the house and her wig to go out, and we even bought a second wig she could wear when she felt so daring as to become a brown-eyed ash-blonde temporarily. If nothing else, a change of wigs reduced the tedium of the long hours she spent at the hospital with a needle in her arm and one or two plastic bags attached to it by hoses, dripping their obnoxius fluids into her mistreated circulatory system.

Thank heaven we could not foresee that Nini would suffer the same hair loss *again* after her hair grew back the first time!

During that series of injections, she began taking cytoxin near the end of February. She repeated the double-entry blood-keeping treatments through March 8, intermittently suffering from nausea and occasionally vomiting shortly after a session at the hospital. The cytoxin, too, was taken, then interrupted, then taken again over a period of weeks. Sometimes she would vomit soon after taking the cytoxin, at other times she felt no ill effects after going back on the drug.

Because Maria went to the laboratory to draw blood for a profile on one day, and then took her chemotherapy treatment the next, we would often reach the hospital, put Maria on a bed, and then wait for an hour, sometimes two, for the doctor to call the hospital nurse to say whether to proceed with the chemotherapy treatment or to postpone it.

This was terribly destabilizing for Nini and demoralizing for me. But when I complained to the doctor, he said his schedule sometimes kept him from looking at Maria's lab results right away, but as soon as he did study them, he let the hospital know which way to go. That explanation definitely left me with the desire to tell *him* which way to go, and the direction I had in mind was not UP.

On another occasion, Maria lay in her bed from 9:00 a.m. to 12:30 p.m. without starting treatment because the 'blood' nurse had to place the needle in her arm, and she was tied up with other duties. After waiting two hours, I went downstairs to see the administrator, and she informed me the 'blood' lady had been extremely busy in the emergency room. When the nurse showed up to place the needle in Maria's arm she apologized—she had spent all morning teaching a class. Emergency room? Hell no: a 'how-to' class, that's what it was, while a nervous Maria waited patiently for over three hours to start her treatment! It then took an hour and a half to administer the therapy, so she was in bed for almost five hours to take less than a two-hour treatment. And of course, I was at her side. That day we definitely were served by the medical *un*profession!

In mid-May Maria took a reduced amount of Methotrexate, only 50 milligrams, accompanied by 10 mgs of Torecan, or thiethylperazine, another anti-cancer drug. Still, the combination forced Maria to vomit after the chemotherapy was completed, and while she was still in the hospital room.

A week later we were back in the hospital to take ultrasound scans of her liver and gall bladder, the results of which were never revealed, only explained as 'Part of the control we exercise during chemotherapy'. The day following the scans Nini ended the Cytoxin schedule.

After a blood test on June 10, we were back in the Oncology Department next day for another round of methotrexate, but without the Torecan. The same routine was repeated a week later, except the saline solution was cut to 20cc.

We had a brief respite from tests and injections until July 3, when Nini had another CAT scan of her head. The very

---

185

brief explanation of that scan was 'To insure that the drugs are not affecting the brain', per the nurse who administered the scan. But my impression, which I did not reveal to Nini, was that the doctor was checking to see if the *cancer* had invaded her brain.

My sixth sense regarding the doctor's devious ways eventually proved to be accurate.

CHAPTER 22

Customarily, I took Maria to church on Sunday morning for Mass; then when I picked her up after the services we had lunch in some restaurant. We had an unusual variation in that routine in mid-September when the car refused to start because of a low battery, just 15 minutes before Mass started.

Maria was suddenly apprehensive. "How can I get to church, Roberto?" she cried, using my name as we'd used it in Brazil. "I hate to miss Sunday Mass." She looked up at me shyly. "I always pray for help from the Virgin Mary," she added softly.

"I know, honey. But don't worry. You'll get there in time for your usual Mass," I said, and was lucky when I quickly got a taxi to take her across the bridge to St. John's. "I'll pick you up at the front steps after the services," I said, as she pulled away. Then I dialed a service station operator to come give me a jump-start, after which I ran on the alternator to K-Mart. There were a number of cars backed up waiting for service, so I bought a battery and installed it myself. Everything went smooth as bunny fur, and I was waiting for Nini when she left the church.

We went for lunch at the Olive Garden restaurant, and then back to the condo, by which time Maria was feeling tired. I think part of her fatigue had been caused by worrying about whether I'd be there to greet her as she descended the church steps; sort of like a bride worries about whether the groom will be there to greet her when she goes up the church aisle.

187

The following week it was back to the needlework routine for my long-suffering redhead with no hair. First the blood test for a full blood profile, then a CAT scan of her head, and then a chest x-ray; then the waiting, followed by the chemotherapy at the hospital. I had long since thumbed through all of the old magazines lying about the various units we visited, and was on a first name basis with the chubby black lady, Lydia who took breast cancer treatments on Wednesday mornings the same as Maria, occupying the bed next to hers in the double room. At least the two ladies could visit while they waited for their respective chemicals to drip glacially slow into their needle-scarred veins.

September 24 Nini had a date with a different output of the pharmaceutical industry when she began the intravenous injection of a new drug. That was Leukeron, or chlorambucil, an anticancer drug which is supposed to interfere with the growth of cancer cells and thus help the body's immune system to overcome the disease. I was shaken up when I looked into my AMA prescription drug guide and learned that Leukeron is used mainly to combat leukemia, or cancer of the blood cells or blood-forming organs, which may cause anemia and enlargement of the lymph nodes. The drug itself may cause lymphoma, which is a painless enlargement of the lympn nodes. Leukeron and lymphoma apparently work hand in glove in the secret recesses of the body to fight their silent war against cancer.

Like most cancer treating drugs, Leukerin has its bad side, and may reduce the production of blood cells by the bone marrow, so that while it helps one malevolent condition, it may set up another in its stead. My beloved would slowly feel the deleterious effect of that drug, and others, on her own life's blood.

Still, Maria was alert and eager to go out and do things, especially to dine in one of the hundreds of eating places that elbow one another for space in the Tampa Bay area, particularly in St. Petersburg with its high density of older people on retirement. Almost every eating or dining spot has an Early Birds program, with discounts off the normal menu prices for folks who dine before 5:00, or sometimes 6:00 p.m.. Their motto seems to be, 'Feed the old folks and get them out of the way before the drinking crowd arrives'. But the program is a blessing to the thousands of people on social security or with modest incomes. Early Bird specials allow the elderly to break the monotony of condo living by dining out frequently, and still not go broke.

Although Nini often felt as listless as a just-fed cat after completing her chemo injections, within a day or two she would be back on her pins, and happy to do anything which took us out of the 'compound' for a few hours and a bit of exercise. Thus it was that in early October, we took the bridge across Tampa Bay and on through Tampa to Ybor City, home of the fascinating old Spanish restaurant, Columbia. Maria exercised her taste buds with *boliche*, the roast beef with the circle of sausage in its center, served with black beans, rice and fried plantain, followed by flan with a few spoonsful of caramely 'juice' ladled over it. I had all the same things, except I ate *pompilla*, the large, thin, quick-fried steak with onions—to me a special treat.

After lunch, we strolled along Seventh Avenue to peak into the artists' digs, and to tour the many shops in the converted cigar factory. Maria bought trinkets for the grandkids, and at a kiosk I bought her a crystal pendant on a silver chain. The new 'jewel' sparkled like a half-inch diamond at her throat!

The following week, we made no trip to the hospital for chemotherapy, for Doctor Able delayed the leukeran injections after her blood tests of October 18 and November 1 and 12. For a short period, Maria had several visits with Doctor Able in his office, plus the series of tests to which she was becoming accustomed and resigned: chest scan, liver scan,

189

x-ray and blood test, all in December. After consultations with Doctor Coe, we returned to the hospital on December 6 at 10:30, where Doctor Coe took a small bit of flesh from beneath her left arm for a biopsy.

We both feared that the cancer had now invaded the lymph nodes on the left side of her body. I joined my beloved in a night of sleeplessness while we awaited the results of the tissue test, but apparently they revealed no cancer. On the 18th, in Doctor Coe's office, he pulled the stitches from the small incision.

The day after Christmas, we visited Doctor Coe again, and he swabbed the incision for a lab test, which again showed nothing, or at least we were not informed of any unhappy discovery. The next day we were back at the laboratory for an EKG, urine test and blood test. One might think that we would be anxious to know the results of every test, and be right on the heels of the doctor or nurse to learn the results; but Maria was not always that keen to hear the outcome, lest it turn out to be depressing.

By now Maria had more needle marks in her arms than a drug junkie, and it had reached the point where even the most skilled nurse might have to 'stick' her two or three times to draw blood. I stayed at her side for all such tests, and winced at every puncture the nurse or technician made with the needle. We asked Doctor Coe about installing a mediport, from which nurses could draw blood, or give injections without sticking her arms.

"I can put in a mediport very easily, Maria," Doctor Coe said. "it will take only a few minutes of surgery. It goes just under the skin above your left breast. After that, the nurse knows exactly where to put the needle to take a blood test or to give you chemotherapy."

"I will talk to Doctor Able, first," Nini said, and she did.

But Doctor Able was not keen on mediports. "I just don't think they're practical," he said, "and each time a nurse uses it, she has to flush it out with heparine. It's too much bother for the little you gain over drawing blood from a vein."

I spoke up for Maria. "But certainly it reduces the pain and nuisance of being stuck several times to draw blood! Her poor veins are already badly scarred from so many drawings. We should try to make such tests as easy on her as possible."

"Well, if you feel you *must* have a mediport, then go ahead and put one in. I can live with it," Able reluctantly consented.

Everything was set for the small surgery to take place on December 30, but when we arrived early in the morning at the 1-day surgery unit we found someone along the line had goofed, for they were not expecting us!

"I wonder if Doctor Coe's nurse screwed up in making the surgery appointment," I asked, "or did the good doctor quietly cancel the operation so he could take his Jaguar in for repairs?"

"Oh, Robin, you are too suspicious!" Nini cried. She hated to hear any criticism of her idol of the operating table.

With so many office visits, and the preparations for surgery which did not occur, our Christmas was not that pleasant in 1991. I had the usual foodstuffs sent to the kids and to Robbie and Larry's family in Marco Island, we traded simple things between us, I took Maria to the special Masses and we walked on the seawall in the evenings if Nini felt up to it, shortcutting so as not to force her to walk too far.

Maria seemed to be standing up well under the battery of tests and multitudinous treatments she'd taken throughout 1991, and except for her missing hair—which was starting to grow back now that she'd been off leukeran for a month and a half—she did not exhibit much of a physical change, which might easily have occurred because of the ordeal which she had endured so stoically over the past 5-plus years.

We went out for Christmas 'dinner' at the hotel on St. Pete Beach again, and when Maria asked the waitress to put some left-over turkey and dressing in a 'doggie box' for us, the girl disappeared for a few minutes and returned with the left-overs wrapped daintily in aluminum foil: the whole package in the shape of a swan with a long graceful neck.

"How charming!" Nini cried, and rose to give the slender waitress a grandmotherly hug and kiss.

"Did you do that?" I asked, for it was amazingly fashioned, and she'd completed it in just a few moments.

"Yes, I did," she smiled brightly. "My hobby is modeling things from clay, so for especially nice people I sometimes do a little work of art when I wrap their take-home food, instead of just tossing it in a box. You two have been so pleasant, I had to do something for you. I hope you have a merry Christmas."

"Well, our Christmas dinner has been most enjoyable, and we thank you for being so kind," I said, and gave her a quick hug the same as Maria had done. The tip I added to the Visa charge was a bit more than 20% that afternoon.

We walked over to the window to look down at the beach and the people without a care in the world strolling or splashing in the sunshine eight stories below, then took the elevator down, and were soon back in our condo, full of turkey and all the fixings. And we had a swan, stuffed with enough turkey for sandwiches that night, sitting gracefully in the refrigerator.

New Years Eve we relaxed at home and watched the noisy crowd in Times Square on TV as they followed the ball in its descent to mark the beginning of 1992. Of course there was a big party up at the Bay Island clubhouse, but Maria was not up to a bash like that. A glass or two of champagne apiece, some dips and some 'finger' goodies completed our celebration of the arrival of what we prayed would be a much happier new year.

In bed we embraced, and as my arms encircled my wife of 48 years, she whispered softly in the darkness, "I love you, Daddy," and increased the pressure of her squeeze.

"I know you do, *querida*," I murmured, "but no more than I love you, my little Brazilian beauty," and I gave her several kisses on cheeks and lips. With those brief pledges of mutual love and allegiance, we relaxed in the big king-size bed until Morpheus could carry us away to that special place where he takes couples who are deeply in love, so they can dream sweet dreams until gentle Eos stirs them to wakefulness at the dawn of their next connubial day.

But before Morpheus overtook *my* mind and thoughts, I whispered a low prayer to whatever God there may be: "Please, dear Lord, let the coming year see real gains in my dear Maria's fight against cancer. She has been so strong and so brave all these years, it seems she should be given a chance to share a life with me for many years to come. In the name of Jesus and the Virgin Mary, in whom she has such deep faith, I ask this great favor. I know that *I* am unworthy . . . but Maria truly deserves Your divine help. Amen."

CHAPTER 23

It goes almost without saying that my final prayer as I drifted off to sleep in the wee hours of the New Year went just as unanswered as did my first prayer for Maria's health. The year 1992 promptly became a dizzying Maelstrom of medical activity for my beloved. We ended the 12 days of Christmas on my birthday, but except for the Greek Orthodox ceremony up in Tarpon Springs, my birthday was a non-event. We didn't even go out to eat, because I turned 74 on Monday, and we'd gone out for dinner Sunday, counting it as my birthday. Besides, paying our share of the medical expenses chewed into our budget like a beaver into an aspen; we dared not run up our Visa card account.

However, Maria's 1992 joust with the doctors began the very next day with a visit to Doctor Coe's office to set a date for the mediport installation surgery. "I can do it on the tenth," Doctor Coe said amiably. "That's next Friday morning at eight-thirty. You can go home that same afternoon, all right?"

Maria looked at me as though seeking approval, and I nodded. "That will be fine," she said, and I nodded again.

"All right, I'll see you in surgery Friday morning, Maria," he smiled at her. "And don't worry. You'll never even know you've got a mediport until the nurse uses it . . . except for the slight bulge over your left breast," he concluded.

The procedure took place as scheduled. Nini checked into the one-day care unit, and shortly thereafter was wheeled away to Surgery. By 10:00 she was back in the reception unit, and after coffee and a roll for both of us, we were home by

1:30. For the next four days, a visiting nurse came to check Maria to see that all was well with her. The 15th we went to Coe's office to remove the stitches from a neat and successful operation. As Doctor Coe had said, Nini's left side looked much the same except for the bulge of the mediport, set in place with a slit in the skin and the opening of a wee pocket for it to slip into. Things were much cheaper in those days, medical-wise, and what documents I can find reveal the cost to be only $1,300.

Actually, I believe there were other costs, for a person could hardly stick his head inside the door of a hospital for less than a thousand dollars. (According to a story on the TV news, it cost one young construction worker several hundred bucks to have a splinter removed from his finger in an emergency room!)

By mid-January Maria was back in the swing of things, having blood drawn on the 16th, via a vein in her arm, (not the mediport!) in preparation for new chemotherapy. That started on our 48th wedding anniversary, January 20, when she began a series of seven injections of leucovorin, 1,000 mgs, together with 1,000 mgs of flourouracil.

The first treatment was supposed to begin at 9:30, but as in previous sessions, the injection didn't begin until almost noon, and we got home at 2:00 that afternoon. Just as sheep struggle through the tick-curing dip-tank at the rancher's pleasure, so Maria got her chemotherapy injection at Doctor's convenience.

Leucovorin is an injectable form of folic acid, vital for the formation of red blood cells by the bone marrow. It appears that the doctor used the leucovorin to offset the ill effects of the flourouracil.

The second such therapy took place on February 3, after the usual intervening blood test, the blood drawn this time from the new mediport. I was greatly relieved when I didn't have to watch Maria suffer through two or three exploratory

195

'sticks' before the technician struck blood. The same routine and injections took place on the 13th, finishing at 12:00 noon.

To be sure that time did not drag for Maria, the doctors scheduled a chest CAT scan on the 19th, and on the 21st we had a visit with Doctor Coe. "You are coming along nicely, Maria," he said. I didn't believe him, but somehow I felt he was doing the right thing by lying to her. I certainly did not think she was 'coming along nicely', but there was nothing I could do about the way the tide was flowing—I could only drift along with it and try to keep my head above water.

Pines of Ponderosa hit us up for a mere $8,388 for their services between February 3rd and 29th.

After her treatment on the 26th, we relaxed with a short drive over to Plant City east of Tampa to take in the Strawberry Festival there. "I know exactly what shortcake and ripe strawberries do to my figure," Nini grinned as she wiped off her mustachio of whipped cream, "but they are so good we have to stay here for another helping in a couple of hours."

"You've got that right!" I heartily endorsed her idea as I waded into my own heaping bowl of utterly fabulous berries, shortcake and whipped cream. After we finished the first round, we strolled the fair, then went to hear a county-western group with whom I was unfamiliar at an outdoor theater. They may not have been great, but doggone it, they were loud!

General Norman Schwarzkopf's command car from the Persian Gulf War was parked near the shortcake tent with a soldier guarding it. Maria posed beside the rugged vehicle, and I took her picture. At least we found comfort in the knowledge that our own Charlie had come through that particular ordeal uninjured. His first war duty was on a carrier off Vietnam. Now with Desert Storm behind him, Charlie was spending his last tour of duty before retirement at Key West Naval Air Station.

By eerie coincidence, Nini and I were visiting the kids in

Key West when that Cuban pilot defected and brought a Russion Mig fighter plane with him. Charlie took us to view it in the hanger of the air station. It looked pretty neat to us, although we were not allowed to climb the ladder to look into the cockpit.

From the command car of the only general who wanted to finish the Gulf War, in opposition to President Bush and National Security Advisor Colin Powell, we went hunting for elephant ears, and found some near a large, open-walled tent under which we munched them noisily while visiting with a family already seated at a long table there; especially with their lovely black-eyed teenage daughter, who was a radiant picture of graciousness. A short time later, after a second go at a mountain of strawberry shortcake, we caught the bus which lugged us back to our parking space free of charge, and we were on our way home.

I was so glad Maria enjoyed the festival, for she was lined up for office visits with two doctors, plus a blood test, before going back on the protocol on March 10, receiving leucovorin and flourouracil for the 5th time. Three more blood tests and three more injections of the same drugs carried us through April 10, and treatment No. 8, during which period we ran up charges of $9,587 at Pines of Ponderosa, to end that series.

What benefit all the coming and going had achieved we had no idea. We'd reached the point of no resistance, a place where resignation set in and we simply let the tests and injections do their job as we prayed for the best.

The next brief hiatus in Maria's many treatments lasted all of 10 days. Then on April 20 it was blood test time again, followed by an office visit with Doctor Able, and a cardiac 'resting' test on the 22nd, which cost over $500. Nini was all set to begin her next 'protocol' of 10 encounters, which would carry through to the end of June.

The first treatment was on April 23, when she received 50 mgs of DoxRubein and 100 mgs of Deca-durabo, plus

197

Zofran. Some idea of the terrible expense involved in the chemotherapy can be gained from the knowledge that the DoxRubein cost $820, the Deca-durabo was $102, and the Zofran, $265. The Leucovorin had cost $2,448 a treatment.

Twice during Maria's dreadful treatments the hospital accidentally billed Medicare for the same treatment two days in a row, although she never, *ever* took chemotherapy two successive days! But one knows how bookkeepers can screw up, right? When I challenged them, the hospital apologized, and said they would make restitution to Medicare and Prudential. Whether they did or not, I cannot say. I was too preoccupied with Maria and her treatments to allow myself to become a CPA for Medicare. I think Pines did give me credit for our share of the excess costs, but I have no record to prove it. There were so many drugs, and each had a number of names, so trying to follow what was going on—especially now, several years later—can be very tedious. A drug may have a chemical, or generic name, and from one to a half-dozen brand names. One doctor will use one brand name, another a different one and a third use the generic term. The poor patient has to stumble along hoping the pharmacist knows what he's doing; and of course most of them do, most of the time. It is my belief that the medical folks use this admixture of names on purpose, if only to make it difficult for a patient to pin them down regarding any given drug or treatment.

Anyhow, my AMA books do not show Dox Rubein; but they do show Doxorubicin, also known as Andriamycin, a drug dating way back to 1974, and 'one of the most effective anti-cancer drugs that has ever been developed', per the AMA drug manual. My question immediately was: If it's so damned effective, why did Doctor Able fiddle around with two or three other drug protocols before giving it to Maria? It had its side effects, such as nausea and vomiting, red urine, and hair loss, but a patient usually overcame the first two symptoms as a protocol progressed, which is what occurred with Nini.

Deca-durabo to me was a mystery drug. Decadurabolin came into use back in 1959, and is an anabolic steroid, a synthetic hormone related to the male sex hormone testosterone, and is normally given by injection. Since this is not meant to be a text on drugs and drug use, I will develop the matter no further, except to wonder why the doctor gave Maria a drug which athletes surreptitiously have used, and in some nations openly used, to increase their weight and muscle strength. Perhaps it was out of pity, because the drug also increases the growth of hair!

As to Zofran, I could find no reference to it in any of my books, including the dictionary and the Encyclopaedia Britannica. But later on I came across an article touting the benefits of the drug which were highly desirable for chemotherapy patients. Using Zofran during the infusion of nausea-causing drugs greatly reduced that nausea for most patients. The item said some people refused to take chemotherapy because of the horrible spells of nausea and vomiting the therapy caused. Now with Zofran, many could be relieved of that misery.

During the 2-month series of 10 treatments, the deca-durabo was omitted a few times, and on one occasion, Able specifically ordered that Nini's blood be drawn from a vein and not from her mediport. On May 20, when Maria took no deca-durabo, she vomited as soon as we got home. On June 2 she had a chest x-ray, and on the 3rd she was nauseous after her treatment. How my dear one managed to endure that horrible period of injections, blood tests, x-rays, nausea, vomiting and general feeling of fatigue I will never know. She was a paragon among cancer patients, to say the least.

"I don't know how you face these treatments with such a brave heart, honey," I said one day early on, just before we headed for the hospital for therapy.

"I don't have a brave heart, Daddy, really I don't," she replied, "but I do what I have to do, and pray that everything will work out, so I can continue to share my life with you."

"I pray to God that your treatments will conquer the enemy, too," I said as I enfolded her in my arms. I would choke on the word 'cancer', so I avoided using it. If nothing else, Maria got more hugging than she'd had in some time as her battle with cancer continued its pitiless progression.

Nini's hair had grown back in quite well over the past weeks, but before the end of this first 'heavy' protocol, Maria called me to the bathroom again. "Look at my hairbrush, honey," she said, and held it out to me. It was full of hair. "I've noticed a little more hair than usual in my brush the past few days, but now it looks like it's all coming out . . . again."

"Oh, *querida*, that's a shame! I knew you might lose some of it, but a few more days like this and you will be my little baldie again."

As I clasped her in my arms to comfort her, I recalled how beautiful her hair had been when first I met her in 1943. Despite the fact that her hair no longer had the beautiful coppery highlights of her youth, but was well tinged with gray (which she kept hidden by periodic 'color baths' at the beauty salon), I could not restrain my feelings, and a deep sigh escaped me.

"I just hate to think of being bald as a newborn baby at my age . . . but at least we'll save money on the beauty salon," Nini wisecracked, and we chuckled at her comparison as we pulled the fistful of pretty strands from her brush and deposited them in the wastebasket. In a very short time, that basket had claimed virtually all of Maria's hair for the second time.

The next major billing by the hospital was for $6,290 for drugs and treatments.

With our continuous comings and goings to the doctors'

offices, the test labs and the hospital, and the hours of wait-ing to know if she were to have chemotherapy on a given day, and when she was, the endless drip, drip, drip of the slow-flowing solutions into her veins, with all those problems, the days flew by almost as fast as a movie reel unwinds through the projector. And although the drugs and treatments were often the same as before, there was no end of minor differ-ences in our cyclical trips for treatment.

Thus it was that we reached the end of June with a visit to Doctor Able's office on the 29th, where he set up two appointments for drawing blood; one for a full profile, via her mediport, and another the following day, July 2, taken via one of Nini's scarred veins. The hospital hit us with another bill now for over $1,250. At the second of the above appoint-ment to draw blood, I winced as I held Nini's hand and watched the nurse make a second probe before striking blood.

Those tests apparently enabled Doctor Able to set up the next protocol, and after some further x-rays, he sched-uled Maria for a new series of chemotherapy treatments start-ing July 15. That particular series turned out to be anathema for my brown-eyed angel.

CHAPTER 24

Before starting a new round of therapy, Maria had a 'cat' scan which cost some $850, which, with other tests and x-rays, ran up a bill of $1,145 at Pines of Ponderosa, plus a few hundred more for visits to doctors' offices. All these expenses were merely preliminaries to the main bout.

We arrived at the hospital Oncology ward at the proper hour September 15, and this time the doctor had cleared the way for Maria to proceed with the therapy. She took the drugs mitamycin (also known as mutamycine—just to add confusion) and vinblastine (or Velban—ditto) in the amounts of 10 mg. each. Mitamycin does a job similar to doxorubicin, as a cytotoxic antibiotic.

Apparently cancer cells are susceptible to different varieties of drugs depending on the type of cancer and which stage the cancer is in. It also seems an oncologist has to experiment with a parade of different drugs to ascertain the right one to use to match the patient's cancer's particular type and stage. Sad to say, the farther we went in Maria's treatment, the less faith I had in her doctors' work.

"How do you feel, Nini?" I asked after this first session with the new drug, fearing the usual nausea and discomfort.

"I feel tired, like always, but at least I'm not sick of my stomach this time," she said, mustering a weak smile.

"Thank God for small favors," I breathed a sigh of relief. I held her arm and helped her from the car into the condo and to her living room easy chair.

Maria repeated this protocol on August 5 and again on

September 2, each hospital chemotherapy treatment preceded by visits to Doctor Able's office, and the usual blood tests taken via the mediport. Along with the treatments the nurse gave an injection of heparin, an anticoagulant used to prevent clotting in the bloodstream. I believe the immediate aim was to flush out the mediport.

We made a follow-up visit to Doctor Able's office the 9th of September. The next day the good luck with which Nini had been blessed in regard to side effects brought on by the last series of treatments came to an end.

She suddenly became very ill in midday, and I rushed her to the Pines' emergency room. There they administered 72 units of halotestin (or fluoxymesterone, an anti-cancer drug) and 16 units of folic acid, vital to the formation of blood cells, both $2.50 per unit.

Maria had low blood counts, and for four days suffered with diarrhea. The drugs she was given would found a pharmacopeia: cefoperazone, an antibiotic for treating serious infections of the respiratory tract, urinary tract, skin and joints; furosin, a topical anti-bacterial good for the urinary tract; tobramysin, another anti-biotic for serious infections; cyprofibrate, a lipid (fat) lowering drug; diphenoxylate-atropine, the former a narcotic anti-diarrheal used to reduce bowel contractions and thus the frequency and fluidity of bowel movements, the latter to guard against addiction to the former; then a combination of the prior two drugs known as Lomatil; plus primaxin, or cilastatin-imipenem, another anti-biotic, and finally, blood platelets and saline solution.

Maria remained in the hospital through the 17th, suffering a fever on the 14th and 15th. As her illness failed to ameliorate and obnoxious diarrhea continued to plague her, I spoke with Doctor Able.

"When we two were in Brazil, doctor, if we caught diarrhea, we took a Lomatil pill and in one day we were cured. Don't we have Lomatil in this country?"

"Yes, we have it; but I want to be sure Maria can take it safely," he replied.

"Well, neither of us ever had an after-effect in Brazil," I informed him, "so it should be safe for her to take here."

Naturally I was not taking into account any possible reaction of Lomatil with the other drugs Maria was taking, but every time I saw Able I twisted his arm. Finally he prescribed the Lomatil. Within one day Maria's diarrhea was gone. The next day, September 17, I took her home with me at 7:00 pm..

Nini was extremely tired, and I had to help her out of the car and she held onto my arm as I walked her to her easy chair in the living room. "I'm sorry to be such a bother, Daddy, but I feel all wobbly inside, and I'm afraid of falling down." "You are no bother, sweetheart. You have *never* been a bother. It's so good to have you back home with me, *querida*. I've worried about you every day since I took you to the emergency room. I know everyone at the hospital was sick and tired of me hanging around all the time like I did. But I just couldn't leave you there alone knowing how miserable you were with that damned infection. And how weak you were from so many trips to the bathroom and so little food to eat."

"I don't know what I would have done if you hadn't stayed there to look after me, honey," Nini said softly. "I was so-o-o tired, and if I rang for a nurse it took too long for one to show up. I think they hated helping me to the bathroom when those sudden urges came."

"I know how you felt, Nini. In Pearl Harbor I got the runs and the doc kept me in sick bay nine days and I lost nine pounds. The doctor finally cured me with a diet of peeled raw apples and unsweetened iced tea. I'm not sure Lomatil existed in 1940. The pharmacist's mates were very caring and helpful. One man was so good to me that when we divers had to go on a diving 'expedition' up in Iceland, we'd ask him to go with us as our emergency medic, sort of a day off for him."

"I remember reading about that in the second volume of your biography," Maria said. "Now I know how you felt!."

"Anyway, I'm more relaxed now, and deeply thankful that you are back beside me here in bed at night," I said.

Her little hand crept across the bed under the sheet to reach my hand and clasp it tightly as she played her little bedtime game with me. "I'm terribly glad to *be* back beside you, Daddy," she whispered, and I leaned over to kiss her goodnight, her sweet lips still dry from her ordeal. "Sweet dreams, Daddy," she ended the tiring day.

"Good night, my little Brasileira," I murmured, and I lay with my eyes open for a long while, worrying about what the future would bring to my dear partner.

Those eight days in the hospital not only took a heavy toll on my poor Nini, they were also a drag on our finances. Bills from various doctors, plus lab and test fees came to over $1,000. The hospital bill was $18,398 plus $600 more for drugs. Of course, the costs were zilch when compared to my darling's health and survival, but they demonstrate once more why I nurse the opinion that if someone were to find a cure for breast cancer this very day, the drug and medical businesses would fight tooth and nail to prevent the Food and Drug Administration from approving it!

Not only are the doctors and hospitals and drug companies reaping huge profits from cancer, there are also the professors and other researchers in colleges and foundations all across the land whose juicy grants for cancer research would come to an end—perish the thought—even before they got their own drug patented.

That Maria was already on the final downhill path still hadn't entered my thick skull, perhaps because she, herself, had so much faith in God.

Some itinerant 'healer' had come to town a few days earlier, and in Maria's church the priest announced that the man had had some miraculous results in curing sick people by holding their hands and praying for them. The man was favoring St. John's congregation with a special session on a given evening, and anyone seeking the help of the Lord in getting well should definitely be there.

"Will you take me, honey?" Maria asked. "They say you should have someone stand behind you during the ritual, because people often faint when the man holds their hands and prays over them." Her eyes implored my assistance even more than her words.

"Of course I'll take you, honey, You know I will do anything to help you. I would gladly give my life if it would help to cure you." I almost said 'to save yours', but I caught myself in time; for in all the months that had passed since the discovery of Maria's breast cancer I had never once spoken of anything except a complete recovery. In the first place, I'd had great faith in her doctors at the beginning, and always told her they would bring about her recovery. I didn't realize that my faith was horribly misplaced.

Now perhaps a deeply religious man, favored by the Lord, might bring about her cure. It was certainly worth trying, even though I had little hope that the good Samaritan would actually succeed where so many specialists had failed.

A few days before the benefactor arrived for his curative ceremony, we found ourselves on 5th Avenue in St. Petersburg which we had never driven before, where we came across the Cathedral of St. Jude.

"Let's park here and go inside," Maria suggested. We entered the church to say a prayer up near the altar, for St. Jude is the patron saint who helps those with hopeless causes, something I didn't know, but with which Nini was quite familiar.

My exposure to Catholic saints had been limited to three: St. Francis, whose small statue with the little white birds we had always kept in the house; St. Patrick, who had driven the snakes out of Ireland, and St. Christopher, whose medal we kept pinned above the center of the windshield in our family car from the day we bought our first 1936 Ford coupe after World War II, to the current day. St. Christopher was the patron saint of travelers; until Pope John Paul II struck his name from the list of approved saints. St. Jude may have resented the demotion, but St. Christopher must have been glad to get away from all the heavy traffic.

The interior of the church was beautifully modern, and we prayed together in silence near the altar. Then Maria picked up a small folder about St. Jude to read as we drove home. We could add the power of St. Jude to that of the man who would lead the coming ceremony at St. Johns on St. Pete beach, and pray their combined strength would have a salutary effect.

By the time the 'healer' arrived in town, Nini was a study in expectancy, her dear heart filled with faith. At the church, those seeking help formed a row across the front of the church near the altar. "Now stay right behind me, Daddy," Maria cautioned, "in case I faint I don't want to end up on the floor."

"I'll stay right here behind you and hold you within my arms, *querida*. You needn't worry about falling down," and I gave her a reassuring hug from behind. We were in ninth position along the line.

Our priest led off with prayers and a call to anyone who was ill to come forward and join the line where the healer would perform his ceremonies. After some shuffling and hurried movement, the line of hopefuls was ready.

At first, Maria was tense, being in the presence of a man of God with a reputation for healing the sick. But as the man moved slowly toward us from our right to left, murmuring his incantations in a low voice, her heart stilled, and she grew calmer. Three or four people fainted and fell backward into the arms of their helpers, but oddly, I felt the fainting was put on, and not real, much like the 'healing' scenes on religious television shows. As for Maria, she listened intently to the man's words, gave the responses he requested, didn't grow weak, and stayed on her feet within my encircling arms.

When the rites were concluded for all those present—and I'd never realized how many sick people belonged to St. John's church, for there was a long line of people up front, many with crutches or walkers or wheelchairs, and several with two or three people to assist them and sustain them from fainting—our priest said another prayer, invoking God to hear the prayers of the sick and of the man who was diligently trying to heal them, and at last said we could go home now, and await our hoped-for cures.

"Oh, Daddy," Maria cried as we drove back across the bridge to our condo, "I do hope this man truly has the power to heal me, for I am so tired of trips to the hospital and doctors' offices, and the endless blood tests and therapies and radiation treatments."

"I pray he has cured you, too, honey. For I suffer with you every time a nurse sticks a needle in you to draw blood or to pump in some miserable chemical. You don't deserve to be so mistreated. You have always been such a kind and wonderful person, not only to your family, but to your friends . . . and to strangers as well. You deserve to be healed."

When we kissed goodnight that evening, I assumed Maria's thoughts were still on the possibility of being quickly cured. My own thoughts and feelings, on the other hand, were far from optimistic. I felt that little, if anything, would come of the ritual we had just taken part in. And that Maria would have to continue her unpleasant treatments in search of a cure or remission of the vicious cancer which continued to gnaw at her body and her mind and perhaps even her very soul. For the cancer was an unrelenting and pitiless marauder, worse than any Hun or Mongol who had ever attacked defenseless people in olden times.

CHAPTER 25

Despite her disgustingly miserable hospitalization in September, there would be no relief for Maria from the ordeals of blood tests and chemotherapy. Each time we headed out to draw blood for testing, I marveled at the staunch manner in which my wife rallied to confront the enemy which was laying siege to her well-being and peace of mind.

I thanked God that hope springs eternal in the human breast, as Alexander Pope so aptly put it, for within Maria's heart lay a hidden warrior, a staunch defender who helped her fight the spreading cancer with all the courage of a U.S. Marine charging up a ridge at Okinawa.

Neighbors encountering Maria at the mailroom of our 32-unit building would ask how she was doing. Invariably her smiling answer was, "I'm doing fine, just fine."

As our neighbors John and Norma put it later on, "Maria never admitted to pain, or fear or any feeling of defeat. She always spoke as though she expected to be well in a few weeks." They were the pair who went on a sojourn to Oklahoma and when they left gave Maria such lengthy, strong embraces I feared they'd squeeze the breath out of her or smother her.

From the day John and Norma bought the unit next to ours, they always greeted us warmly, with strong hugs and kisses on the cheeks, just like family. Even better than family, for Norma usually grabbed me to plant a kiss squarely on the lips. No fooling around with pecks on the cheeks for her!

She was cute, and considerably younger than I, so I didn't mind.

We grew deeply fond of them, and admired John for fishing so faithfully off our sea wall without ever hauling in a fish over eight inches long. The pelicans loved him, for although condo rules said not to feed the birds, John cheerfully gave his fruits of the sea to the happy pelicans which paddled about awkwardly with a noisy shaking of wings and their big bills flapping open and closed in hopes of a piscatorial reward.

Eventually I learned why John and Norma were so warm and enthusiastic in their goodby hugs and kisses when they left that day for Oklahoma.

It was back to the salt mines as of October 1, when we went to the lab for a blood test to prep for Nini's coming round of chemotherapy. The nurse insisted on drawing the blood from a vein. Sadly, the test showed Nini was in no condition to accept or endure a chemical invasion so soon after her dismissal from the hospital. We made the unsettling trek again on October 6, and this time the nurse drew the blood from Maria's mediport, after which she 'flushed' the port with heparin. Again the doctor found her blood to be 'unsatisfactory' for the administration of chemotherapy.

"I wish they would make up their mind, Daddy," Nini cried impatiently. She was not petulant, though she deserved to be. "This playing around and back-and-forth stuff is driving me crazy!" That was the strongest complaint I can recall from my little Brazilian during all her campaign against cancer, from the day of her mastectomy until now, six years later.

"They're trying to insure that everything in your blood is in balance before risking any more injections, honey," I explained as best I could. "As soon as your blood builds up to its proper resistance, you'll begin your new protocol."

Her next test, of Novembber 2, with the blood drawn via mediport, was *still* unsatisfactory! During the ensuing office visit, Doctor Able said we probably should wait until after the Thanksgiving holiday to pursue the new protocol. Those last three 'sticks' to draw blood, the lab tests and the visits to Doctor Able cost almost $2,500 and were of no assistance whatsoever other than to warn us that Maria should not start the next round of treatments yet.

"At least you can enjoy Thanksgiving, Maria," Doctor Able said kindly. I wondered if *he* planned to go away for the holiday?

"That's good," Nini replied, "because my niece and nephew on Marco Island invited us to dinner at their house. They build homes on contract, which is a high-pressure job, and they really relax during the long Thanksgiving weekend. Now we can drive down to see them." Maria gathered up her things and we were on our way to the car. "I really do look forward to some time off from doctors and hospitals and labs," she said, clinging to my arm as we walked slowly along. "They get so boring!"

"Especially the nurses with those big needles!" I said, and for the first time in ages we laughed at a quip about Nini's multi-round bout with the 'blood' nurses at Pines of Ponderosa.

Although Maria had a keen sense of humor, I deliberately avoided making jokes or puns which touched on her operations or cancer, on chemotherapy or on scans and x-rays or other tests. To me, the awesome battle which Nini was fighting with body and mind and emotions offered no opening for humor or joking. If anything were sacrosanct, it was Maria's tough struggle against cancer.

It was more than a two-hour drive each way between our condo in South Pasadena, and Robbie and Larry's home in Marco Island, located on the island bearing the same name, the town and the island being synonymous. We left home at 8:30 and arrived at Robbie's house close to 11:00 a.m.. Robbie is such a buoyant spirit and happy soul that she soon had Maria overlooking the fact that she was tired.

"You look very nice, Aunt Maria," Robbie said after hugs all around. "How do you feel?"

"I feel fine," Maria gave her stock answer. "I just feel tired from the long drive, for even in a Mercury the trip through pine trees and cabbage palms is boring and tiring."

"Well, you do look very nice, Maria, just like Robbie said," Max cut in.

My widowed sister, Maxine, came to Florida from Vancouver, Washington after her daughter Robbie and family moved here because there was so much construction going on in the area. Larry studied Florida rules and regulations, and soon passed the exam and became a licensed General Contractor. He and Robbie then sent for Sis, who now had her own small apartment nearby in a beautiful complex with a lovely pool which mirrored royal palms.

Sis was in poor physical condition, with her lungs so plugged up she could barely breathe at times. Her lung problems were brought on by smoking, which began when she was 15 years old. Apparently my folks had no problem with Sis latching onto the nicotine habit; and I was far away in the Navy most of the time, so I couldn't watch after her.

When a trip to the hospital in 1985 shortly after she arrived in Florida almost killed her, Sis stopped smoking. But she had quit too late, and now was almost an invalid. Robbie bought a wheelchair for her, and when they went shopping together, pushed her in it down the aisles of the grocery stores, and wrestled it among the racks of clothing in the department stores.

Sarah and Laura, were home during the holiday, so we had a fine visit, touring most of the homes Larry had under various stages of construction, and wading heavily into the superb dinner which the three Taylor women had whipped up with a bit of help from Sis. We rented two movies and watched them in the big den that evening, I drove Maxine to her apartment around 10:00, and before it grew late Maria and I were upstairs in bed, this time in Sarah's room.

The next morning we all went out for breakfast in a small cafe in a shopping center, then returned to the Taylor home to throw our gear into the Mercury's roomy trunk, including a tin-foil package of goodies. "I know Uncle Bobby loves cold turkey sandwiches," Robbie exclaimed as she made up the package.

My name, of course, is Robin, but at home all of my family called me Bobby as I grew up, so I have always been Uncle Bobby to nephews and nieces and grand nephews and nieces. When Maxine named her daughter after me, it was convenient to call her Robbie, and me Bobby, to avoid any misunderstanding as to who was supposed to jump at a call for help!

We left Marco Island around 3:00 and drove home, passing over the beautiful Skyway Bridge across the mouth of Tampa Bay into the south end of St. Petersburg and around the water to the west to reach our condo on Boca Ciega Bay. "I truly enjoyed or visit with Robbie and Sis and the family . . . and the dinner was fabulous. But I am terribly tired, honey," Maria said as she slumped into her recliner. "But riding in the Mercury is as comfortable as riding in any heavy car we've ever owned since we bought the Cadillac in nineteen fifty-five."

"You're right, *querida*," I said, "but how did you remember we bought our first Caddy in nineteen fifty-five?" I asked.

"That's easy," she replied. "That was the year you became head of the Purchasing Division at State Farm Insurance in Bloomington, Illinois. Remember how one of your friends remarked that it was interesting how shortly after you became the company Purchasing Agent you began driving a Cadillac?"

"For gosh sakes, Nini, you *do* have some memory! I didn't tell him the Caddy was two years old, and cost me no more than a new Chevrolet sedan would have cost, and that the President of State Farm had suggested the purchase to me. I let him stew in his own suspicions!"

Because Maria kept going so strongly over the many months of treatments, and virtually never complained, other than when we had to wait extra hours to start her therapy, the reason for her 'tiredness' still did not penetrate my thick skull to impress itself upon my brain. She enjoyed going out for lunch or dinner, and ate heartily, whether it was filet mignon or pizza. She went to Mass every Sunday, played bridge one or two afternoons a week, and watched the afternoon soaps and evening news on TV. When she had hair, she made a trip every week to the beauty salon.

Because so much of Maria's life was the same as in the past, I did not realize how debilitated my sweetheart was becoming. But the realization would soon be impressed upon me when she reached the point where she could no longer walk alone without falling.

On the first day of December Nini had a blood test, and this time her blood was in that part of its vacillations when she could go to the hospital December 2nd and begin her chemotherapy anew. This time she took vinblastine, 10 mg. and mutamycin 20 mg, plus the Zofran, plus Periactin, an antihistmine used to treat allergic reactions. The drugs cost from $104 for Zofran, to $134 for vinblastine, to the princely sum of $2,359 for the mutamycin, which I can only guess had to be specially brewed. Maria felt some nausea, and was very tired after the therapy was completed, but did not seem unduly affected by the treatment.

As we drove across the causeway to our condo gate, she admired the spread of Boca Ciega Bay and the wee island maybe 50 yards from the road. "That island with its tiny beach always seems like something someone anchored there, and not a real island," she observed.

"I know," I agreed, "but they don't come by and take it

home at night. It's always there when we go past, so it must be an island . . . or perhaps just an islet."

Christmas day we went to the Pier in downtown St. Pete and had a lunch of Spanish food in the Columbia Restaurant on an upper floor of the inverted pyramid, enjoying the view of the downtown area, of the yacht club with its adjoining yacht-filled marina and of the sailboats frittering about on the open bay.

We both dined heartily on crisp Cuban bread with ice cold 'real' butter on it, something we rarely ate; the butter, I mean. Then came boliche, the slabs of roast beef with the red sausage insert, and black beans with rice and fried plantain, plus mouth-watering flan dessert with an extra dollop of rich caramel sauce dripping tauntingly down its succulent sides.

Through the huge picture windows we could see the snowy egrets and blue herons stalking wee fish among the rocks below the seawall over near the yacht club, and watch the brown pelicans waiting on the pier for visitors to buy a pail of fish and toss to them. Fishing in the bay was difficult now for the big brown birds, for as the waters grew colder and the fish swam lower in the water, they were too deep for a buoyant pelican to reach in his normal diving attack.

We exchanged Christmas cards and small gifts, so unimportant I can't remember what they were. We really didn't feel like it was Christmas except when we looked at the calendar, for our fear of the future hung like a heavy dark cloud over our thoughts. The new year would begin with more chemotherapy, and God only knew what else, as we passed through the holidays into 1993.

We both prayed the new year would see some real improvement in Maria's health, and a remission in the cancer which gnawed at her breast, and apparently at her lungs, as the oncologist studied her scans and x-rays over the weeks.

215

He never went into much depth of discussion after he got the results of the tests and exams he had ordered.

"There appears to be a lesion on the breastbone, he remarked laconically, "and perhaps on the left lung."

"What are 'lesions', Daddy," Maria asked back at home, and I did my best to answer without revealing what I feared was the true state of affairs. With her overpowering, lifelong dread of death and anything connected with it, I could never bring myself to tell her what the word truly meant. Instead I obfuscated.

"I think they're something like a scar or blemish, querida," I'd say, "which is why the doctor keeps such a close tab on them, constantly adjusting his therapy protocols."

"I sure hope he knows what he's doing," she said pithily. At her words, that awful feeling welled up from my shoelaces through my total anatomy, almost tearing things loose as it passed them en route, and by the time it reached my throat and began to choke me, I was in tears, for the words of our son came back to me clearer than a bugle call: "Tell him to hit the cancer with everything he's got, and not to use half-measures!"

I fled to the bathroom to conceal my collapse, and washed my face with cold water and dried off so I could return to Nini. "For some reason I was feeling all sticky," I said, then forced myself to continue. "He must know, querida, or he would not be so greatly admired by all the hospital staff."

How could I possibly tell her that I thought the lesions were spots where her original breast cancer had metastasized, or spread, to other parts of her body? That the pains she felt occasionally were probably where the unrelenting cancer had opened shop in another area, always pushing out the boundaries, always striving for new conquests, always insatiable, and quite likely unstoppable by now?

On December 29 Maria endured one more session of blood tests, office visits, and the same chemotherapy as above, again without any undue adverse effects beyond the horrible probing to find a vein willing to part with blood for the tests. The hospital bill for the two sessions was $4,741, enough to stagger a longshoreman.

Between those two sessions at the laboratory and the hospital Oncology ward, I took Maria for drives, and to dine out at Steak and Ale and for seafood at Leverocks's to reduce the strain of waiting for that treatment of the 29th. That therapy went well for a change, and we were out of the hospital by noon after Maria's last chemo for 1992.

We went to Mass together on Sunday, and then to lunch at a family restaurant on 34th Street, the Kissin' Cuzzins. We had been going there from time to time either for lunch or for breakfast, for they made superb pancakes. 'Pancakies', Nini called them, following the Portuguese rule to pronounce the final 'e' on any word in their language. We'd ask for a waitress named Karla, who was a cute little server, with a bright smile and a quick sense of humor despite the fact that she was almost blind in her left eye, a condition brought on because her mother had had a cat in the house during and after her pregnancy with Karla and the cat had an allergy-type effect on the retina of Karla's eye. "It's a rare occurrence," she said, "but it had to happen to me!"

December 27 Maria went to Mass. I drove her there and picked her up afterward, and we proceeded to the Chinese Delight restaurant in South Pasadena where we knew the young couple who owned the place, The food was excellent, with almost no MSG, and we enjoyed the owners who always came to chat with us. It began one day when I said I'd like to have pepper steak, but I preferred snow peas instead of peppers. Her cute response came quickly, "We can do that, Robin, but it will be twenty-five cents extra."

"That's fine," I agreed, as Maria ordered egg fu yung and rice. We had delicious fried bananas for dessert, so delicately crafted that they melted in our mouths in a flood of delight and sips of plum wine.

When the hostess brought our fortune cookies, Maria selected hers, and when she cracked it open the tiny slip read, "You will soon be crossing the broad waters." When Nini handed me the slip to read, I felt like I'd been hit in the face with a bucket of ice water. '*My god!*' I thought, '*what an atrocious fortune cookie: and it has to end up in my darling Maria's hands!*'

Maria interrupted my jangled thoughts. "What does that mean, Robin?" she asked.

I certainly couldn't tell her what most people, especially church-goers, mean when they say someone has crossed the broad waters, but I had to come up with something, and I latched onto our often-discussed trip to Brazil. "I think it means we are going to take that trip to Rio before too long. We'll fly over broad waters to get there, you know."

"I never thought of that," she smiled. "Now the cookie makes sense," and she had such a happy look on her face I almost burst into tears.

The last day of the year Maria had a CAT scan early in the morning, and at noon we drove to Kissin' Cuzzins for lunch with Karla, dining on amberjack sandwiches, which were a special treat there because one of the owners went out in his own boat to bring them in fresher than morning dew. We both thought amberjack was tastier than the fabled Florida grouper. We didn't even squeeze in a dab of Key lime pie: at Kissin' Cuzzins an amberjack sandwich is a meal and a half!

We wound down the year quietly, not even exercising our noisemakers on the seawall which constituted our front yard. The lights from the condos and apartments across the bay gleamed softly on the water, paths of fairy moonbeams sprinkled gently there. We walked down to a nearby wooden bench and sat for a while listening to the noise of traffic on

South Pasadena Avenue, punctuated by the racket of an ambulance coming down the street to pull into the emergency room. The faint odor of marine bare space created by the ebbing tide caressed our nostrils as we quietly held hands into the New Year.

The night was idyllic, and we would have been superbly happy were it not for that miserable cancer gnawing away at Maria. After a half-hour we went inside for the final sips of champagne. I stowed away the leftover snacks while Maria prepared for bed. I followed her to brush my teeth, and we were soon side by side in the big bed. We clasped hands, hugged, kissed one another gently and without slobbers and soon drifted off to sleep.

To close down 1992 was a blessing, because for the most part it had been a miserable year for Maria. Again I whispered a prayer for my dear mate before falling to sleep, asking Someone out there in the vast beyond to take pity on her and let her be healed in 1993.

But my prayer had about as much chance of being answered as we two had of winning the Florida lottery.

CHAPTER 26

New Years Day 1993 fell on Friday, and to start the year right I went with Maria to ten o'clock Mass at St. John's across the waterway. Returning home we had the great pleasure of sitting in the car atop the drawbridge for 10 minutes while a pint-size sailboat dilly-dallied through the opening toward the gulf. Congealed into quadruple lines of waiting automobiles, hundreds of us resented that one guy drifting nonchalantly through the upraised bridge while we wasted our gasoline. I disliked such pests for two reasons: first, they held up what I was doing by keeping me from where I was going; and second, because I couldn't afford a boat myself to do the same unto others.

Five days later the two of us celebrated my 75th birthday in a most restrained manner. Nini brought a birthday card to the table at breakfast, we then enjoyed a hug and a kiss. She put on her ash-blond wig and we drove up to the Homestyle Cafeteria for lunch. The cafe was in a shopping plaza nearby, and served excellent food in wide variety. Nini loved to pick and choose, and have free seconds on drinks. I was no slouch at the table, myself, so we truly nibbled our way well into the owner's profit margin at that luncheon.

Maria's hair had vanished, so there was no need to visit her beauty salon for a wash-and-set for some weeks now, and except for that, it was as though our lives were back in their old rhythm. Because she felt weak when she walked. I knew Nini was very sick, and yet her iron will, and the kindness of the Fates kept her from *appearing* ill. Only the loss of her hair would serve notice to anyone checking on her health. She never complained of pain (thank the Lord), she had a good appetite, she slept well and she enjoyed going out for drives to visit or revisit scenes of the area which had charmed us so much when we first arrived in 1980. She couldn't walk around as well as before, but still she enjoyed our small sightseeing trips.

There was, however, some inner voice which whispered to me to do as much for, and be as kind to, Maria as I possibly could. 'You may not have her much longer', I could sense, rather than hear, the small voice cautioning me. So I took her to dine out as often as possible, and for short drives, so she could unwind away from the condo and get some respite from the tests and drugs she constantly contended with. The amount of activity in relation to Maria's cancer had grown from an occasional test during the months which followed her mastectomy, to where now she had something to do, some medical appointment, some test almost daily.

I helped her in any way I could. She used to walk with her friend, Gail to the clubhouse some 150 yards away to play bridge, for she was President of the Bridge Club and one of the top players. She could cite Culbertson and Goren by heart, and frequently won Club prizes. But now, instead of walking, she would come to me and ask, "Will you drive Gail and me to the clubhouse for bridge, Daddy?" in a voice which showed she knew it was only a short walk, but she would appreciate the favor greatly.

"Of course, honey, Is it time to go?" I would reply, and rise to the task.

"Well, I go a few minutes early, because I get out the cards and put them on the tables with score pads and pencils, so we can begin playing on time. I'll call Gail." She'd dial Gail's number. "Gail? Maria, honey. If you are ready to go to bridge, come on down. Robby is driving us to the clubhouse."

It was the same situation regarding church. She had

reached the point where she didn't trust herself to drive through the thick traffic over the bridge to St. John's, so I would take her there, help her up the steps and to her favorite pew, then return home, and at the proper time, go back and pick her up and bring her home or take her to lunch somewhere.

I am not a religious man, and don't place my faith in any particular sect, be it Christianity, Islam, Judaism, or whatever. I have no quarrel with any of the many churches and would-be churches which fill America. I just don't particularly care to take part in their ceremonies. That is the reason I rarely stayed with Nini to take part in the Mass.

We truly enjoyed dining out. It wasn't just the food which gave us pleasure. We had fun with the servers and receptionists, we visited with the folks sitting nearby, we toyed with their children and played cootchy-cootchy with their babies. We savored the drives to and from the spot we'd selected for the meal, and of course we took pleasure in the food. To go out for lunch or dinner was not just to go out to eat; there were so many little side benefits which turned 'dining out' into a small adventure.

The day after my birthday We went to dinner at the Pasadena Steakhouse, a modest but pleasant restaurant just over the bridge from our condo. Their steaks were delicious, but they also served superb lamb shanks, for the owners were Greeks. We had never eaten lamb shanks until we settled in St. Pete, when we soon discovered how savory they are. And that's what we had for dinner the day after my birthday.

Then on Saturday we went to the mall to buy a couple of things Maria needed, and at Burdines department store took the escalator up to the restaurant to enjoy another simple meal we fancied: a bowl of black beans and white rice with minced onion, accompanied by four different types of ladyfinger sandwiches and a fresh fruit salad. It didn't look like that much food when it came, but by the time we'd polished it off we were sated.

It was a special treat for Maria, because black beans and rice is a favorite dish of all Brazilians. Saturdays all over Brazil the restaurants will serve the combination cooked with several meats and sausages, along with a variety of veggies of indigenous origin, and refer to the whole meal as a *feijoada*, a sort of bean banquet. The meal is unbelievably delicious!

We passed the first three weeks of January with simple rounds of bridge, church, light shopping (though I now did the grocery shopping alone, it was too tiring for Maria), short drives and lunches and dinners out. It was lunch at Kissin' Cuzzins with Karla after Mass on the 10th; lunch at Bennigan's the 12th, and again on the 17th at Kissin' Cuzzins, where Karla made us feel so welcome and was always so sweet to Maria.

Our 49th wedding anniversary, January 20, fell on Wednesday, and we went to the lovely dining room of the newly-restored Vinoy Resort Hotel on the side of the bay in downtown St. Pete. It was expensive as the devil, but somehow it seemed I just had to take Maria there for lunch. The food was superb, the service impeccable and our waitress a very sweet young lady who made a fuss over us to help us celebrate. We finally ordered just one desert to share. Obviously it did not upset the chef, for he placed the fancy cut of French silk chocolate pie in the center of a huge plate, and in chocolate syrup delicately wrote 'Happy 49th Anniversary Maria and Robin' surrounding the pastry, all very artfully done.

A good lunch in 1993 could cost less than $5.00, and our lunch that day was over $25, plus the tip, so one can judge that it was a marvelous treat, and that my pet adored the meal and the setting. I made no note of what we ate, and can remember only the exquisite pie.

I'm glad that lunch was such a happy 'event', with chauffeur parking and the whole cubic metric system, for it was the last wedding anniversary meal we would share.

On the 26th it was back for an office visit with Doctor Able, when he set up an appointment for a new blood test, preparatory to chemotherapy on the 27th. Between the office visit and the blood test, I drove Nini to Mass and to play bridge, where she won first prize, and took her to Kissin' Cuzzins restaurant for a great lunch served by Karla. Our daily activities at home were as routine as my early life aboard ship in the Navy.

The blood test by vein was on Tuesday, with the therapy to be administered on Wednesday. But when we got to the hospital, we learned that Maria could not have chemotherapy that day; her blood platelet count was only 17,000. Apparently the platelet count was so low Doctor Able decided against chemotherapy by IV. He switched to oral medication, pills which Maria could swallow with less dire effect on her blood chemistry.

"I'm so glad I don't have to take my chemotherapy through a vein now, Daddy," Maria sighed with relief.

"I know what you mean, Nini. I'm thankful, too," I sympathized, and swept her into my arms for a hug which she was not expecting, but which I had to give. For in the back of my mind a tiny voice was whispering, '*If Nini can't take chemotherapy any more, she must be terribly ill, even though her actions belie it*'. But I could not bring myself to reveal my doubts and trepidations to Maria.

As Nini grew constantly weaker and less spirited, she would complain a bit about the nausea and lack of animation which she felt, and would worry that she wasn't getting any better. "It just seems that no medication is any help, Robin," she said, "and it makes me almost want to give up." Her words truly held a touch of resignation as her voice fell for the final phrase.

I offered her reassurance as best I could, using the first

reasonable excuse I could think of. Usually I would tell her to be of good heart. "I think you will feel better once you complete the course of pills the doctor has you on now," I encouraged her.

"But that fluebestering, or whatever it's called, comes in a big bottle! I don't know if I can fight it that long," she sighed in a voice with a tremor.

"We'll just do a day at a time, sweetheart, and pray the Lord will help you. And I will do all I can to help. I would gladly take the cancer to myself if that would relieve you of it, *querida*. But since that is impossible, I am your sworn slave until you are healed."

Some time later my sister said to me, "Once Maria told me, 'You're brother is a saint, Maxine. He waits on me hand and foot, and does everything to try to cheer me up and keep me brave. I adore him, for I know for certain he does his best to keep me from worrying'." When Sis repeated Maria's words, I knew at last that I had not deceived Maria into believing she was going to get better. She was on to my tricks. Tears flooded over at Max's words, and I turned away to go towel them off.

On Wednesday, we went out for lunch at Chili's, putting away a combined order of beef and chicken fajitas, which were exceptionally tasty. Despite a shortage of blood platelets, my partner did a pretty good job tucking away her quota of the food. We shared a big scoop of ice cream served in a crisp tortilla shell using two spoons. That was just to hold the fajitas in place and keep them from bubbling up.

On the 29th we returned to Doctor Able's office, and after he examined Maria, he prescribed new pills for her: fluoxymesterone in 10 mg. doses, to be taken three times a day until she finished them. We were both worried about how the pills would affect her, but she suffered no heavy consequences. She got a light headache now and then, and was nauseous at times, but it was never to the point of vomiting.

She still went to Mass and played bridge, even if she felt a wee bit queazy.

"I know I'm not quite up to par, but I think I can bid and play my hands. Do you think Gail will mind if I foul up, Daddy?" and she smiled a soft smile for me.

"Of course not. Just tell her about the drug you're taking, and blame it on the medicine," I said.

"Will you write the name down for me?" she asked, "because I can't pronounce it." When I complied, she tucked it in the corner of her purse. Now she and her three bridge-playing widow ladies would have something to talk about and conjecture upon. I kept my fingers crossed that none of them had been married to a medical doctor and might know what the drug was and what its use signified for Maria.

The 6th of February we varied our dining-out routine, and drove to a barbecue place on the north end of St. Pete. I won't name the spot, because their barbecue sure couldn't hold a candle to the mouth-watering barbecue we'd eaten when we lived in Texas. Of course in Texas, barbecue isn't just a meal, it's more like a religion. A good bait of Texas barbecue, doused with a bowl of Tex-Mex chili, can keep your innards in a tizzy for two days and nights!

By the time I drove Maria to Mass on February 7th, she had developed a slight limp in her left leg, and I had to help her walk. She also had difficulty in standing up, so she'd call me, and I'd go to her assistance when she wished to rise. Once up on her pins, she did well, although she felt weak, and always worried about her balance, which is why I wouldn't let her walk alone. We had gotten a cane for her, but she didn't trust it enough to walk alone with it.

Because it was so difficult now for her to sit down on the stool and to rise from it again when she went to the bathroom, I got a 'booster seat' to attach to the toilet. It raised the stool about six inches higher, and helped her greatly in sitting down, although she still needed help to stand and to tidy up.

These extra 'nursing aids', and Nini's almost overnight dependence on me to help her suddenly struck me as ominous flags signalling a swift deterioration in my darling's mobility and freedom. Her reliance on me to help her out of the car, and into and out of her seat at a restaurant, and now to go to the bathroom, had suddenly banged me on the head with the force of a pile-driver pounding in a 16-inch concrete piling.

'Oh, my god!' I whispered to myself, *'I've been blind as a bat while Nini has been drifting downhill faster and faster. I have got to pay even more attention to her, and be of more help and cheer whenever and wherever I possibly can!'*

From then on my speech and ministrations and demonstrations of love and affection grew ever more delicate, ever more frequent and ever more tender, while at the same time, down inside, I grew ever more bitter and heartstricken over the horrible way the gods were mistreating my only possession I really cared about.

In bitter anguish I cried out silently, *'Lord, You may take my home, take my car, take everything that I have, but please don't take my Maria. Don't take the girl I fell in love with in Brazil; so deeply in love that I learned a lot of her beautiful language just so I could court her. Please don't take her from me now.'* But my supplications fell on deaf ears, or vanished into empty space, for they were cruelly ignored.

It doesn't hurt me when I'm criticized or even browbeaten; but lord how it hurts me to be ignored!

CHAPTER 27

It was February 10 when our family doctor, Jones, injected himself back into the proceedings concerning Maria's progress or lack of same. He ordered her to take an MRI of her brain. The scary-looking Magnetic Resonance Imaging machine came to the hospital in a big truck and parked outside a door where patients could enter it from within the hospital. As I got the picture, instead of every hospital paying a fortune for an MRI machine, the owners of a big semi-truck with an MRI inside it worked with the hospitals and handled patients for several of them.

With the MRI scheduled to be at certain hospitals on given days, doctors could set up appointments for their patients. By sharing the mobile machine, the care providers could economize greatly on the cost of an MRI, which savings of course they passed on to their patients. In a pig's eye! In those days to own an MRI machine was *better* than having a gold mine, for the owner didn't have to dig; the gold flowed in with virtually no effort!

Maria's appointment with the infernal machine—which scared me just to look at it—was on February 11 at 10:00 a.m.. Although Maria faced up to the huge apparatus with a brave heart, the scan results showed that it was indeed a diabolical device.

Since the report of the scan would not come through until next day, Maria proposed lunch at Gigi's Italian Restaurant in South Pasadena. After which I took her and Gail to the clubhouse for bridge. Also on that day, Maria began taking dexamethasone in 4 mg tablets, two pills every six hours. Now there's a drug to conjure up conflicting emotions. Dexamethasone came into use in 1958. It's a corticosteroid used in treating various skin, soft tissue and gastro-intestinal conditions caused by allergy or inflammation. The drug may also be prescribed for certain blood disorders and brain swelling due to a tumor. Low doses taken for short periods seldom have side effects; but like other corticosteroids, dexamethasone can cause unpleasant or dangerous side effects. Prolonged use can lead to glaucoma, cataracts, diabetes, fragile bones and thin skin. (One of my bosses at State Farm Insurance was thin-skinned. Maybe a doctor along the line somewhere had put him on dexamethasone and failed to take him off soon enough!)

The following day, we visited Doctor Able, who told Nini to stop taking flouxymesterone, but to continue the dexamethasone. He also quietly mentioned, almost as an aside, that the MRI scan seemed to show a lesion on the right side of her brain. Back home, Maria again inquired as to what Able meant by 'lesion'. I forced myself to fib just a mite by saying I thought it was like a scar on her brain. Obfuscating like that tore at my very innards, my heart skipped a beat with the lie, and my spirit cried out against the perfidy, but I absolutely could not force myself to say, "I think it means the cancer has attacked your brain, honey." All I did was fight like hell to keep from breaking down in front of her, for tears shoved at my eyeballs like steam pistons, my head throbbed like a heavy-metal band in full cry and my vocal cords were tauter than E-strings. The bad news was like a knife in the heart, it hurt so much.

The bill for that little bout with the MRI machine and the auxiliary services rendered therewith came to $1,900, with no discount for the patient to offset its obnoxious revelation.

As bad as I felt at the moment, when Nini suggested we

go to K-Mart for some minor shopping and to have hot dogs for lunch, I was happy to go along with the idea. When we got home, we called Kathy and Nini told her what we'd learned from the MRI scan. I held my breath, fearing that Kathy might unthinkingly blurt out a cry of alarm. But if she knew what a lesion was, she didn't say anything to her mother, bless her heart.

The cancer's drag on Maria's strength began to show ever more clearly now. Her habits changed to reflect the cancer's sapping of her vitality, and the tenor of our lives slowed perceptibly as the monster hidden within inexorably worked its wicked ways on my battle-worn sweetheart. The notes she put on her calendar each day, from which I was able to reconstruct much of this story, are just as revealing of Nini's deterioration as any diary would have been.

For example, her usual notes about her visits to the beauty salon, and what her beautician did: wash and set, trim, color bath, no longer appeared on the calendar, for with most of her hair missing for the second time, she wore either a turban or one of her wigs in lieu of visiting the beauty parlor.

For another example, she did not go to Mass on Februay 14. The next day she went to have blood drawn, although the trips to the lab were now an atrocious ordeal for her. And on the 18th she did not play bridge with her group. "I'm too tired to sit on a hard chair for that long," she explained.

Her comment about the 'hard chair' led me to recall one of her little quirks. She played bridge with three other ladies, and as they went through their games the women changed chairs from time to time. Maria took a thin little cushion to sit on, and as they moved from chair to chair she moved her cushion with her.

"I don't like to sit on a chair that is still warm from the person's bottom who sat on it before," she told me, "so I use the cushion to insulate me from the body heat . . . and sometimes the perspiration."

"That makes sense to me!" I agreed warmly, for Maria had always been the fastidious one.

Then one day Nini forgot her cushion after the game. When I went back to the card room, it was gone. "Somebody must have taked it," Nini cried in disgust. "Now I have to find anozzer one."

"First I'll try an experiment," I said, and typed a 3 x 5 card saying Maria had forgotten her cushion in the card room Wednesday, and would whoever picked it up to look after it for her please call us. I put the card on the game room bulletin board next morning, and that afternoon a lady called to say she found the cushion but didn't known whose it was. So Maria got back her precious bottom insulator within 24 hours.

It was February 19 when I finally unloaded my wrath on poor Doctor Able. We were in his office for the routine checkup. The doctor finally spoke to me aside from Maria. "The cancer now appears to have spread to Maria's chest wall, her lungs and her brain, Mr. Leatherman," he said in a flat tone of voice, looking off nervously into space rather than meeting my eyes.

My blood began to boil within me, and I felt like slugging the older man. For a moment I was back on the battleship *Maryland* taking a poke at the Fleet runner-up boxing champ who had the temerity to call me an SOB. I didn't know he was a boxer when I slugged him, but became aware of the fact soon after.

Here with Doctor Able, reason ruled over rash action, and although my fists were clenched in pain and sudden anger, I controlled myself, and merely gritted out my fury in a low voice.

"Doctor Able, when I told you some time ago in this very corridor what my son had said, to hit Maria's cancer with a tough, hard blast, you said, 'We don't want to use an elephant gun to kill a mosquito'. Well, you have pussyfooted around all these months, until now you have an elephant on your

231

hands . . . which I am certain you're no longer able to kill . . . with *any* kind of gun!"

He recoiled from the force of my words and my explosion of anger, quite possibly fearing bodily harm, but after five seconds of silence he looked at me, almost pleadingly. "I've done everything possible, Mr. Leatherman," he said softly. "Maria is such a sweet person it breaks my heart that I have been unable to cure her. Believe me, sir," he ended softly. I could see a threatening trace of tears in his eyes.

Suddenly I felt horribly miserable, from the illness which was chewing at my Maria, from all the pain she had endured, apparently for naught, and from the thought of how much Doctor Able must hate to watch another of his patients fail to conquer the formidable enemy. A wave of guilt swept over me. "I realize that, Doctor," I said, "I'm sorry I blew my stack. I apologize. I know it's just the constantly increasing pressure on me that led to my outburst." There was nothing I could do but place my arms around the slightly built man and give him a forgiving embrace. Then he put one arm around me and gave me an understanding squeeze, his clipboard clutched in the other hand.

Without further words, he went in to check on Maria, and I went back to the waiting room: a waiting room filled with hopeless patients and their mates, a waiting room which seemed ugly despite the pleasant decor, a waiting room I had come to fear and detest worse than a pit full of rattlesnakes.

By an eerie coincidence, as we shall see, Doctor Brown, the slender woman in charge of the radiation department at Pines of Ponderosa was setting up a display in the Radiation area to better acquaint cancer patients, their friends and relatives with the facilities of the unit, and with one another, while they visited together and enjoyed punch, coffee and cake—the only thing they ever enjoyed in that sparkling-clean venue.

The 'party' was on February 20, from 10:00 a.m. to noon,

and I was amazed at the number of people who were there: not only patients and their relatives and guests, but the working staff, secretaries, technicians, doctors and specialists. Considering the significance of the area, and the apprehension with which most patients approached their first radiation treatments, I was surprised by the smiles and general air of bonhomie which permeated the department as we mingled and enjoyed the comestibles.

Despite her bright smile for her patients and guests (and particularly for Maria, whom she gave a long hug, for she knew Nini was from another land, as was her own husband), Doctor Brown appeared weary and haggard, her eyes seemed sunken, there were tiny new wrinkles under her makeup, and she moved at a slower pace than I remembered her during Maria's first chest radiology treatments in 1987.

The reason I began this portion of Maria's story with the words, 'By an eerie coincidence . . .' was because of the dreary fact that in four days, Maria would begin another bout with Doctor Brown's infernal machine. The three doctors had consulted after the MRI scan and decided Maria should be given more radiology treatments. This time the treatments would be even more delicate, for they would be on her brain.

How Maria could be so vivacious and warm at that party when she knew that on the 24th she would begin what had to be a worrisome series of treatments once again? She was an absolute paragon of courage.

The mere thought of the docs shooting their magic bullets into my beloved's brain was enough to curdle my blood. How much more frightening it must have been for Maria! Yet she never flinched, never wavered and never showed fear. My Brasileira had apparently become inured to all aspects and phases of the many treatments against the marauder which had set out to destroy her.

Like Chief Joseph of the Nez Perce Indians, who battled the U.S.Army to a standstill with a handful of warriors as he strove to move his small tribe hundreds of miles north through the rugged, mountainous country of Idaho and Montana into Canada and asylum, only to be caught and defeated by a greatly superior Army force just a few miles from the Canadian border, just like Chief Joseph, Maria was standing up to vicissitude and travail with the heart of a lion. In spite of the daily anguish I felt for my failing helpmate, I was prouder of her than Ike was of his whole Army when he brought the men home from Europe.

Maria also gained courage from her visits to St. John's Church, And on Sunday the 21st, three days before her radiology series was to begin, I stayed with her for Mass, for she was very weak, and leaned on my arm even more than usual.

The day before at the condo, as we came home, she had grasped the handrail beside the walkway to step up about four inches onto the carpeted patio outside our door. But the effort was too much for her. She fell before I could run and grab her. John, our great neighbor, saw her fall, and rushed to help me lift her to her feet and assist her to her easy chair. All the while, Nini was apologetic for being such a nuisance!

From then on, I stopped the car three doors away from our own condo, where there was a wheelchair ramp and a handrail, and no 'step' to negotiate. With Maria growing so weak, it was no wonder that I dreaded the radiology treatments she was about to endure again.

'*God bless your dear courageous heart, my darling,*' I whispered to myself about an hour later as I watched Maria nodding off in her easy chair, her little paperback romance story lying open beneath her hand on her lap.

CHAPTER 28

During an office visit with Doctor Brown on Tuesday 23, she reduced Maria's dosage of dexamethasone from two pills to one pill every six hours. She wrapped up all the preliminary measures which she had to take care of before Nini's coming treatments, and our more-than-patient patient was physically prepared for brain radiology the 24th. It appeared she was also psychologically prepared for the attack on the center of her mentality.

"I know they are going to be messing around with my brain on that scary machine," she said. "but I'm not as afraid of it as I was the first time . . . now that I know it doesn't hurt when they microwave me in it."

"Thank heaven for that," I said. "Let's just hope that the radiology erases the lesion they saw on the MRI. Apparently they caught whatever it is early enough to do something about it, which is some consolation." Actually, deep down inside, I feared that since the day of Maria's mastectomy they had not taken *any* of their actions early enough! It seemed we were always a few steps behind by the time her phalanx of doctors came to a decision to take action, whether it was surgery, radiology, or chemotherapy.

Maria continued, interrupting my dark musings. "Oh, I hope they caught it soon enough, Daddy. I *pray* they caught it soon enough, and now we can take care of it quickly. A thing like that worries a person even when she tries not to worry," and she put her hand on my arm as we drove across the causeway back to the condo.

It was a pretty day, the water flashed multitudinous signals to the sun, and a young couple with a small boat were puttering around on the dime-sized island off to our left.

God, how I wished Maria and I could be so carefree. And suddenly I was fighting back the tears, for the dark thought hit me like a hard-thrown medicine ball in the stomach that our own carefree days were over. We could try to relax, and watch TV and go out to eat and maybe take in a movie, but we'd never be carefree again. The specter of that nemesis lurking within my loved one would always be there to diminish our enjoyment of whatever we were doing.

To shake off the cloud of gloom which had settled over me, I made a suggestion to Maria. "What do you say to some seafood at Leverock's, and then a little drive down to Pass-a-Grille?"

"I say it sounds very nice. Just remember, though," she reminded me, "I can't walk on the beach with you after we're there. I get too tired walking in sand."

"Of course not. We'll drive down past the seagulls and pelicans perched on the pilings along the inland waterway, circle the south end of the island and find a parking place in the area of the sandspit where there aren't many people on the beach."

Sated with excellent clam chowder and broiled flounder, we made our gentle way south onto Pass-a-Grille beach. The beach is little more than a long sandbar smeared over with houses. It was once lined end to end with a row of Australian pines which offered a touch of shade to the hot seascape in summer. But the pines were all destroyed by the last big storm, and now the main attraction along the beach was the ugly string of parking meters, which could gobble up a tourist's quarters faster than he could say 'grouper sandwich', the specialty of one of the beach's more notorious places to eat, and more particularly, to drink.

To restore the dunes after the storm, they moved the

sand around a little, and planted more sea oats to hold it in place. If you think it's against the law to molest girls, don't even dream of molesting a sea oat! They'll throw the book at you, plus rocks and seashells! Every so far along, they built an arched 'bridge' from the street over the dunes and down onto the beach to give access to the water without walking on the sea oats or dunes.

"It's a shame you can't stroll the beach right now," I said to Nini. "Remember that sunbather you saw one time when we came down and strolled along the shore?"

"What sunbather?" she asked with unguarded curiosity.

"The guy who had fallen asleep lying on his back, and while he was snoozing his loose swim suit had formed itself into a teepee tent. Remember him? You pointed him out to me as we went by."

Maria blushed. "*Oxente, menino!*" she cried, and poked me on the arm. That handy Brazilian phrase in this case could be interpreted, 'Knock it off, kid!'"

Arriving at the end of the island, I doubled back north a couple of blocks to the end of one of the footbridges, fed the alligator next to my radiator, helped Maria out of the car and made our way slowly up the gentle incline of the walkway and down onto the sandy beach beyond the dunes. I had my camera slung over my shoulder. As I had said several times in our family, 'I have a picture of Maria standing in front of everything important in the United States, from its geographical center to the world's deepest hand-dug well, and from Rainbow Bridge in Utah to the Black Canyon of the Gunnison in Colorado.'

"If you plan to take a picture of me, Daddy, you have to remember I can't stand up alone," my little buddy cautioned.

"Don't you worry, I'll take care of that problem," I said and I helped her walk a few steps to where she could lean against the railing of the 'bridge' we'd just crossed, touch that railing with her hands and be safely stabilized to pose for a snapshot.

I helped her move a few feet twice, and got three shots from different angles, one of which is included in this volume. It was a bit breezy and cool, but Maria was warm enough to pose happily for me, wearing her white turban. We stayed only about 15 minutes, but it gave Nini a chance to revisit Pass-a-Grille, let the sea breeze caress her, and stretch her legs in the afternoon sunshine. For a lady going back into radiation again the next morning, she was a picture of high spirits that afternoon.

Those were the last snapshots I ever took of Maria.

Wednesday we were up early, breakfasted on toast, dry cereal and coffee, Maria donned slacks and a blouse and we were in the waiting room 15 minutes early. After an eternity, the pleasant young technician came for Nini. I walked with them down the corridor as far as the door to the radiation unit, and gave Maria a long hug. She squeezed me in return with such power as she had. "Don't worry about me, Daddy," she admonished, "I'll be just fine. I'm scared, but I know if other people can go through this, then I can do it," and she released me.

The patient young man led her through the door into the room housing the big machine we had visited only a few days earlier during the open house party, when it had only a dummy lying on its table-like treatment platform.

"God bless you and care for you, Nini," I whispered as she left my arms, although somehow I knew in my heart that God was not involving Himself in Maria's case, If He were, He'd have been of some help long before now.

At 9:15 Maria moved toward the slick machine that awaited her. As I chewed my fingernails in the lobby, Nini endured exactly two minutes of treatment on each side of her head. Between the make-ready work, the radiology itself, and the release of the prisoner, the technician used most of Maria's allotted quarter-hour before helping her back to me.

"Do you feel all right, honey?" I asked as soon as she was in my arms again. And what do you think her weak reply was?

"I'm fine, Daddy, just fine," she tried to smile as she spoke. But her chin was trembling, and I knew she had been deeply frightened as she stoically met Big Beta in head-to-head combat.

Maria took those frightening brain scans every day through March 4 except for the weekend. That made a total of seven visits to the machine in nine days, for a few minutes on each side of her head. The last remaining hairs on her head were almost invisible as she became teetotally, absolutely, completely bald and the skin of her bare head turned slightly pink from the frequent exposure to radiation.

During that series of treatments, Maria turned 73 on March 2, and decided that in spite of her weakness, she wanted to celebrate by eating at her favorite spot, the nearby cafeteria. "Wouldn't you rather go to a regular restaurant for lunch, where the waitress will wait on you?" I asked.

"No, I enjoy seeing all the different salads and hot dishes and desserts laid out so pretty, and trying to pick the things I think will taste best. I'll hold onto your arm and we'll fill my tray and you can carry it and help me to a table. Then you can go back and get what you want. It will be a lot of fun that way," and she laid her limpid brown eyes on me and mustered a touch of a smile. Her coy little look melted my heart.

"Okay, sweet, it's your birthday. We'll do it your way," I said and gave her a warm squeeze.

But we shouldn't have.

When we arrived at the restaurant, there wasn't an empty parking space for 100 feet in any direction. After I'd run every row of the parking lot for several minutes, I headed back to the cafeteria entrance. "I'll help you out of the car and you can stand by that post for support while I park the car. Does that sound okay for you?"

She nodded affirmatively. "Just fine."

I stopped at the curb, which was only about two inches high, helped her out of the car, and with some effort assisted her up the slight step and a couple of paces over to the stanchion supporting the porch roof.

"Now, you hang onto this column and wait for me, and I'll be back in a minute or two. I'll run over and park at the far end and jog back." Maria nodded, and I jumped in the car and did the quick trip. As I cleared the last row of cars on my way back, I saw a small crowd standing in a circle on the sidewalk by the cafeteria door, and no Maria in sight. My heart sank like a lead weight in my chest as I ran toward the group. Had Maria had some kind of an attack? I was desperate. Why had I dared to leave her alone by a stupid post? Then I reached the circle of people and saw Maria was lying on the concrete in the middle of the crowd. She was already trying to sit up.

"We'll have to call an ambulance," a lady cried out excitedly, "she may be having a stroke or a heart attack," and she headed for the cafeteria.

"No, honey, don't call an ambulance," I said. "She's my wife, and is only weak from radiation treatments. I'll take care of her." I broke though the spectators and another man and I lifted Nini to her feet. "Are you all right, Nini?" I cried. "What happened?"

"Yes, I'm all right. I shouldn't had tried to walk into the restaurant. I got half way, and lost my balance and fell. I'm sorry, Daddy, but I broke my glasses and skinned my knees," she said. She was trying to brush herself off as she spoke, and her cute little face was perspiring. The same man helped me take her inside and put her on a chair near the cashier where she could recover from her fall.

I sat down beside her and helped her put herself in order.

She was wearing shorts, and the light bruises on her knees were seeping a touch of blood. After all was calm, and she seemed to be her normal self, I left her for a moment and got a damp paper towel from the men's room and lightly cleaned her knees, then blotted the bruises gently with a dry towel. "Do you want to go home, or to another restaurant, Nini?" I asked.

"No, Id like to go down the line and pick what I want to eat. I'm really hungry, and I feel all right, except my knees hurt a little and my cheek, too." The frame of her glasses had put a tiny cut on her cheekbone, but nothing serious. I straightened her glasses so she could see well enough to eat, then helped her up, and we negotiated the serving line together. She selected her dishes, we paid for her tray, I escorted her to a comfortable booth and then returned and took her tray to her. I made the trip to select my own chow, and soon we were munching happily on our lunch. She knew the deserts by heart, and told me which kind of cake she wanted, with a bit of soft ice cream beside it.

"I'm sorry for being so dumb, Nini" I said as we ate. "What I should have done was help you inside, and let you wait for me while sitting down comfortably, instead of leaving you clinging to a pole on the sidewalk! The older I get the stupider I become. This is all my fault. Do you forgive me?" And I took her hand in mine for a moment.

"But there are big signs saying 'No parking' all along the curb. You could had been arrested for parking there."

"Sure, I might have. But by leaving the doors open over the sidewalk and leaving the motor running, everybody would know a person was being helped inside the restaurant, the car was only stopped, not parked."

"And some teenager could had stealed the car while you were inside!" Maria said, a tad ungrammatically, and shook her bewigged head. "You did right, Daddy. I just tried to do too much, instead of obeying your orders."

241

In the end, the birthday was a big success, for we both gorged ourselves on entrees and accessories, and had double desserts. There was no limit on desserts. They were displayed in the center of the dining area, were all priced the same, and the cashier rang up the desserts when she tabulated our checks.

My beloved endured the brain radiation treatment from March 1 through the 5th. On the 4th, her dexamethasone dosage was changed to three times per day, 8:00, 2:00 and 10:00. The next day we talked to Bobby and Kathy on the phone and brought them up to date on Maria's activities, including her fall at her birthday luncheon. We also got a bill from Pines of Ponderosa for over $4,400 for services rendered. But the For Eyes Optical company replaced the cracked lens in her glasses free of charge.

Maria decided to skip Mass on Sunday, "I'm just too tired, Daddy," she said. She was also having more difficulty walking and standing. She stayed in bed almost an hour longer than usual, so I knew she was extra tired, for Maria was never one to lounge away the day in bed. She liked to be up and doing things.

She was introduced to a new drug, Zantac, or ranitidine, on March 8. My dictionary says it is used to reduce or treat stomach and doudenal ulcers. Because ranitidine promotes healing of the stomach lining, there is a risk it may mask stomach cancer, so it's normally prescribed only after stomach cancer is ruled out. Just why the drug appeared on Maria's pill menu I cannot say, but she took 150 mgs. of it twice a day.

I remembered how my mother's mother, my Grandmother Smith, suffered and died of stomach cancer in her small home in Oak Creek, Colorado back in the 1920s. She lived on morphine the last few weeks in order to bear up under the agonizing pain. Ranitidine would not come into use until 1983, almost 60 years after Grandma died.

Nini had the 10th radiation treatment on March 10. Her

blood pressure that day was 160 over 106, and she weighed 146 pounds, down almost 50 pounds from two months earlier. With two minutes on each side of her head, for 20 days, she had endured a total of 40 minutes of brain radiation. She drew blood for tests on the 10th; and on the 12th we visited Doctor Able in his office. It was clear to me now that Doctor Able knew Maria's blood tests were bad, but he said nothing to me about them. Meantime he hit us with bills for over $900. The hospital managed to get by on $4,482 for Nini's treatments.

From then on, it was a series of blood tests and office visits to Doctor Able, who would change Maria's pills, or change the dosage, or tell her 'stay on steroids', until finally, on March 17 the doctor sent her to the hospital for an injection of blood platelets which lasted from 9:00 to 3:00 p.m. that day.

My darling was having greater trouble walking now, and could not stand alone for more than a few seconds, yet her face showed almost no signs of strain or great illness. It was Maria's lack of pain, her good appetite and her fortitude which was so disarming for those last few days of March, although her steady loss of weight should have been a bold clue to me.

I realize now that it was clear to her doctor. "Are you on a diet, Maria?" Doctor Able had asked once, and she replied, "Oh, no. I eat like a horse, Doctor!"

And he said, "Fine. Don't try dieting without talking to me first, all right?" And Maria promised she wouldn't. It was the sneaky cancer which was pulling down her weight, along with her strength.

Friday evening of the 26th, we went to the Pasadena Steak House just over the bridge, where Maria dined heartily on her favorite dish, lamb shanks and mint jelly. The young bartender there had once been a waiter for the Olde World Cheese House and usually waited on us, referring to us as his 'Kids', like coming up to our table and asking, "Well, how are my kids doing, everything okay?" and giving Maria a hug, which she obviously enjoyed, for he was a handsome lad.

Now as we entered the steakhouse, he came from behind the bar to hug Maria like his mother, and to shake my hand. "How are my kids tonight? Everything is all right, I hope," he exclaimed as he hugged Nini. We replied in the affirmative and he went back to work behind the bar. Maria had always engendered that kind of friendliness from people for as long as I could remember. In all truth, it was exactly as the ad says, 'Nobody didn't like Maria'.

We had a fine dinner, with me chomping on steak and Maria enjoying a lamb shank. She ate about half of it, but obviously relished the tender meat. When it was time to go, it took all of my strength to help her out of the cramped booth so she could stand up. Clearly she was much weaker that evening. Of course I worried about her loss of normal strength, but I said nothing. I simply helped her to walk and to stand, the same as I'd been doing over the past few weeks.

CHAPTER 29

The antepenultimate day of March found me up at the usual hour. I set up breakfast in our small kitchen, then went to help Maria to the bathroom. I picked up the paper at our back door and brought it to the living room to browse until Maria called, "I'm ready, Daddy." For years she had used the title 'Daddy' rather than my name; and at times she'd say, 'Roberto', a Brazilian style 'Robert', and of course '*querido*' or darling.

"Coming, honey," I called back immediately, for Nini would grow restless if I didn't go promptly and help her to semi-rise from the toilet and to peal off the tissue for her.

"I feel more tireder this morning, for some reason" she said as she washed her hands and rubbed them on her bare head and face before taking the towel from my hand to dry all three.

"I know, Nini. These last few days must have been a terrible strain on you. Every time I pause to think about them, I want to cry. It just seems so doggoned unfair for such a great little girl to have to undergo all these troubles, when you have never been anything but nice to everyone. It's a damned shame, that's what it is!" and for a moment I let my feelings show through to Maria, even against my will.

"But you have made everything much more bearable. I could not put up with all this without your precious love and great help, you know that, honey." And she put her arm around my waist and I enfolded her in my arms to hug and kiss her.

245

Then we made our tedious way to the kitchen, where I helped her sit down, and pushed the lever to put the toaster to work.

I walked her back to the shower, and helped her wash herself as she leaned against the side of the bath and clung to the faucet handles for support. I washed gently over the scar of her mastectomy, though it had long been healed. I think I was extra gentle in loving memory of her beautiful bosoms as they were when we first married in Brazil during the war. After her shower, I helped her out of the stall, and she hung onto the towel rack while I dried her with the big fluffy towel. Then I took the puff and powdered her body all over. She sat down on the toilet and I put her anklets on her feet, helped her into her panties and into her bra and its prosthesis, then her blouse and shorts, and finally her shoes. I held a mirror while she put on a bit of make-up to became the lovely lady she was once more.

I helped her outside and into the car, and we drove to the lab at the hospital so Maria could take the blood test the doctor had prescribed prior to her office visit on the 30th. The lab visit filled me with anguish, and tested the endurance of my love, for the nurse 'stuck' her twice in her veins and got no blood, so she cut a 'butterfly' in her arm, and then managed to draw the life's liquid she needed for the tests. I winced at each prick of the needle, and doubly so when the nurse made that tiny cut, but Maria was either completely inured to the procedure, or somehow had lost her sensitivity to the drawing, because she showed no reaction.

The next day, Maria and I went through the same program we'd pursued the day before, because today she was to visit Doctor Able in his office. When I first woke her she was quite listless, and was obviously very tired after we'd finished breakfast and the bathroom routines.

"I think I'll stretch out in bed for a few minues, I get so tired just from cleaning up each morning," she sighed, "Will you help me?" and she fixed those big brown eyes upon mine.

"Of course, I'll help you," I said, and we soon had her tucked neatly under the sheet on the king size bed. I bent and gave her a kiss. "You relax and rest while I read the paper," I said, and she nodded and closed her eyes obediently.

By the time I'd read the paper it was time to head for Doctor Able's office. I went back in the bedroom, and touched Maria's shoulder. "Wake up, *querida*, it's time for your office visit."

She stirred slightly, but then made no effort to push back the sheet. "Oh, Daddy, I feel so awfully tired. I just don't want to go see the doctor today."

But I knew she had to go, so I insisted, gently pulled back the sheet, took her upper body in my arms, and raised her slowly to a sitting position on the side of the bed. Then I put her tiny shoes on her small feet, helped her to stand and to briefly visit the bathroom again. I helped her put on her wig and take a few passes at it with a brush, she put on a touch of lipstick, and we went arm in arm to the door, her purse clutched in her right hand as she clung to me with her left. It took a long time to cover the 75 feet to the car, and it was only with great effort that we got her seated and the seat belt fastened around her.

When we arrived at Able's office, 10 minutes away. It seemed even more difficult to help her turn in her seat. She didn't try to rise. "I think you should go bring a wheelchair," she said, and I did. It was difficult to lift her from the car seat and move her into the wheelchair, but I managed to do it and still have my darling in one piece. Meanwhile my mind was in turmoil over the extreme deterioration of Maria's strength.

Then oddly, in a flash, my mind ran back 40 years to when we took the children, when they were five and seven, to the Colorado National Monument, an area of spectacular formations carved like a deep bowl into the side of the plateau, with a variety of huge pinnacles rising from the basin floor to reach our level as we drove along the canyon rim. Maria was afraid the kids would fall into the chasm, so, per her orders, at each viewpoint the kids would pile out of the car on the right side—away from the abyss—take our hands, and walk around the car to lean over the guardrail or barrier and peer at the splendor below. As we drove the 22-mile semi-circular tour, we must have opened and closed the car doors and jumped in and out of the Ford, with lots of chatter and much banging of doors, at least 40 times.

Now, in the flit of an instant I could see 'Mama' jumping up and out of the car in a flash at each overlook, to be there when the kids' feet hit the ground! How vivacious she was, compared to today! Tears tried to rise up and overflow, but I forced them back. I reached for my handkerchief and blew my nose to hide my face from Nini.

Maria stayed in her chair until the nurse called her, when I wheeled her back to the consultation room. "She can't stand up by herself," I cautioned the nurse, and we both helped Maria step onto a low stool and then to sit on the examining table. As I turned to push the wheelchair out of the way, the nurse tried to turn Maria on the table so she could lie down, but Nini slipped from her arms and fell back against the partition behind the table. Her poor head bumped against the wall with a dull thud.

She was not hurt, but Doctor Able came running. "What was that?" he cried, for the sound was like someone hitting a kettle drum, with the noise reverberating throughout the examining area.

I let the nurse answer. "Maria slipped out of my arms and fell backward, and her head bumped the wall, doctor," she said.

Maria lay there, looking at us apologetically, and saying nothing.

Doctor Able instantly checked Maria's head, her pulse and her blood pressure. Finally he turned to me. "Maria is very weak, Robin," he said, using my first name for the first time I could remember. "I want you to take her to the Oncology unit at the hospital immediately. I'll call and notify them you're on the way. I'll be there as soon as I finish with my patients here." Maria lay there, listening and totally unconcerned, so I knew she was not hurt. She was just insufferably weak.

"I'm sorry, little partner," I said to her, "we have to get you up again."

"Que sera sera!" she assayed a weak grin, repeating the words of one of Doris Day's popular hits. What will be will be.

The nurse and I helped her up and into the wheelchair and out to the car, where we both worked her into the front seat, which was almost more difficult than if I had done it alone. Arriving at Pines of Ponderosa, I asked a male volunteer to help me put Nini in a wheel chair and we took the elevator up to the Oncology unit. Just as we arrived in the unit, my long-suffering sweetheart had an uncontrollable bowel movement while still in the chair.

"Doctor Able sent Maria here to be put to bed. He says she is very ill," I told the three women at the nurse's station when we arrived.

"You can put her in the bed next to the window in room 207," the supervisor said. Her remark pissed me off! They had all cared for Maria during her chemotherapy treatments, and I knew they all liked her, yet they acted as though *I* were the nurse, not they! Perhaps it was the slight odor which perturbed them. I could almost hear them thinking to themselves: *'He could at least bring her in clean!'*

Whatever they were thinking, I interrupted their thoughts. "No, *you* can put her in the bed next to the window, *I'm* almost pooped just getting her here from Able's office, She needs to be tidied up, for I think she had an accident on the way here." Still those women stood glued to the floor.

"We believe in letting the patient's friends and relatives

help with the nursing. It's a practice we follow here," one lady in white said calmly. I was aware of that, for during Maria's chemotherapy sessions I always helped her, brought her ice water and held the glass for her to sip, washed her face with a damp cloth and plumped her pillow. But this situation was different.

"Look, I expect you nurses to clean Maria up this minute. I don't give a damn what your 'practice around here' is. If at least two of you aren't washing my wife, putting a gown on her and getting her into bed in the next ten seconds, I'll be on my way to the Administrator's office to find out why the hell not!" Then I was suddenly overwhelmed with grief as patient little Maria sat in her chair watching us and listening to us. I could not be sure she was conscious of what was going on around her, but if she were, she was seeing her husband about ready to knock some heads together if someone didn't move. And *still* there was no action on the part of any of the three nurses.

I tried another angle, for the fire was reaching the end of my fuse. "Look, I am so distraught from Doctor Able's assessment of Maria's condition, that I'm about ready to fall apart. If you girls don't take care of Maria immediately, I swear you're going to have to put both of us in bed!"

As I forced back tears of desperation, one girl finally set to work, and a few minutes later Nini was ensconced in her bed, as clean and sweet-smelling as she normally was, the head of the bed raising her into a semi-sitting position. They then began to administer an infusion of blood platelets, per the doctor's phone orders, while I tried to calm down in a chair at the foot of her bed. I felt as tense as a huge clock spring, and was afraid I'd suddenly unwind or explode if I didn't try to relax.

Suddenly I was as beat as I'd ever felt in all my life. The physical and nervous strain of getting Maria to the doctor's office and then to the hospital and finally into bed, coupled with the horrible realization that my darling Maria was terribly, desperately sick, had stretched my nerves to the snapping point.

Happily, the neighboring bed was unoccupied: no Lydia today.

One of the nurses ordered lunch for Maria, for it was the noon hour when we hit Oncology. I followed 'the practice' and helped my darling eat hers. She did not eat with much appetite, so now I knew for sure she was very sick, because her appetite had always been great until this meal. I spooned some thin soup into her mouth, which she swallowed and enjoyed, she drank some juice and a sip of water, and finally she ate a few bites of scalloped-like potatoes. "That's enough, Daddy" she said, "I need to rest a little," and lunch was over.

I lowered her bed part way, and she closed her eyes and took a nap. I ran down and ate a bite of something in the cafeteria, but I can't recall what, for it was an aimless meal, used mostly to pass the time. When Maria awoke I washed her face with a fresh cloth and dried it gently as she smiled a rather crooked smile at me. I think she had to concentrate to achieve a smile, I don't believe it came of its own natural force.

We spent the afternoon together, with Nini dozing off now and then, and suddenly coming awake, like when a person is reading on the sofa and drops off into dreamland and awakens with a start to find the book on the floor, and ponders the situation sleepily for a moment to puzzle out what happened.

When dinner came it was delicious pot roast with some pretty bites of potato and some green beans alongside. Again Maria ate only a few bites. She refused any pot roast, which had an aroma most enticing, but she took a few dabs of potato, and finally some green beans as I patiently forked them into her mouth. "What would you like next?" I asked.

"Beans," she answered softly, so I put two bits of beans

on the fork, and when she opened her mouth for them, I saw that she still had beans in her mouth. She had chewed them, but hadn't swallowed them!

"You have to swallow, *querida*," I said. She looked at me and repeated the word. "Swallow," she said, and made the motion of swallowing, but when I gave her the next tiny bite, she still had a touch of green on her tongue.

"Would you like some pudding or ice cream," I asked, trying to find something easier for her to work on.

She looked at me and said, "No, sanks," and shook her head slightly, having more trouble than normal with the 'th' sound so foreign to her native Portuguese.

She drifted off to sleep, I lowered her bed, and at 10:00 p.m. went home. I was not hungry, and threw myself onto the big bed and wept uncontrollably. I know I fell asleep, because all of a sudden I awoke and was lying there all rumpled, my face in a big damp spot on the bedspread. All of the previously repressed tears had sprung from between my lids in a great gush, like Old Faithful in Yellowstone Park spouting one of its eruptions.

I rose, brushed my teeth, washed my face and went back to bed, this time with my face on my pillow. "My god, what will tomorrow be like for my little darling?" I worried aloud, this time thinking numbly about Maria alone in that sterile hospital room across the narrow inlet of Boca Ciega—Blind Mouth—Bay.

Mouth. Green beans. Swallow. No sanks. The words drifted idly across the screen of my tired mind as I drifted off to sleep after another one of those deep sighs escaped me, followed by a quick, involuntary quiver.

CHAPTER 30

Wednesday morning I awoke from a troubled sleep, feeling both desperate and fatigued. The events of Tuesday had finally registered in my conscious mind, leaving me deeply grieved and doubly afraid. Could it possibly be that my sweetheart, my helpful life's companion, my cherished idol among all women was on the verge of leaving me? Was the clock ticking away the final seconds of her waning life? Was I about to lose the mother of my children into the void of infinity? I stared at my haggard reflection in the mirror, and dolefully shook my head. "I'm afraid so," I said aloud, and grabbed my electric razor and whacked furiously at my whiskers, as though they were the cause of my pain.

I hadn't seen Doctor Able since our encounter in his office Tuesday morning, so I still was not 'professionally' informed of the reason he had ordered Maria to the hospital, although it was obvious from the events of yesterday that she was very ill. Tears dripped into the cereal bowl as I scooped out the last spoonful of oat circles floating in the shallow layer of skim milk.

As I drove across the narrow bridge to the hospital parking lot, I was still trying to clear my vision, quiet my nerves and pull my rioting thoughts together. *'Stay calm, Rob!'* I ordered myself, and tried to obey. But that was like asking Mt. St.Helens to un-erupt and restore her Fujiyama-like peak to its prior pristine beauty. It was simply impossible to do.

By the time I'd made my way to the elevator and up to Oncology, I had simmered down enough that I could walk into Maria's room and present a decent face to her. It was only 6:30, and she seemed to be asleep, but she stirred when I put a light kiss on her forehead.

"Is that you, Daddy," she whispered, her eyes still shut, her voice a trifle hoarse.

"No, querida, it's that handsome fellow who walks you to the radiology room," I murmured.

Her eyes came open, and she smiled at me. "I like *you* more," she said, and took my hand in hers to kiss it tenderly, though lifting it to her lips was clearly an effort. Had I realized at the time the condition of her blood, I'd have called it a miracle.

"Well, I'm glad to hear that. For a time there I was afraid he was going to steal you away from me," I bent down and gave her a hug as best I could. "Now *minha filha* (my daughter), let's get you tidied up to be pretty for the doctor when he comes."

We visited almost normally as I fetched a basin with warm water and a clean washcloth and washed her face and little nude head, then did her hands and arms and dried them all. I'd brought the stuff for chapped lips, and gently applied some, for her lips were very dry; and I put drops I'd brought from home in her eyes to make her more comfortable.

"Bathroom?" I asked, though I dreaded the thought of moving her to the portable stool in the corner. I'd call a nurse to help me, assuming it didn't conflict with good 'nursing practice'.

But Maria relieved my worries on that subject. "No, I'm fine now. They put a tube in, and I can go whenever I want, without calling anyone . . . which is very handy." She seemed truly content to know she could handle minor bathroom demands without assistance. But I suddenly felt an ache all through my chest and midriff.

"Then I guess we're ready for breakfast when it comes," I managed, "so I'll sit here in the chair while we wait for it."

Food soon arrived, and I helped her with some oatmeal mush, juice and a dab of soft-boiled egg. "Remember to swallow, honey," I encouraged her, and she did better than she did with the beans at lunch Tuesday, and with the few bites of supper she'd managed to get down last night.

Not long after breakfast the nurse came to give her a bath, "You can go to the oncology lounge down the hall while we take our bath," she told me. I looked at the nurse's over-filled figure, and decided her suggestion was my choice, too, if indeed she were going into the tub with Nini. Of course, she gave Nini a sponge bath, not a tub bath!

Later that morning Maria was propped up in bed with me seated in the chair at the foot of it, and I was gazing intently at her, more fixedly than I realized, as one miserable thought after another eddied around in my head, as though wanting to escape from my skull.

Suddenly Nini brought me back to reality. "Why are you staring at me, honey?" she asked, and then I realized how deeply I had been immersed in acrid contemplation of losing my beloved wife.

Naturally I could not reveal my true state of mind, nor my dark, lugubrious thoughts. Instead. I smiled softly, and spoke the truth, "Because your eyes are so absolutely beautiful today. Even clear across the room they glow like big brown opals. You knew very well how thrilled I was by your sexy figure when I met you, so you may not want to believe this, *querida*, but the reason I married you was because your gorgeous eyes mesmerized me. We've both changed a lot in the last fifty years, but I swear your eyes are just as dazzling and hypnotic as they were the night I met you in Bahia."

"Really?" she actually smiled at me.

"Absolutely!" I said, and went to the head of her bed and leaned down beside her, nuzzled my cheek up against hers, and enjoyed a long embrace, with my face turned to the pillow. There were two reasons why our hug was so long; I felt

255

more serene so near to her, and I had to wait for the tears to subside.

Nini dozed on and off all day, and each time she awoke she was thirsty and I gave her cold water and held the glass so she could sip through the bent straw, then I gently dried her chin because oftentimes some water escaped from her lips. When I brushed her teeth, and held the crescent-shaped pan under her chin, I told her, "Spit," and she thought she did, but in actuality all she did was open her lips and let the fluid dribble down her chin. My angel wasn't too good at swallowing now, and she couldn't spit either . . . .

Doctor Able came that morning and checked Maria carefully. "Her tests reveal high blood sugar, Mister Leatherman," he said, "so I am prescribing insulin for her, four times a day." Then he led me into the corridor and told me what I, myself, had finally realized. "Maria is very sick. I don't think she has many days left. You probably should call your children and loved ones. I plan to draw bone marrow from her hip this evening for a biopsy. Then we'll know her exact condition. One of two things is likely to happen; she will either slide gently into death in a few days, or she will lapse into a coma and perhaps live for two or three weeks." He was looking up into my eyes, and I thought I felt remorse eating at him as he spoke.

'How can anybody ever want to be an oncologist?' I wondered to myself. Then to Able, "I'll do as you suggest, Doctor. I'll call the kids, and my niece and her family from Marco Island, and tell them of Maria's sudden degeneration. It's still impossible for me to comprehend, though, despite the fact that she has grown steadily weaker. Imagine this, Doctor: we went to dinner at the Pasadena Steakhouse Friday evening, and only five days later here we are with Maria on her death bed? I just can't believe that since her mastectomy her condition has weakened to this low state." My voice had risen uncontrollably to a high pitch and was almost inaudible at the end, so I squeezed Able's arm and turned to head for the rest room to clean up my face and regain control of my voice. 'Able,' I thought as I dried off. *'It was Abel who was slain by Cain.'*

I thought Nini was napping when the doctor led me into the hallway, but I soon realized she was well aware of our actions. She knew we were not discussing Able's golf score in low voices out in the corridor. I'd only been back in my chair a few seconds when she opened her eyes and studied me with an air of resignation across her face. "I'm very sick, aren't I, Daddy?" she asked, simply, more as a statement than a question.

I almost went into meltdown. *'Heaven please help me!'* I wanted to cry out, *'how can I reply to that simple question when all of her life Maria has been so afraid of anything to do with death?'*

For Maria suffered badly from necrophobia. She loathed funerals, would never put a wreath of any kind on our door, and would even make me remove an empty carton from the room after I'd unpacked a purchase from the store. "A box with the top open like that looks just like an empty coffin, and is bad luck!" she'd say, and give an irrepressible shudder. So I would quickly remove the box.

Now I was in a soul-searing dilemma. Should I say 'Yes' and have her know she was dying, when I knew how much she feared death? Or should I lie, and say 'No, you're going to be all right, honey,' and perhaps have her think I was crass and uncaring at a time when she most needed my love and strength and sympathy; that is, in the event she *knew* she was dying. I resolved the problem with a few simple words of truth, spoken as I snuggled my face up against hers and held her hand in mine.

"Yes, querida, you are *very* sick. But we're still fighting."

"I know, Roberto . . . I know, for I'm getting too, too tired. Thank you for being so caring with me. I love you very deeply, you know," she spoke with a tone of voice almost as if to verify that I truly knew how much she loved me. Then she slid her hand across the sheet to touch mine, much as she used to play that little game at bedtime. I was totally wiped out, and for the first time during all her illness that I could remember, I sobbed openly in front of her, with my head beside hers there on the hospital pillow. Her tears flowed copiously at the same time.

When at last I found my voice, I spoke, for I understood that now it was Maria who was the serene one. "I know you love me, darling. And I love you just as deeply, and have suffered right along with you in this long crusade. We just have to tough it out together," and I kissed her drenched cheeks and lips, for her emotions had overflowed along with mine.

"Together," she whispered, as our tears blended, and she squeezed my hand tenderly but prolongedly, as though pulling sustenance from the handclasp. Outside, a siren vented its noisy wrath into the night as an ambulance roared up to the emergency room entrance and then drooled into silence.

The nurse came in to interrupt, and draw blood for tests per doctor's orders, taking it from the mediport rather than her bruised and battered veins. Now that the blood tests had revealed high blood sugar, the nurse also administered insulin, per Doctor Able's instructions. Even as Maria slipped inexorably away from me, there was no cessation of the damnable tests and medicines. And there was the bone marrow biopsy still to go, which worried me no end.

Doctor Able performed the biopsy there in the room a short time later. Using a needle a foot long—I'm almost positive it was a foot long. He drove it into her hip and on into the hip bone, I think it was. I winced, but Maria didn't flinch, so apparently the procedure was painless. Perhaps the doctor had deadened her hip, but I didn't see him do it. He stayed at the hospital to get the results of the biopsy from the lab downstairs, then came to me with his heart-wrenching news.

"I'm sorry, Robin," he said, "but the biopsy shows that Maria is even worse off than I thought. She has very few white corpuscles [to fight infection], even fewer platelets [which will help to stop blood clotting], and virtually no stem cells."

"And without stem cells," I cut in, "no red corpuscles are being formed, which is why Maria is so tired . . . because she has nothing in her blood to carry oxygen to the cells throughout her body. So in a way she is being slowly asphyxiated, isn't she?"

"Yes, you could say that," the doctor acknowledged. "That is why I suggest you call your dear ones right away, or they may never see Maria alive again."

"Can't she have a bone marrow transplant," I asked, my heart in my throat but little hope in my heart. *A bone marrow transplant is the final resort, and even that probably would not save my beloved,'* I thought to myself.

Doctor Able confirmed my thoughts. "No, it's too late for that. Besides, that's a very expensive procedure, even if a donor could be found." His comments were such as to discourage further thoughts along that line.

Now everything seemed clearer to me, like a color slide in a projector warms up and then suddenly snaps into focus on the screen. The medical staff which had been attending to Maria for years most certainly had been aware of the deterioration of her bone marrow, from the evidence which they found in all those blood tests they had administered. Otherwise, why had they given her platelet infusions on two occasions that I can recall? In my opinion, it was to prop up the work of the bone marrow itself, which by now had been invaded by the nefarious cancer.

Until that moment, with all the pressure and worry over my Maria, such a thought never came to me. But now, as I write this seven years later, I begin to understand. A bone marrow transplant is very costly; so if the patient isn't wealthy, and Medicare and the insurance company have to pay for it, for god's sake avoid any reference to the subject, and never suggest it to a dying patient. That's what I believe is the truth. I invite any medical person who wishes, to offer up his or her facts or arguments to refute my belief. I don't expect to hear from many medics, except perhaps some who secretly agree with me.

After absorbing Doctor Able's gloomy prognosis, it took me a few minutes to recover my equilibrium, but at last I spoke up. "I'll call the children right away," I said, and turned brokenheartedly away.

With Nini sleeping, I rushed home and called Kathy in Key West, who burst into tears, making my terrible task even more difficult. After I had calmed Kathy down and given her as much of the picture as I understood, I called my niece namesake in Marco Island, who also grew tearful and distraught. Then I finally made the call I dreaded to make, the one to Bobby in Rochester; for his mother had always been inordinately fond of him, and he deeply loved his mother. But I couldn't get hold of Bobby, because he was at work, and I didn't have his work-phone number.

When granddaughter Sheila answered the phone and she couldn't find his number, either, I told her about her *Vovo*, that Grandma was dying, and that she had to call her Daddy and tell him the sad news, and that he should come quickly if he wished to see his mother alive for the last time. Sheila was weeping as she acknowledged my instructions and said she would carry them out immediately . . . if she could find her daddy's phone number. They had never been the most organized family, so I prayed Sheila would work things out and Bobby would call me back.

Within a half-hour, Bobby was on the line. "I'm so upset

with the news of Mama's condition," he said, and I could feel the sorrow in his voice.

"I'm sorry I couldn't call you sooner, honey," I said, "but believe it or not, we went out for dinner Friday at the Steakhouse, then Tuesday Mama had an appointment with the oncologist, and he sent her to the hospital, and today he took a bone marrow biopsy, and it revealed that her blood is virtually useless now. So she has the cancer in her chest wall, in her lungs, in the right side of her brain and I guess in her bone marrow. She has certainly fought a brave fight, and as much as I hate the thought of losing our dear Mama, I am thankful she hasn't been in a lot of pain, and that the end is coming quickly and gently."

"I know, Dad," Bobby said, "it sounds terrible to say, but in truth Mama is much better off if she can slip away peacefully in the night. The sad thing is, I have no money for a plane ticket, so I will leave as early as possible tomorrow morning and drive straight through, which takes twenty-two hours. I'll call her tomorrow so she'll know I'm on my way," and we hung up.

As tired as I was, I tossed and turned most of a sleepless night, a hundred unhappy visions of things to come swirling in among a thousand fond memories. I was filled with dread of what inevitably had to be, and simultaneously was soothed by recollections of the happy times which had comprised so much of our lives as a couple together, and as a family.

We'd had bitter times, too, such as when my pregnant Maria arrived in America and I had to leave her alone in a hotel in Norfolk, Virginia at 4:00 a.m. New Years Day, 1945, and head for the Pacific on the light cruiser *Vicksburg* at 08:00 that same morning. There Maria remained alone, not speaking our language, pregnant with our son, not knowing when she would see me again, if ever, nearly 3,000 miles from my family out in Washington state, and with very little money with which to make her way to them. And filled with dread all the while over what might happen to me, 'out on that big ocean full of Japanese' as she so aptly phrased it.

She had some cause to worry, for my ship lay just off Mt. Suribachi and gave fire support to the brave Marines who hit the mushy black sands of Iwo Jima a month and a half later. We provided vital firepower during that entire battle. Then after raids on Japan itself with a Navy Task Force, we did the same job for the Marines again throughout the battle of Okinawa. That scrap began on April 1, Easter Sunday (and April Fools Day), the final battle of World War II, which finally ended what Hitler began on September 1, 1939, after 2,194 days of warfare.

This last day of March had been an ordeal for all of us; Maria, the doctor, the kids and me. I was thankful we'd all made it through that miserable Wednesday, and I was ready to turn my back on it whenever Morpheus called on me. My mind felt as though it were drugged, as anxiety over tomorrow reacted with happy memories of the past, and thoughts of my nine Navy years crowded each other from whichever spots in the mind handle each type of recollection and preoccupation. I know I eventually dozed off, because the alarm clock jangled me awake at 5:30 Thursday morning.

CHAPTER 31

Suddenly I hated that stupid clock and wanted to throw it out the door into the bay, and would have if it hadn't been anchored to the wall by its long tail behind the headboard. As I moved to open the draperies in the living room, I was so lost in space and so lethargic I had no appreciation of the sparkling bay gleaming in the morning sun, nor the beauty of the trim white egret standing just outside the door, nor of the blue heron looking for all the world like a Baptist preacher, so erect and disdainful under the tall echeveria shrub to the right of our porch. I couldn't even find any humor in the poses of the brown pelicans standing on the seawall patiently awaiting a fisherman, and looking like a panel of staid judges regarding me from the bench.

I threw a hasty piece of toast, some cereal and some cold milk at my truly empty stomach, and headed for Room 207. Maria was awake this time, and I collected a hug and some kisses right away. "How do you feel this morning, *querida?*" I asked.

"I feel just fine . . . except for being so tired. I wish I could get rested up for once." She put her brown eyes on me as though she thought I could do something about it.

"Well, now that the bone marrow biopsy is over with, you can probably relax a little more, and catch a few winks of sleep now and then without somebody disturbing you. Breakfast will soon be here, and one way for you to rest up is to eat," and I went about washing her face and hands in preparation. To me it was genuinely incredible how Nini could be

---

263

so coherent and so aware of what was going on around her. Except for her missing hair and the cloak of lassitude which enfolded her, Maria seemed almost normal, though a bit slimmer, for she had lost almost 50 pounds in the last couple of months.

I had barely finished brushing her teeth when the phone rang. It was Bobby on the line. I placed the receiver by Maria's ear on the pillow. "It's somebody you know, Mama," I said.

"Hello?" Nini said. "Bobby! Oh, Bobby, you don't know how happy I am to hear from you! You're on your way here? That's wonderful!" She looked at me with glowing eyes. "Bobby's coming, Daddy. He'll be here in the morning. He had to drive. He didn't have money for a plane ticket," and she told me most of those things of which I was already aware. With her adored son on the line, my little wife was a new women, her fatigue seemingly banished, at least for the moment.

They talked for several minutes, but one thing Maria said will stand forever in my memory. "I remember that trip, Bobby," she said regarding some bygone day which Bobby mentioned to her. Then, in a moment of obviously deep nostalgia, she continued. "We had a lot of fun over the years, didn't we?" By now I had nestled my ear down close enough to Maria's that I cold hear Bobby speaking. "Yes, Mama, we sure did, because you were always so caring of us kids and so deeply interested in whatever we were doing. We had great fun over the years . . . a thousand wonderful, marvelous experiences."

As they talked, I saw that Nini had brightened considerably, and didn't seem as weary as before. After they said goodby to one another, I added my own goodby, said "See you in the morning," and hung up the phone. But it was Nini's words, "We *had* a lot of fun, didn't we?" putting it in the past tense, as though she expected no more such great times, which told me definitely and convincingly: Maria knew she was about to die, and was ready to face the fact without dread. She had reconciled her dislike of anything funereal, and in my opinion, was ready to meet in heaven with her mother and father and three brothers, all of whom had passed away at too early an age. Suddenly a heavy weight was lifted from my shoulders. I could be at ease with my beloved Brazilian wife now, for she was obviously reconciled to her future.

As if to verify her amazing transition, one of the priests from St. John's Church came in about ten o'clock to visit with Maria. He didn't say specifically what he was doing, but Maria knew, and listened with a haunting look in her eyes as he performed the Last Rites beside her bed. "Thank you, Father," she said simply, and he held out his hand and she kissed it lightly. Then the warm look in her eyes mesmerized him, and he bent down and kissed her on the forehead, disregarding her baldness.

As though it were an omen, a Protestant minister also came through that morning, and asked if he could say a prayer. "Of course, Reverend," Maria said, "please do," and closed her eyes while the pleasant minister offered up a very comforting prayer of hope and regeneration in a most pleasant tone of voice, and then like the Padre before him, bent and kissed her.

Right after Nini's scarcely-tasted lunch, Robbie and Larry, with my sister Maxine and girls Sarah and Laura arrived to hug and kiss Maria. They sort of milled around until Lydia, the black lady who today occupied the second bed, and who also had breast cancer, told Larry, "Take my chairs, honey, I'm not using them." She had come in early that morning, and Maria greeted her warmly, for they had taken chemotherapy infusions together several times. Her cancer was not yet that far advanced, but if her case was like Maria's, her cancer would never go into remission.

It was mid-afternoon when Kathy and Charlie arrived from Key West with Cindy and Terry. Now the room overflowed

with family, even after the four children went to the oncology waiting room to visit and watch TV. I knew they all loved
Maria dearly, but happily, at 10 to 17 years of age, they were
too young to be plunged into deep sadness over the passing
of a great-aunt or grandmother.

We visited together, with Maria taking an active part in
the conversation, for she was quite lucid. When she dozed
off soon after lunch, we all went out to eat at a place on St.
Pete Beach where we could watch the light surf coming in.
With all of his years at sea as a Navy pilot, Charlie still enjoyed the beach. I was so preoccupied that I have no idea
now what we ate, nor the name of the place, but we managed
to tuck away enough calories to carry us through the afternoon.

We went to the condo to talk, and then about an hour
before Maria's dinner time, I returned to the hospital, while
the visitors went out to procure lodging in a motel. They
found a place with rooms for one family, so Kathy and crew
took it, and Larry and gang found another half a mile away.
When they arrived at the hospital just at Maria's dinner time,
they were set for the night. I was so distraught I failed to ask
them the names of their motels, and their room and telephone numbers.

With Maria's supper on the table, I helped her take a few
spoonsful of custard or pudding and drink a few sips of cold
milk, which she enjoyed, even though she couldn't hold the
straw, and she leaked a bit of milk on her chin for me to tidy
up. After doing the best she could, my little redhead said,
"I'm not very hungry, Daddy. Take the tray away, please, so
I can see everybody better."

Our large assemblage eddied about in the crowded room,
and some even sat on Lydia's bed, for she had gone home
after her therapy. Maria talked with all of us, including the
children. It was Robbie who spoke of a past incident which
brought a smile to Maria's face, and a chuckle to the rest of

us. "I just thought of the time, Maria, when you were telling us how angry you got with a salesman who knocked at your door and refused to go away. You told us, 'He made me so mad I was ready to boil my top!'"

"I remember that," Nini smiled. "He was such a nuisance!"

Maria appeared highly pleased with everyone's presence, in total disregard of why we were there. Yet I knew the significance wasn't lost on her. She knew why we were gathered, beyond question. She knew the reason, yet she absorbed it, and didn't let it nag at her. During the past few days she had conquered the terror of death which had besieged her all of her life. I was positive this was true, just as sure as I knew that the day was April 2nd, 1993.

It was 9:30 in the evening, almost exactly, when Maria spoke softly to the gang: "I'm feeling very tired, everybody, and very sleepy. I hate to send you all away, and I apologize. But I will see you all tomorrow, okay?" Everyone murmured 'Yes', 'Of course', or 'We understand, Maria', and each went to Nini's side and kissed her goodnight, including the children.

Of course I was the last to go. I gently adjusted her bed the way she liked it, fluffed up her pillow, gave her a sip of cool water, and then bent down to hug and kiss her tenderly. She opened those magnificent eyes and regarded me with a look of affection in her gaze. "I love you very deeply, Daddy," she said simply, and kissed my cheek. Her eyes were moist, but no tears broke through, and I forced back the ones which wanted to flood my own tired face.

"I love you very deeply, too, my *querida* Maria," I said, and squeezed her to me. "Have a good rest, and I will see you in the morning." I kissed her once again, and caressed her cheeks and hands gently before rising and forcing myself to walk away.

Suddenly I remembered the day I kissed her goodby in

Recife, Brazil when I got Navy orders sending me back to America in 1944 during the war, and I recalled how she sobbed the whole night before my departure, and was still weeping next day as the elevator doors closed and separated us while she stood in the doorway of the room we had shared for several months. And again, on New Years Day, when I left her all alone in the small hotel at 4:30 in the morning in Norfolk and headed back to my ship which before 8:00 a.m. was on its way to the battles of Iwo Jima and Okinawa. She was a crumpled, broken-hearted young lady at both those farewells, because at each parting she never knew if she would ever see me again.

Now, I paused at the door, for her shining eyes had followed me as I left. "Good night, darling," I whispered silently, then blew a kiss to her. She formed the same soundless syllables with her lips, made a little kiss with her lips and closed her eyes peacefully, as I left. That bitter-sweet moment would be tucked away forever in my memory.

I was already dozing off in bed at home when suddenly I remembered something: I'd forgotten to eat dinner. "Tough luck," I whispered, "I ain't about to get up to fix something," and rolled onto my other side to go back to sleep.

CHAPTER 32

The alarm clock beside my bed ripped open the early morn, and half-asleep I turned and cut off it's yelp. *'I'm so tired, I can't believe how fast the night shot by,'* I complained to myself.

But the stupid clock kept ringing. By then I'd stirred enough to realize I shouldn't be picking on the poor clock. It was the telephone which was demanding my attention. I lifted the receiver to my ear and gave it a tentative, 'Hello?', still not fully aware of what was going on until a voice came over the line.

"Mister Leatherman, this is the night nurse at the hospital. Your wife passed away just a few minutes after midnight. They will move her body to our morgue very soon now. What should I do with her diamond rings and bracelet?"

Dear god, what a lugubrious way to be stirred awake in the middle of the night! She didn't even say, "I'm sorry—", just dumped the shocking news on me like a garbage truck unloading at the county landfill! I studied the clock through already-flooded eyes and managed to make out the numbers. It was a few minutes to 1:00 a.m.. Finally awake, I replied foggily. "Please remove them for me; I'll be right over."

As I pulled on my clothes, I kept asking myself, *'How can this be? How can I lose Maria in the space of three days? How can she have left my side . . . forever, after such sweet goodnights just a few hours ago?'* While these thoughts, and the rush of sudden loneliness they brought with them, ran through my mind I was sobbing as though I were being beaten. Before I donned

---

269

my shirt I went into the bathroom and washed my face with cold water to try to regain my composure.

There on the little shelf which ran across the bathroom beneath the mirror, were all of Maria's little things awaiting her return: a brush and comb, the box of face powder with a puff inside, three small vials of perfume . . .

'Nini will never need those things again,' I thought, *'nor her dresses and slacks and blouses . . . '* and I looked at the long rows of her clothing suspended in the walk-in closet or folded neatly on the small shelves on the back wall. I gave a shudder. *'You have to stop thinking like this!'* I chastised myself. Then I wondered just how I would manage that? For starters, I washed my face with cold water again.

When I arrived 15 minutes later at the oncology ward, the sheet was pulled up over Maria's head. I ignored the nurse, and went directly to the head of the bed to pull the sheet down and look at my sweetheart's face, now wrapped in the peace that comes with death. I broke down for a few moments as I put my arm under her head, squeezed her to me and kissed her cheeks, her eyelids, her sweet lips and even the top of her precious bald head.

When I rose and covered her face with the sheet again, the nurse eyed me casually, reached into her uniform pocket and drew out Maria's diamond engagement ring, her diamond wedding ring and the modest gold bracelet set with small Brazilian aquamarines which I had given to her many years ago and which she never removed from her wrist, not even when going into surgery. The nurse was obliged to cover it with tape, for Nini absolutely forbade its removal.

"Here is her jewelry," the provider of Tender Loving Care stated in a flat, unnecessarily detached voice.

I took the items and tenderly put them into my pocket. "Poor Maria," I said to the nurse, "the little darling still has traces of the injury to her knees when she fell down on her birthday . . . just a month ago," and I moved to raise the corner of the sheet to show her the small scabs.

"You can't do that, Mister Leatherman!" the nurse cried out, as though I planned to commit some heinous crime, and moved as if to stop me from lifting the sheet.

"For god's sake! I'm only showing you that Maria died before her knees healed from a fall exactly a month ago," I said, and showed her the tiny injuries and put the sheet back in place.

Then I paused to look at my bearer of bad news. "You know, I don't believe a damned bit of that story about my wife dying just after midnight. You said you checked her at ten o'clock, and she was sleeping quietly. You heard no sound from her, but when you checked her at twelve-thirty she was dead, 'so she *must* have died just after midnight!' That reasoning doesn't follow, you know, and I'm virtually positive she died *before* midnight. But I suppose the hospital can squeeze out another day of income by recording it as a death after midnight."

The nurse blinked, but didn't say a word, either in denial or in confirmation of my theory. But I have always considered that Nini's death came on April 2, exactly one month after her 73rd birthday and our luncheon at the cafeteria.

I was moving in a daze, mostly, my vision blurred by tears, but I gathered together Nini's personal items from the little drawer and the few clothes she had worn to the doctor's office Tuesday morning, the nurse put them in a plastic bag and I took them home, alone in the middle of the night, my thoughts in chaos, my head aching madly, my chest constricted with the pain of sorrow.

"I know we expected Maria to die soon, but I still can't believe it was this soon, so suddenly, so very . . . final!" I cried out aloud against the world and all those gods who take such pleasure in the sufferings of we mortals.

Maria's and my kisses just prior to my leavetaking the

271

night before, and our salutes to each other when I was in the doorway, those were the last hugs and kisses we would ever share together, and our last farewells. That was the last time I saw my darling's bewitching brown eyes; flashing eyes which haunt me to this day, more than seven years since I lost my dear Bahiana.

Back in the condo, I reset the innocent alarm clock, dropped onto the bed in my shorts and spent the rest of the night crying and trying to comfort myself. In a blurry haze I regarded Maria's side of the king-size bed with anguish, a bed which seemed more massive than ever now, with Naria's side henceforth to be forever empty.

While I was tossing and turning, my mind struck on one little incident which occurred about a month earlier. Maria was in her easy chair, and as I was coming from the bedroom when she called me. "Come here a moment, Daddy," she asked. I went and stood before her expectantly. She turned her tiny face up to look at me, her shining eyes regarding me intently. "After I die, will you marry again?" she asked, in a sort of casual, matter-of-fact voice. But behind the casualness I sensed her preoccupation.

I dropped to the floor at her knee, took her hands in mine, and looked at her steadily and calmly. "In the first place, honey, that time is many years away. And if you *should* die first, the answer is, No, sweetheart, there could be no other woman in my life after all the joys we have shared together . . . and all the sorrows, too, for that matter. If you should die first, when my day comes to cross over into the Beyond, I will still be an unmarried widower, *querida*."

The soft smile and warm look she bestowed on me proved how deeply she felt about not having a successor in her home. "I knew that, Daddy. But I longed to hear you say it, anyway."

Another thing I suddenly remembered: I had forgotten to ask the kids where they were staying. *'How dumb can a man be?'* I bitched to nobody in particular. *'Now I can't even call and tell them Mama is dead.'* I rose early next morning, shaved and took a cold shower. I tried to eat a dab of cereal but the tasty oat circles were reluctant to go down, so finally I stopped nagging them and washed the dish and spoon.

Not knowing what time Kathy would arrive at the hospital, I made my way to the parking lot at 6:30, parked in the space closest to the hospital entryway, and waited for the Starnes family to arrive. Fortunately for me, they rose early, ate breakfast and pulled into the parking lot just after 7:00. They parked nearby and started toward the entry. I rose to meet them.

"Mama died a little before midnight, *Boneca,*" I said simply, using the nickname, Doll, that I had used so often with her when she was a child, for she was indeed a pretty little creature, crowned with a pitchfork full of blond hair and blessed with a bright, ready smile. Now she went from darling doll to wilted woman in an instant.

She stumbled toward me, almost losing her balance. Most assuredly the awful news hit her as hard as it had hit me, for she and her mother had always been very close together, often playing with the ouija board for hours on end, talking to the spirits of Bela Lugosi and Eric the Red time after time.

"Oh, no, Daddy!" she cried, and Charlie joined us in a three-way embrace until Kathy recovered from her first shock, and managed to slow her tears. "But we can go on up to see her, can't we," she implored, her grey eyes tearfully beseeching. "No, honey, they already took her body to the hospital morgue, and I gave them instructions to call the funeral home across the waterway on St. Pete Beach to handle arrangements." It seemed as though by talking about the coming interment I eased the pain in my head and relaxed my swirling thoughts. "I think both our wills call for cremation, so that's what we'll do. We won't have a funeral, we'll have a memorial Mass at St. John's on St. Pete Beach. You went there with Mama for services, I believe."

"Yes, I remember it well. It's very pretty, inside and out," Kathy said.

As we spoke, Robbie and Larry and girls showed up without breakfasting first, and all were very broken up by Maria's swift passing. The instant grief which my sister Maxine registered surprised me, for I had never known for sure whether she was fond of Maria or not. She took Nini into her home in San Diego before Bobby was born and looked after them both while her husband and I were in the Pacific helping to end World War II. Her tearful reaction to my words answered that question. It was obvious that she was very fond of Nini.

After we pulled ourselves together, and apart, we made our way to a family restaurant and had some breakfast, although my French toast tasted like day-old cow chips. Kathy and crew drank coffee or juice, but didn't eat again. Then we headed to the condo, where always-well-organized Kathy took command. I was in such terrible shape I couldn't have taken charge of an unattended coin laundry, let alone the arrangements for a funeral and the amenities with friends and neighbors. Kathy took the names of people who came by and who attended the memorial service, and later on, when I was beginning to see the world without peering through saltwater, I wrote the traditional Thank you notes.

Kathy took me grocery shopping to be sure she was buying things I liked, and I posted a note on our condo bulletin board saying Maria had died the night before, and soon neighbors were coming by to express their condolences and next morning to drop off a cake or a salad or some hot dish, always saying how sorry they were, and how much they would miss Maria, until the whole operation began to spin around me with only the corner of some occasional mental image cropping to the surface like the flotsam in a huge eddy in a river after a storm, and before I knew it, day had ended and I was back in bed, alone with the all-consuming despair which had engulfed me when I got the nurse's midnight call.

Bobby had arrived with Sheila, his eldest daughter, in mid-morning, too late to see Maria alive. But he'd seen enough of death, for he'd killed a number of men in Vietnam as the head of a 4-man liaison team which led a company of South Vietnamese in frequent skirmishes north of Saigon, up toward the North-South Vietnamese border.

Sheila burst into tears and was very nervous, but Bobby did not appear too sad. or unhappy. He had a rational explanation. "I cried when you called to say Mama was very ill, Dad, and I was a bit leaky on the way down, for I was almost certain Mother would die before I could get here." He paused. "Exactly like happened to you when you flew to Seattle from Bloomington, Illinois during that winter storm, took the ferry to Bremerton and got there just after Grandma passed away." How he remembered the details of that sorrowful trip I'd made alone in 1950 when he was less that five years old I don't know!

Much like Kathy, my son proved to be a great help, a gentle comforter, and a stabilizing influence on the rest of us over the next few days.

CHAPTER 33

In brief summary, Maria had undergone a mastectomy on April 17, 1986, with the hope that all the cancer had been removed. But many months later the doctors realized the cancer had spread, or metastasized. Then it was weeks of radiation, followed by weeks of chemotherapy. Then more surgery, more radiation and more chemotherapy, until the list of strange-sounding chemicals which Maria had absorbed would fill a book.

Then there were CAT scans and MRI scans and x-rays and biopsies and hundreds of blood drawings, injections and infusions until her blood vessels could no longer cope with the needles so a mediport was installed above her left breast to permit easier entry to her bloodstream. She bore up under it all with few complaints and the courage of a Trojan warrior.

Treatment after treatment, Nini engaged in an increasingly ferocious war against the vicious intruder, losing all of her hair twice as the insidious foe inexorably spread to her chest wall (causing the pangs which she had often felt after the mastectomy), then to her lungs, then to her cerebrum, and finally to the very marrow of her bones, where it destroyed even the stem-cells, bringing on her death on April 2nd, 1993, seven years from the date of her mastectomy and one month exactly after her 73rd birthday.

After her unbelievably gallant acceptance of the many phases and types of treatment, my beloved Brazilian wife, wearied by the intense and prolonged struggle, finally succumbed to overwhelming odds, and passed away peacefully in her sleep—just a few months before our golden wedding anniversary.

Maria's long war with breast cancer was over and her soul was with her previously departed loved ones.

As I reflected early that morning of her death, while waiting for Kathy and crew, my mind went back to Chief Joseph of the Nez Perce Indians of Washington.

When an unbelievably superior force defeated his small tribe just before he reached Canada and amnesty, the Army demanded his surrender. With the decimated remnants of his band starving, ill, some of them dying, Chief Joseph stood before the Army commander, and made a very simple statement: *From where the sun stands now, I will fight no more.*

My dear wife of 49 years ended her own last battle with that same deep dignity.

She had reached the point where, despite her courage and stamina, she could fight no more.

Now it was time for her mourning survivors to try to adjust to the great loss in their lives, to try to fill in the void which had so swiftly appeared in their days.

Almost every reader would be familiar with funerals and the pain of making burial arrangements, so I will only touch on those points which made Nini's interment different.

First, we made arrangements for Maria to be cremated, and selected and paid for a beautiful spot in the cemetery where her ashes would be buried in an urn. But when a neighbor told me Catholics would consider it a mortal sin to be cremated, I decided I'd best check her will to be sure it called for cremation. Of course it did not! *My* will does, with my ashes to be scattered at sea; but Maria's did not speak of cremation. I don't know where I came up with that asinine notion! Of course I wasn't thinking that straight anyway.

I immediately called the funeral parlor to stop the proceedings, after which we all drove up to the funeral home which had the crematory, where they would hold Maria's body temporarily until we picked a new burial site. We had a family viewing, with Maria's body swathed in a sheet temporarily. Robbie and Larry and Sarah and Laura stayed in the back of the room, and nothing would persuade them it was all right to come up and say goodby to their Aunt Maria, who had loved them so deeply.

Kathy and Charlie and Bobby and I then went to the funeral parlor adjoining the cemetery on 1st Avenue South to choose an open-air mausoleum where Maria would be laid to rest in a nice crypt. The local director had shown us a beautiful 'chapel mausoleum' in the North St. Pete cemetery. They were in the process of building one similar in the cemetery where Nini would be interred. It was a charming arrangement, with two banks of crypts facing each other under a broad canopy roof supported by tall columns, with a terrazzo floor, planters between the crypt walls, and both ends of the 'chapel' open to the view.

Our funeral guide explained to us. "The new addition to convert the current large mausoleum into a chapel mausoleum in your cemetery won't be ready for about four months. However, if you wish, we can put Maria's body in another crypt nearby, and move it when the new chapel is ready."

With the payment of about $1,500 more, of which Charlie gave me $500, bringing the grand total up to about $4,500, we accepted the director's kind offer. Originally thinking that Nini's ashes were going to be buried under the trees that afternoon, we had all ordered flowers and they were already in place beneath the gorgeous tree, since we were not having a funeral, but only a memorial service in the chapel at St, John's Church. Such memorial services were a common practice in our condominium group as the old ones passed away. So Bobby and I went by and moved the flowers to the temporary mausoleum where Maria's body now rested.

During my 75-plus years, I had moved over 70 times between babyhood and adulthood and through the naval service and postwar years, living in several states in the US, and various places in Brazil. After Maria and I were married, we moved numerous times, from coast to coast and almost from border to border. Now it gave me an eerie feeling to realize that even in death, Maria's body would move once more, from a simple crypt to a chapel mausoleum.

The new location had gray granite crypt closures, except for the outline of a cross in the center of each wall, which was done with tannish-brown granite. When the new crypts were ready, Maria's body was placed in the crypt which forms the right arm of the cross, the location which would have been beneath the right hand of Jesus.

'And sitteth at the right hand of God the Father . . . 'the words would insinuate themselves into my consciousness for days after we moved Maria's body to its final resting place that fall.

I was picking up my mail at the Saratoga Building mail room, when I bumped into Johnny, my next door neighbor. "Hi, Robin!" he cried, and grabbed my hand to shake it warmly. "How is Maria?" Then I realized he'd just returned from his Oklahoma visit, and hadn't heard the doleful news yet.

"My darling Maria is dead, Johnny," I said quietly. "She died April second." He immediately swept me into his muscular arms and joined me in a flood of tears as our bodies rocked back and forth there in front of the mailboxes for many seconds.

Yet he was not as surprised as I expected him to be. "I'm terribly sorry to hear that, Robby . . . you know I am. But when we left for Oklahoma, and we four shook hands and hugged goodby, Norma and I gave extra strong hugs and extra warm kisses to Maria, for I told Norma we would never see Maria alive again. I knew the cancer had about done its dirty work. I realize you are still in shock, but I pray the Lord will give you as much peace of spirit as possible very soon."

"Thank you, Johnny. Maria was always particularly fond

of you and Norma, and I know you'll miss her bright face."

"We most certainly will. She never once complained. We'd ask her how she was, like people do, and she'd say, 'I'm fine, just fine'. I will never forget those sweet words as she spoke then in reply ... to me and to everyone else,"

At the memorial service, at least a hundred of our condo friends came to pay their respects. One lady of Spanish descent presented me with a beautiful card which she had artfully lettered with the names of all our building residents, along with a hundred dollars those same neighbors had given to me, and which I in turn gave to the church for the memorial service in their chapel.

During the service, the priest set up the keyboard of the Hammond organ ready for use in the chapel, and I played 'Just a Closer Walk With Thee', one of Maria's favorite hymns. I played it first in the key of F, then modulated to B-flat to replay it. Oddly enough, as well-known as that sweet hymn is—especially in New Orleans, where it goes to almost every funeral—it's composer is unknown.

I was blinded by tears, and was unfamiliar with that organ, and I play only by ear, so I was fearful of how the hymn came out, but our neighbors in the building next door said it was very beautiful and most touching. Deep inside I felt a little better after personally playing that final tribute to Maria, to her love and to her everlasting memory.

CHAPTER 34

Larry had several houses under construction which needed his attention, so he and Robbie and girls headed for Marco Island right after the services. Kathy and Charlie had bought a home which was just being completed in Orlando, ready for his coming retirement from the Navy. Charlie had to check on something there, so I quieted my roily thoughts by going along with him and Terry, as did Bobby. Back to the condo that afternoon, Charlie took off on another obligatory duty for the night, and Kathy and children stayed with me.

Kathy's fear was that I would run out and get married again right away. "Now, Daddy! Don't you go doing anything rash," she urged. "Give yourself time to adjust to your new life without Mama. You were together fifty years, and no one else would be quite like her, and might ruin your life instead of making you happier. A few years down the road you might consider marrying again, but you shouldn't do it now."

"I understand what you are telling me, honey," I hugged her to reassure her, "but you don't have to fret about your poor old Pappy. He's seventy-five years old, and doesn't plan to rush out and get married. Like one of the Marx brothers said, I think it was Groucho, the kind of woman I want wouldn't have me, and any woman who would have me, I wouldn't want. So you needn't worry your pretty blond head over that problem," I hugged her and kissed her cheeks again to reinforce her belief in me, and chase away her fears.

The next day Charlie picked up Kathy and Cindy and

281

Sheila and drove home to Key West. The following morning Bobby left for Rochester, going by way of Key West to see Kathy's Navy quarters and to pick up Sheila. At Kathy's he called to see how I was doing, and told me he'd made it to Key West in eight hours, which was excellent time, considering it's mostly two-lane highway down that long string of small islands. Kathy got on the line to comfort me and caution me, and after she hung up I felt all alone for the first time since Maria's death.

Now I was totally lost in the condo. I'd wander from one bedroom to the other, from one bath to the other, into the kitchen, and back out through the enclosed patio porch to the seawall, and back through it all again. I was trying to do things, but was making no progress. The burden of my sorrow pressed down too suffocatingly upon my tired spirit and body.

Once I paused in my listless rounds, and remembered a pair of robins which had nested in one of our pear trees near the country road which passed our tiny Oregon farm when I was a child. They were both busily searching for food and bringing it to their four fledglings, which were almost ready to fly out on their own, when the female was struck and killed by a passing pickup. The male saw his mate lying beside the road, and stayed near her for several hours, back and forth, hopping about and hovering over her. I left the little body there for two days, for the male seemed to be in mourning for her. Then he disappeared, and the little ones fled the nest, and I buried the crumpled mother in the corner of the garden. Now I realized how much my little feathered namesake had missed the company of his mate those soft spring days in the shadow of beautiful, snow-capped Mt.Hood.

I had told the kids that I might move to Guadalajara, Mexico to live, for expenses were much lower there, and my income was reduced to about $1,500 a month when Maria passed away, for *her* social security payments stopped, of course. So that thought was intermingled with my other thoughts and memories as I wandered aimlessly around the condo.

Every day I made the dolorous drive to the cemetery, parked before Maria's temporary crypt, and murmured a prayer for her through my heartache and tears. After a quarter-hour beside her crypt, I drove the lonely drive home. As the weeks passed, I went to see Maria's burial place every second or third day. Eventually I went once a week, and after I moved to north St. Pete I went by at least once a month, as I still do.

The most incredible thing that happened shortly after Maria's death occurred in the condo bedroom in the middle of the night. I heard, or sensed, someone in the room as I stirred from a deep sleep. When I sat up in bed, there was Maria, sitting on my side of the bed, near my feet, as beautiful as she could be, her dark eyes filled with love and compassion.

"Maria!" I cried out, "You've come back! Oh, thank God!" and I slid to her side and threw my arms around her to hug her voraciously. She didn't speak, but squeezed me in her arms, too. And then as my heart overflowed with joy, my *querida* Nini faded from my grasp, and I was sitting alone on the big bed.

In an instant my elation faded to deep despair, and I fell backward in an uncontrollable spasm of sobbing and tears.

Next day I called Kathy to tell her of my unbelievable experience, and was amazed by her reply. "I know exactly what you mean, Daddy. Mama came back to me two nights ago in precisely the same manner, sitting on the corner of the bed at my feet in the middle of the night!"

I make no attempt to explain this eerie experience, except that I take it to mean that somehow my beloved Maria had returned in order to give me the strength and courage to go on with my life.

For several months before Maria died, I had suffered frequent pains in my chest, but I never mentioned them to her, for she already had too heavy a load to carry, especially in the late stages of the cancer. Within three months of Nini's death, I took the usual tests, with a wire poked up an artery to my heart, from an entry in my thigh. The doctors and I watched my heartbeat on a TV screen, and could see the constrictions in three cardiac arteries. They performed open-chest surgery, and pulled veins from both my thighs and one from my throat area to replace, not three, but four, plugged arteries, one of them hidden from view during our probe. They finished re-wiring my chest Thursday night about 5:00, and Tuesday morning I went home and fixed my own lunch at the condo.

There was still some vinegar left in the old cruet.

My niece and her gang came up to visit me in the hospital. "How are you doing, Uncle Bobby?" little Robbie cried. "I know it's terrible to be in the hospital, especially alone." As she spoke, a very pretty blonde came in to check on me.

"Oh, it really is, Robbie," I agreed and turned to the nurse. "Honey, will you please bring in my other caretakers so my niece can see how I'm suffering here?"

"Of course, I'll be back in a moment, Robin," she replied very seriously, and scooted off toward the nurses' station. In a few seconds she was back with her two cohorts in tow. They formed a little line for inspection near the foot of my bed: three absolutely delightful, beautiful, affectionate blondes, each of whom then came to give me a kiss on the cheek before going back to work. Their cute little leader spoke up as they were about to clear the exit. "Remember, Robin, if there is *anything* you want, just push the buzzer!"

"I will!" I cried. "But right now I can't think of a thing!"

Larry looked at the fabulous girls, then at Robbie, and finally at me. "No wonder you want to get out of here early. That galaxy of gorgeous girls must be driving you crazy!"

As the days passed, I realized the condo was too unhappy

to live in; its walls crowded down upon me despite its 1,100 square feet, and I constantly saw and remembered things concerning Maria, and my eyes flooded and overflowed the banks until I calmed down. As I cleared things from Maria's dresser and bathroom drawers and her desk, I grew bluer every day. I put the condo up for sale, and a lovely lady from New Jersey bought it.

I bought a small house in north St. Petersburg, using the money from the condo to pay cash. It's in this quiet, pleasant neighborhood with lots of great trees (except on my lot!) that I have worked now for over five years on my autobiography, of which this story forms one section. It was four years after Nini's death before my heart would let me begin these chapters.

When I was emptying her desk and dresser drawers in the condo I put some of her papers in a cardboard box. I kept the box in my clothes closet. Seven years passed before I could open that box to take care of its meager contents.

This volume tells the story of a sweet, brown-eyed immigrant girl from Brazil, and of how she battled cancer for seven years. I pray it will prompt other women and girls to be super alert, and take the time, REGULARLY, to check for any sign of breast cancer. It is imperative that you check every month, so that in the event a lump appears you can stop the vicious, skulking SOB in its tracks before it can spread and ruin your life.

The latest statistics I have seen, published by the American Cancer Society, are contained in a report for the year 1993, the year Maria died, in which it states that 1 out of 9 women in America will get breast cancer during her life. And that in the US there were 182,000 new cases in 1993, of which 11,300 were in Florida. In 1993, when Maria died, there were 2,900 deaths from breast cancer in Florida, and 46,800 in the nation. What a horrible loss of life, and love, and wealth to our society.

In the nation, the death rate per 100,000 in 1993 in Florida was 165, and for the whole country it was 172; so women in this state shared a slightly better experience than the nation as a whole. But all women must work diligently, nationwide, in order to keep these figures coming down, and hopefully, to chop them substantially.

So all of you ladies take the time to make the regular self-examinations which may save your lives, moving meticulously over every square inch of your breasts, and trying to reach deeply with your fingers. For Maria undoubtedly missed her 'lump' when she checked herself because it was more deeply embedded than most.

I pray that none of my readers will ever have to battle cancer as Maria did, in hand-to-hand combat. But if any reader *is* obliged to wage a similar war, I pray that she will have beside her someone who loves her deeply, who will offer her as much tender love and care as possible, and who will sustain her and give her strength in her war against a secretive, implacable and unrelenting foe.

POSTSCRIPT

Several years after Maria died, I came across a type-written page containing this story which she had begun, in English, sometime in the past. Just when, I cannot say, for it is undated. I admire so much her courage in starting an autobiography (something she *never* revealed to me!) that I have to insert what she wrote here at the end of this book to add something from Maria herself to brighten the final pages. I type it exactly as she wrote it while she was still learning our language. The reader will note instances in which Maria put adjectives in the plural when their subjects were plural, carrying over into English the Portuguese use of such grammar:

How a Brazil Girl Was Raise—1st Part

We arrive in Soledade, a small comunity in Parahiba State, in the year of 19—. The whole Family (my Father, my Mother, five Brothers and I, and a very young negro girl that my mother had 'adopted' about 8 years ago) stayed in the house of the Mayor of the town, Colonel Paulino. My father came to this town to manager the telegraph. I was only 4 years old, but, I still remember several episodios of our first mountain town.

I remember the house we move in, to wait until the house that belong to the telegraph had finish been redecorated. Lots people were very concern when heard that that nice family was going to live in the Sills house. Why, this house was haunted . . . everybody knew that. Was such a big house . . .

---

15 rooms, and the 'toilett' was outside. We took only 5 rooms on the south side of the house and we let all the other rooms stayed closed.

To go to the kitchen we had to go by a nero, dark and long hallway. And in the way we could see the others rooms all close(d) up. The kitchen was something enormous, dark and cold. The only thing bright was the huge wood stove on the middle of the kitchen.

I remember how my old brother, Jose, one day open one of the close rooms and found it full of cactus, big heads of cactus that they call 'cabeca de frade', Monk's head. The head is green and full of neddles and between the neddles small red buttons. How long we stay in this house I cannot remember. But one thing I am sure, my life start in this little town, I just cannot remember anything before that. Even our trip from the big city (We lived before in the capital of Parahiba State) I can not remember. So this town is where I begin.

I don't believe that anybody had a begin of life so mix up as I had mine. I was raised a little wild animal full of my own thoughts and believes.

Everyday after breakfast I went with Toni, (a neighbor girl of my own age) to play on the big rocks and corn fields. From our back yard we could see the small cemetery on top of the knoll. To go there we had to cross a small creek, the "Lava Pe," or Wash Feet. That was our destination every day after we ate our lunch.

We never used any shoes until we came home, and the day was almost over. About 5:00 or 5:30 P.M. after we wash ourselves we always change clothes and put our sandals on. The family always stayed together at 6:00 P.M. listening to the Bells of the church playing the hours. After that we had supper and go to bed.

Nora, our negro girl always put me in bed and told me stories about princes and princess. About the good fairies and the bad ones. I enjoyed so much this stories, sometimes she had to repeat the sames stories over and over to see if I could fall asleep. I never could go to sleep right away but nobody never pay any attention because I was too young to have insomnia . . .